ETHICS AND PROFESSIONALISM
For CPAs

Mary Beth Armstrong, CPA, Ph.D.
Professor of Accounting
California Polytechnic State University

COLLEGE DIVISION   South-Western Publishing Co.

Cincinnati, Ohio

Publisher: Mark R. Hubble
Marketing Manager: James Sheibley Enders
Sponsoring Representative: Sandra Luce
Production Editor: Sue Ellen Brown
Cover Designer: Graphica
Production House: Bookmark Book Production Services

AZ65AA
Copyright © 1993
by South-Western Publishing Co.
Cincinnati, Ohio

The text of this publication, or any part thereof, may not be reproduced or transmitted in any form or by any means, electronic or mechanical, including photocopying, recording, storage and information retrieval system, or otherwise, without the prior written permission of the publisher.

Library of Congress Cataloging-in-Publication Data

Armstrong, Mary Beth.
Ethics and professionalism for CPAs / Mary Beth Armstrong.
  p. cm.
Includes bibliographical references and index.
ISBN 0-538-82301-1
1. Accountants--Professional ethics. 2. Accounting--Moral and ethical aspects. I. Title
HF5657.A75 1993
174'.9657--dc20

92-37500
CIP

Printed in the United States of America

1 2 3 4 5 6 7 MA 9 8 7 6 5 4 3

*This text is dedicated
to my son Chris
and to all the accounting students
who may benefit from it*

Preface

Introduction

Not since the Watergate era has the topic of business and professional ethics been so popular. During the mid- and late 1980s the financial press was filled with stories of management fraud, scandals on Wall Street, and unethical behavior in government. Is it any wonder, then, that the public cry for an increase in ethical thought and behavior has filtered down to our institutions of higher learning where tomorrow's leaders are being prepared to take on their leadership roles?

Cynics often doubt if ethics can be taught in schools. They believe that people make good and bad choices based on personal character traits that are instilled long before students reach their college or university years. Recent research in the psychology of moral development, however, shows the contrary to be true. Individuals' conceptualization of right and wrong, good and bad, and how to reason when confronted with difficult moral choices continues to develop throughout the years of formal education, and often beyond.

The business and government leaders who have recently made the headlines because of their illegal or unethical behavior probably do not see themselves as evil people. Rather, they were people caught up in an environment that rewarded achievement based on a single goal (often "the bottom line"). The environment did not challenge them to critically analyze their choices from the viewpoints of other affected individuals or institutions. They often did not even recognize that they were stumbling into a moral arena. In other words, their moral problem *spotting* skills and moral problem *solving* skills were deficient. Those skills can, and indeed must, be taught in our academic institutions. Thus, the goal of this text is to enhance moral problem spotting and solving skills in students who are preparing to enter the field of public accounting.

This text is designed for use in a second auditing course, in a capstone or policy course in accounting, or in a stand-alone ethics course for accounting students.

Contents

Certified Public Accountants must be concerned both with personal ethical decision making and with the ethics of the profession itself, since the profession is composed of individual CPAs and their firms.

The disciplines to which CPAs might turn for a deeper understanding of ethical issues facing themselves and their profession are as follows:

Individual Ethics	Professional Ethics
Philosophy	Sociology
Psychology	

The first two chapters of this book are based on the ethics of the individual and are designed to aid the student in developing moral problem *solving* skills. Those chapters introduce alternative ways of viewing ethical situations and solving ethical dilemmas. The third chapter, based on the sociology of professions, is designed to give the student a clearer understanding of the nature of professions and the role of ethics for professionals. The remainder of the book is designed specifically to help accounting students develop their ethical problem *spotting* skills. At the same time, Chapters 3 through 13 are also designed to enhance a sense of professionalism in students. What does it mean to be a professional? What are the unique characteristics and problems of the profession of public accounting? What is the recent history of the profession and where is it headed? The author hopes that each reader, after completing this book, will have a deeper understanding of professionalism; be more committed to the profession of public accounting; and be able to spot, and effectively reason through, ethical issues related to the practice of public accounting.

To aid the student throughout the text, a list of additional readings is included at the end of each chapter. In addition, each chapter concludes with a number of mini-cases and/or questions. The following section presents a model useful in analyzing the short cases, or ethical dilemmas.

Case Analysis

The nature of ethics is such that experts might disagree about the "right" or "wrong" solution to those dilemmas. Nevertheless, the quality of the solution depends on how one *analyzes* the problems. Following is an outline of one model of ethical decision making. It will not lead all decision makers to the same answer, but it will help ensure that each decision maker has considered all important elements of the problem.

Components of Ethical Decision Making

1. Identify the facts: who, what, when, where, why.
2. Identify the accounting issues, if applicable. Include a reference to official guidance related to the issues.

3. Specify the ethical issues:

   a. Identify the stakeholders and their duties/rights/claims to rights.

   b. Identify major principles, rules, norms, and values.

   c. Specify the problem (for example, conflicting rights or duties, rights versus claims, safety versus rights, and so on).

4. Specify the alternative actions and their probable consequences.

5. Compare the alternatives listed above with respect to ethical considerations:

   a. As they relate to principles, rules, norms, values.

   b. As they relate to the consequences (short run and long run).

6. Decide the best course of action and defend it.

Although the dilemmas in this text do not have one "right" answer, instructors may benefit from the author's reflection on the issues and her use of the ethical decision-making model shown above. Hence, an *Instructor's Manual* is available for instructors' use.

About the Author

Mary Beth Armstrong, a Professor of Accounting at California Polytechnic State University in San Luis Obispo, California, is a CPA. She has experience with a large international CPA firm as well as with small local CPA firms. She received her Ph.D. from the University of Southern California, where she minored in Social Ethics. Dr. Armstrong is the author of numerous articles relating to ethics in accounting and has served on the Professional Conduct Committee of the California Society of CPAs and the Professionalism and Ethics Committee of the American Accounting Association.

Contents

Preface	v
PART ONE	
ETHICAL ORIENTATION	**1**
1 Philosophical and Ethical Theories	**2**
Introduction	2
Ethical Philosophies	3
The Dilemma	3
Egoism	4
Utilitarianism	6
Act Utilitarianism	6
Rule Utilitarianism	7
Rule Deontology	8
Conclusion	9
Cases and Questions	13
Additional Readings	16
2 Developmental Psychology and Moral Maturation	**17**
Introduction	17
Lawrence Kohlberg	17
Level One	19
Stage One	19
Stage Two	19
Level Two	22
Stage Three	22
Stage Four	23
Level Three	24
Stage Five	24
Stage Six	25
Conclusion	26
Cases and Questions	26
Additional Readings	27
3 Professional Ethics	**28**
Introduction	28
Characteristics	29
Public Service	29

The Accounting Profession	30
Expertise	31
Monopoly	31
Public Service	32
Self-Regulation	33
Summary	33
An Integration	33
Questions	33
Additional Readings	35

PART TWO
THE AICPA CODE OF PROFESSIONAL CONDUCT   37

4 Principles	38
Introduction	38
Responsibilities	39
The Public Interest	40
Integrity	42
Objectivity and Independence	43
Due Care	45
Scope and Nature of Services	46
Cases and Questions	48
Additional Readings	49
5 Rules	50
Introduction	50
Rule 101 Independence	52
Interpretations of Rule 101	52
Rule 102 Integrity and Objectivity	60
Interpretations of Rule 102	60
Rule 201 General Standards	60
Interpretations of Rule 201	61
Rule 202 Compliance with Standards	61
Rule 203 Accounting Principles	61
Interpretations of Rule 203	62
Rule 301 Confidential Client Information	63
Interpretation of Rule 301	63
Rule 302 Contingent Fees	64
Interpretation of Rule 302	65
Rule 501 Acts Discreditable	66

Interpretations of Rule 501	66
Rule 502 Advertising and Other Forms of Solicitation	68
Interpretations of Rule 502	68
Rule 503 Commissions	69
Rule 505 Form of Practice and Name	69
Interpretations of Rule 505	70
Cases and Questions	70

6 Monitoring and Enforcement of the Rules — 73

Introduction	73
Peer Review	74
Quality Review	76
Joint Ethics Enforcement Program	78
Joint Trial Board	79
Conclusion	80
Cases and Questions	80
Additional Readings	81

PART THREE
ETHICS IN TAX PRACTICE, CONSULTING SERVICES, INDUSTRY AND GOVERNMENT — 83

7 Ethics in Tax Practice — 84

Introduction	84
Public Service Ideal	84
IRS View	85
Other Views	85
AICPA View	86
Summary	86
Treasury Department Circular 230	87
Duties and Restrictions	87
Penalty Provisions	91
AICPA Guidance	92
Statements on Responsibilities in Tax Practice	92
SRTP (1988 Rev.) No. 1: Tax Return Positions	92
SRTP (1988 Rev.) No. 2: Answers to Questions on Returns	94
SRTP (1988 Rev.) No. 3: Certain Procedural Aspects of Preparing Returns	95
SRTP (1988 Rev.) No. 4: Use of Estimates	96

SRTP (1988 Rev.) No. 5: Departure from a Position Previously Concluded in an Administrative Proceeding or Court Decision 97
SRTP (1988 Rev.) No. 6: Knowledge of Error: Return Preparation 99
SRTP (1988 Rev.) No. 7: Knowledge of Error: Administrative Proceedings 100
SRTP (1988 Rev.) No. 8: Form and Content of Advice to Clients 101
Conclusion 102
Cases and Questions 102
Additional Readings 104

8 Ethics in Consulting Services 106
Introduction 106
Consulting and Auditors' Independence 107
    Independence in Fact 107
    Independence in Appearance 108
Responsibilities of Profession vs. Firms 109
Statements on Standards for Consulting Services 110
Statement on Standards for Consulting Services No. 1 110
Cases and Questions 113
Additional Readings 114

9 CPAs in Industry and Government 116
Introduction 116
Management Accountants and Financial Executives 118
    Standards of Ethical Conduct for Management Accountants 119
    Code of Ethics of Financial Executives Institute 121
    Statement of Responsibilities of Internal Auditing 122
    Institute of Internal Auditors Code of Ethics 125
    Association of Government Accountants Code of Ethics 126
Foreign Corrupt Practices Act of 1977 129
Whistle-Blowing 130
Cases and Questions 131
Additional Readings 133

PART FOUR
CONGRESSIONAL AND PROFESSIONAL INVESTIGATIONS — 135

10 Investigations During the 1970s — 136
Introduction — 136
Congressman Moss — 136
Senator Metcalf — 137
    The Accounting Establishment — 137
    Final Recommendations — 139
AICPA Response — 140
    Institutional Changes — 140
    Cohen Commission Report — 141
Conclusion — 142
Questions — 143
Additional Readings — 143

11 Investigations During the 1980s — 144
Introduction — 144
Congressman Dingell — 144
Congressman Wyden — 146
Congressman Brooks — 148
Professional Responses — 149
    Changes in Professional Standards — 150
    Changes in Auditing Standards — 151
    Treadway Commission — 153
Questions — 156
Additional Readings — 157

12 Governmental Actions to Increase Competition — 158
Introduction — 158
Department of Justice — 158
Federal Trade Commission — 159
    Advertising and Solicitation — 159
    Commissions and Contingent Fees — 160
    Efferent vs. Afferent Ethics — 161
State Action Doctrine — 162
Cases and Questions — 164
Additional Readings — 165

13 Public Opinion Surveys — 166
Introduction — 166
POB Survey — 166
Harris Poll — 170
- Moral and Ethical Practice — 171
- Performance — 172
- Three Kinds of Accountants — 172
- Attributes — 172
- Challenges from the Outside — 173
- Qualifications and Preparation — 174
- Enforcement of Professional Standards — 174
- Services CPAs Ought to Offer — 175
- Commissions and Contingent Fees — 175
- Nonaudit Professional Roles — 176
- CPAs Vs. Lawyers on Tax Matters — 176
- To Whom Are Auditors Responsible? — 177

Conclusion — 178
Questions — 179
Additional Readings — 180

APPENDIX
CASE STUDY — 181

Parker Bros., An Accountancy Corp. — 181
Part One — 181
Part One Questions — 190
Part Two — 191
Part Two Questions — 194

Index — 197

PART ONE
Ethical Orientation

1
Philosophical and Ethical Theories

Introduction

Ethics is the study of morality. Ethical thought, therefore, is the process of trying to determine morally acceptable behavior. Ethicists reflect on the nature of good and evil, of right actions and wrong actions. Ethical philosophers attempt to perfect the art of moral decision making.

Certified public accountants (CPAs), like doctors and lawyers, often must make moral choices in the practice of their profession. To make those choices well, CPAs need to acquire or sharpen at least two complex intellectual skills. First they must be able to recognize ethical issues when confronted by them. That is, CPAs need to recognize the moral implications arising from situations. Their ethical consciousness needs to be heightened such that they have a highly developed "issue-spotting" ability. Second, CPAs need the ability to reason properly. If the moral situation they have perceived is a choice between an ethical option and a nonethical one, the problem is easy to solve, since the solution simply depends on the strength of the CPA's commitment to ethical principles. No complex reasoning powers are required. Often, however, the decision is not one of good versus evil. Instead, two goods or two evils present themselves to the decision maker. The CPA must isolate and evaluate competing ethical claims and values, a complex thought process requiring the following qualities: understanding of the principles involved; application of the principles to the situation at hand; analysis of competing interests of stakeholders and values inherent in the decision choices; and evaluation of the various alternatives, including the ability to predict the consequences of each choice to all stakeholders.

The purpose of this text is to help CPAs and accounting students attain increased abilities in both of the ethical proficiencies listed above. Accounting professionals need to be good issue spotters, as well as problem solvers with heightened reasoning abilities.

But where do professionals look for guidance in achieving the above skills? Traditionally, guidance has come from philosophers, since ethics, the study of morality, is a branch of philosophy.

Ethical Philosophies

Normative ethics deal with questions of "ought." For example, "What ought to be valued?" or "What ought to be considered a person's duty or obligation?" Some normative ethicists are concerned with value. They ask questions such as, "What is good?" Other normative ethicists assume that one knows what is good or bad, and they therefore theorize about what makes actions morally right or obligatory. It is these latter "theories of obligation" with which we will be concerned. Figure 1-1 shows the relationship between various ethical theories and outlines those theories of obligation that we will consider. Because this is only an introduction to the subject, not all normative theories are presented. We have limited our study to those theories most applicable to CPAs. To be able to apply each theory to concrete dilemmas faced by public accountants, an example of such a dilemma is now presented.

The Dilemma

Ed Thick was not in a happy mood. He had been under pressure to increase his marketing activities for his firm's services for some time now. Ever since he became a partner last year, his client load seemed to be contracting instead of expanding. He lost two large audit clients to mergers and was underbid on his last three attempts to secure new audit clients. Now he was facing the prospect of losing another long-time client, Benders Department Store. Benders was a local department store in a large regional mall. Although fees from the annual audit were only average for his office, Ed was aware that substantial management advisory service opportunities would soon open up for Benders because their new aggressive manager had already spoken to him concerning the possible installation of new computer systems and new

Figure 1-1. The Relationship between Various Ethical Theories.

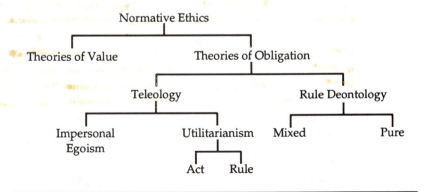

inventory control procedures. That same manager, Harvey Ball, had just stormed out of Ed's office. He was angry at Ed's characterization of an unusual transaction involving his company.

Benders was the largest lessee in its mall. The owners of the mall and Benders had amended their lease early in the year such that the owners obligated themselves to undertake extensive remodeling of the mall's exterior, a doubling of the mall's square footage, and the addition of extensive new parking areas. Benders agreed to modernize the interior of its store and to pay an increase in monthly rents. The lessor paid Benders $1,500,000 for revising the old lease, which still had 10 of its original 25 years remaining.

Harvey Ball argued that the $950,000 difference between the present value of the increased rent expense and the $1,500,000 payment already received should be treated as revenue earned this year, since Benders had substantially completed its interior remodeling and no other performance was required of it by the contract amendments. Both Ed and Harvey agreed that $950,000 is a material amount in Benders' financial statements.

Ed Thick's initial reaction was to amortize the $950,000 difference over the remaining life of the lease. Ed did not believe that revenue recognition theories should apply to this case because he characterized the payment from the lessor as a rent reduction—a decrease in expense. Therefore, the net rebate should be amortized over the life of the related lease, since it is a reduction of rent expense over the next 10 years, not just during the year of signing and receipt.

After Mr. Ball left his office, Ed admitted that this was a technical area where experts might disagree. He also admitted to himself, though, that in his heart of hearts he believed the item was an expense reduction and should be amortized over 10 years.

Egoism

The theories of egoism and utilitarianism are both subsets of teleological ethics. Teleologists assert that a given act or rule is morally right or obligatory insofar as it tends to produce some desired end, such as happiness or pleasure. Egoists contend that an act is moral when it promotes the individual's best long-term interest. Personal egoists claim that they should pursue their own best long-term interests, but they do not say what others should do. Impersonal egoists claim that everyone should follow their own long-term interests. Students of economics should recognize the theories of Adam Smith as impersonal egoism. Adam Smith contends that, in a "perfect" market situation, the pursuit of one's own long-term interests by all buyers and sellers is guided by an "invisible hand," which acts to bring about equilibrium and benefits to each individual while also benefiting society by achieving the most efficient allocation of scarce resources. This rough interpretation of the theory of Adam Smith is often what students incorporate after taking an economics class. Actually, Smith does not say what everyone "should" do, but asserts that, in fact, this is what everyone "does" do. This "fact" is disputed by many empiricists who point to such "irrational" behavior as leaving a tip in a restaurant where one does not intend to return, or voting at great personal inconvenience. Smith's assertion about the "fact" of personal behavior is no more valid than his other assertions needed to illustrate his theory (for example, perfect information, ease of market entry and exit, and so on).

Most moral philosophers do not include egoism, in either form, as valid ethical theories because they both deny the "moral point of view," which briefly states that interests often conflict and that it will be necessary, on occasion, to act against one's own interests to preserve the moral order of society. Egoism is included in this text because of the prevalence of economic theory in business schools, and because of the widespread failure to distinguish between Smith's assumptions needed to formulate his theories and actual human behavior.

Let us now attempt to apply the theory of egoism to Ed Thick's dilemma. Since Ed's long-term interest is the only factor to consider, we need not analyze the interests of other stakeholders in the decision, such as Benders, Ed's partners, Ed's family, the profession, or even users of the financial statements involved. Ed perceives that his short-term well-being depends on keeping Benders as a client. The pressure he is currently feeling to maintain (indeed, expand!) his client base as well as the contribution each audit makes to his share of the firm's profits dictates that the loss of the Benders account would be painful at present. But Ed must also consider long-term consequences. Might investors be harmed, opening the door to litigation? Might his reputation for objectivity and integrity be damaged? On the other hand, what kind of reputation would he have within the firm if he continued to lose clients? Would his career goals suffer if he achieved a reputation as a poor marketer?

Ed decided that the accounting principles involved were gray enough that experts might disagree in this case. Even though, in his heart, he believed the money received should be allocated over 10 years, he knew he could construct a convincing argument to the contrary, thus reducing the risk of damaging his reputation for objectivity and integrity to a minimal amount. He also believed the risks of litigation were minimal in this case because the nature of the $950,000 receipt would be fully disclosed in the footnotes to Benders' financial statements. Therefore, he decided to allow Benders preferred handling of the item, since to do so furthered his own short- and long-term interests the most.

Utilitarianism

Utilitarians are the precursors to modern decision scientists. The basic concept of utilitarian ethics is the idea of utility: an act is right if it produces at least as much net good as any other act that could have been performed. The right, therefore, depends on the good. We can know whether an act is morally right or wrong by determining the intrinsic goodness (or badness) of its consequences. Two classical proponents of Utilitarianism are Jeremy Bentham and John Stuart Mill.

Act Utilitarianism

Act utilitarianism is concerned specifically with how a particular act in a particular situation will maximize the good in the world. Each situation is unique and must be analyzed afresh with little or no guidance from rules or laws.

In the case of Ed Thick, the consequences of his choice must be reasoned through to their logical conclusions for *all* stakeholders. The choice that maximizes the overall good should be chosen. Ed might, for example, draw a decision tree for each stakeholder. He must carefully consider all possible courses of action, the probability of their occurrence, and he must assign values to the probable outcomes. His own decision tree might look like the one in Figure 1-2.

Ed's decision, to agree or disagree with Benders' position, leads to the possible outcomes shown in Ed's decision tree. Each outcome must be assigned a probability (shown in parentheses). The value column is very subjective. On a scale of –10 to +10, Ed must assign a value to each path of the decision tree. The values include such considerations as monetary reward (or cost) and increase (or decrease) to one's self-esteem, reputation, and so on. For example, the first path of Ed's tree asks what value he places on keeping the client if he has to agree with

Figure 1-2. Ed Thick's Decision Tree.

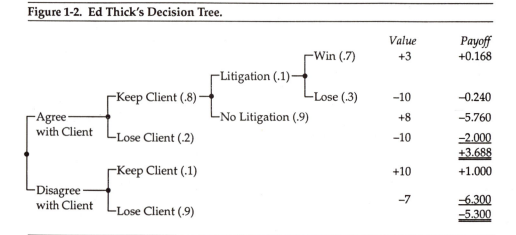

its position (contrary to his own) to do so and that decision is challenged by litigation, even though his firm ultimately wins the litigation. The payoff for each path is computed by multiplying the value times the cumulative probabilities for each path. Again using the first path for an example, the value of +3 is multiplied by .8 ¥ .1 ¥ .7 to arrive at +.168. The payoffs for each decision are then summed. Since +3.688 exceeds –5.300, Ed's choice would be to agree with his client if he were the only stakeholder. Since he is not the only stakeholder, he should construct similar decision trees for his partners, for his profession, for users of Benders financial statements, and even for Benders itself. The value column can change drastically for different stakeholders, thereby causing the payoff column to also change. Since all stakeholders might not have an equal stake in the outcome, each stakeholders' payoff could be weighted to indicate relative importance of that stakeholder. Finally, all of the payoffs for "agree" would be summed and contrasted to all of the payoffs for "disagree."

In practice, act utilitarians seldom construct formal decision trees. Nevertheless, they do intuitively include values, probabilities, and the roles of other stakeholders in their decision analyses. The tree is just a formal tool for organizing all of these very important considerations.

Rule Utilitarianism

Rule utilitarians theorize that one could specify all the alternative rules to guide various courses of action open to a decision context and then calculate the probable consequences of each choice. When the calculations are completed, the results are compared for all possible rules and that rule is chosen that maximizes intrinsic value and minimizes intrinsic disvalue. Choice of any other rule in a given situation would be morally wrong.

Utilitarians further argue that no limitation on human freedom is justified unless it serves a good purpose (that is, maximizes utility). If a society is to have rules that require people to refrain from doing what they might want to do, there must be some consequence thereby brought about whose goodness outweighs the intrinsic badness of the restrictions themselves. This calculus concept is the underlying justification for laws or codes by which societies or groups regulate themselves. Since the laws or codes are justified only if they maximize society's welfare, and since moral actions are those that maximize society's welfare, to obey society's laws or codes is to act morally. Obeying laws or codes is morally right not because of the intrinsic goodness of obedience, but because the consequence of obedience is the maximization of society's well-being. Thus, when a society such as the American Institute of CPAs (AICPA) promulgates a code of ethics for its members, it is explicitly stating the rules which, it believes, will result in more utility to both the members and society at large than any other set of rules.

Hence, if Ed Thick is a rule utilitarian, he need not construct his own decision trees since the AICPA has already decided what rules will maximize all stakeholders' utility.[1] Ed need only apply the rules to his particular problem situation. Ed need not be unduly concerned with Rule 101 of the AICPA Code of Professional Conduct because that rule pertains to independence, or relationships. Neither Ed nor members of his family own stock in Benders, he does not sit on its Board of Directors, and so on. Ed believes that he, his firm, and his family have no relationships with Benders that might impair independence in fact or in appearance.

However, Rule 102, "Integrity and Objectivity," is more to the point. It states that "in the performance of any professional service, a member shall maintain objectivity and integrity, shall be free of conflicts of interest, and shall not knowingly misrepresent facts or subordinate his or her judgment to others." Deep in his inner self, Ed believes that Benders should amortize the $950,000 over 10 years. To agree to do otherwise would be to subordinate his judgment to others. He would therefore choose to stand firm.

Rule Deontology

Advocates of deontology, such as Sir David Ross and Immanual Kant, hold that the rightness of an act (and our duty to perform it) is either *not entirely* determined by the intrinsic value of its consequences (mixed deontology) or *not at all* determined by such value (pure deontology). The basic principle is that the right (what we ought to do) does not entirely depend on the good (what we judge to be intrinsically valuable), and this principle contradicts the basic principle of teleological ethics.

Rule deontologists believe that morality is a function of rules dictated by one's sense of duty. Particular acts, to be moral, must conform to a particular moral rule or set of rules. In this sense, rule deontology is similar to rule utilitarianism. In both cases, it is a rule or set of rules that defines what moral behavior is. These philosophies differ, however, in two aspects: First, they differ in the extent to which consequences are allowed an impact on moral determination. Pure deontologists would not consider the consequences at all, while mixed deontologists would allow consequences to impact the decision making somewhat, but would deny that they are the only relevant consideration. Second, the rules of deontologists are usually broad, universal principles, while the rules of utilitarians are often detailed prescriptions.

---

[1] See Chapters Four and Five for a discussion of the AICPA Code of Professional Conduct.

In the case of the AICPA Code of Professional Conduct, both general principles and detailed rules are presented. If Ed Thick is a rule deontologist he will look to the Code's general principles for a source of guidance. There he will find six articles outlining the essence of professional responsibility for CPAs. He will reflect upon his responsibility to the users of Benders' financial statements. Although he has responsibilities to his client, to his partners, and to other possible stakeholders, Ed's responsibility to the public is paramount. The public's continued reliance on companies' financial statements, and hence the market's ability to efficiently allocate scarce financial resources, is predicated upon trust in the accounting profession. Ed owes it to the public to maintain his integrity and objectivity. Even though honest, objective professionals might disagree about how Benders' $950,000 net rebate should be reported, integrity demands that Ed, after thorough research, consultation with other professionals, and careful evaluation of all opinions, facts, and circumstances, must make the decision without subordinating it to others. If he is a pure rule deontologist, Ed's choice is clear: He must stand firm in his decision to require amortization of the rebate over 10 years. If, however, he is a mixed rule deontologist, Ed must perform the steps outlined above to achieve his *tentative* decision. He would then allow himself to consider other aspects of the problem. For example, he might ask, "What harm might befall stakeholders, especially the public, if I subordinate my judgment in this gray area where room exists for honest disagreement?" He might conclude that, in this case, there is little likelihood of harm to stakeholders since the complete nature of the transaction in question would be disclosed in the footnotes to the financial statements. On the other hand, he might conclude that great harm would result to himself and his family if he does not give in to his client. Therefore, his conclusion, as a mixed rule deontologist, could be as follows: "Normally I should not subordinate my judgment to others. But in this particular case, because the technical issue is so gray and because little harm could result from a flexible stance, I will therefore agree to Benders' preferred method of reporting the item." However, he would only allow the impact of consequences to change his deontological decision if he believed the harm to Benders, his firm, and himself would be great, while the harm to users of the financial statements would be minor.

Conclusion

Depending on one's ethical theory, a CPA might reach very different conclusions when presented with a dilemma such as Ed Thick's. Logically, then, the student of professional ethics might ask, "Which theory is best?" Unfortunately, a definitive answer cannot be found among ethical philosophers, since each ethical theory has advocates claiming that *it* has the best method for arriving at moral truth. Yet other moral philosophers advocate their own brand of mixing the above theories (for example, the ethical decision-making model in the Preface to this text). Professor Norm Bowie, a professor of Business Ethics at the University of Minnesota, asserts that "accountants are deontologists in a utilitarian world." By that he means that the *role* of the accountant is to examine principles such as truth telling, revenue recognition, matching, conservatism, and so on in a world where management is concerned with the bottom line and the consequences of various reporting alternatives. In the next chapter we shall expand our inquiry to include the psychology of moral development in an attempt to identify additional ways of reasoning through moral dilemmas.

In the Preface to this text a model of ethical decision making was presented. By now, students should recognize the deontological and utilitarian components of that model. In this section we will apply the model to the Ed Thick dilemma.

1. Identify the facts: An auditor disagrees with a client about classification of a significant transaction. This is not a clear-cut accounting issue; CPAs could disagree. The auditor needs the client because of recent losses to the auditor's client base and because this audit client may soon have additional consulting business for the auditor's firm. The client is adamant about how this transaction should be recorded.

2 Identify the accounting issues: Is the receipt of a lease rebate a revenue item or a reduction of expense? The rebate was received as consideration for terminating the old lease prematurely and entering into a new lease with higher rents. If the net rebate is a revenue item, all revenue recognition elements are met (performance is complete, a market exchange has taken place, collection is complete) and the entire net rebate should be recognized immediately (*SFAC* 5). If the net rebate is an expense reduction, the matching concept would require its amortization over the remainder of the lease term, since the rebate represents a reduction of rents over the entire life of the lease (*SFAC* 5 and 6).

3. Specify the ethical issues:

   a. Identify the stakeholders and their duties/rights/claims to rights.

      (1) Users of financial statements: Users need information that is "presented fairly" if they are to rely on that information in the market place to optimally allocate society's scarce financial resources. (Right = "fair" information.)

(2) The client: Because the manager is so adamant and angry, he must believe that Benders will benefit by having the rebate reported as revenue, in its entirety, in the current year. (Claim = right to any choice among GAAP.)

(3) The firm: The firm must be protected against loss of reputation or possible legal liability, but also needs a larger client base and increased revenues. (Duty = objective, independent audit; claim = prosperity.)

(4) The CPA (and family): Ed Thick must maintain his personal integrity, but also needs to please his partners in order to prosper in the firm and provide well for his family. (Duties = audit with independence, objectivity, integrity; loyalty to firm; provide for family: rights = to be treated fairly by firm and client.)

b. Identify the major principles, rules, norms, and values. Rule 102 (AICPA *Code of Professional Conduct*) requires the CPA to maintain integrity and objectivity, defined as "... not knowingly misrepresent facts or subordinate his or her judgment to others." Thus, CPAs are expected to use their professional judgments in difficult cases, not just look to written technical rules or the opinions of others.

Duty to client may not require satisfying all of the clients' desires, especially if those desires conflict with other duties.

Duty to firm and family is complex. Their short-run needs may conflict with their long-run needs. For example, enhancing revenues in the short run, by appeasing the client, may lead to long-run reductions in revenue, due to litigation and loss of reputation.

The claims of the client and firm may or may not be valid rights. For example, does a client have a "right" to report items as he or she wishes if GAAP does not specifically prohibit that re porting?

The principle of the public interest (AICPA *Code of Professional Conduct*, Article II) states that members who encounter conflicting responsibilities should resolve the conflict with integrity, "guided by the precept that when members fulfill their responsibility to the public, clients' and employers' interests are best served."

c. Specify the problem. The auditor's primary duty is to those who use the financial statements, but he or she also has a duty to the client, to his or her firm and to his or her family. The auditor's duty to those who use the financial statements requires independence, integrity, and objectivity while auditing the client's financial statements. These principles do not allow a CPA to subordinate his or her judgment to others. The duty to the client requires the CPA to aid the client in achieving its long-term best interest. The duty to the firm requires the CPA to be diligent in upholding the firm's reputation and protecting it from legal liability while at the same time increasing its client base and revenues. The duty to family includes providing for their well-being. These duties appear to conflict in this case.

The client seems to be asserting a claim to a right to report items however he or she wishes so long as the letter of GAAP is not violated. Since the lease rebate is not specified within GAAP precisely as a revenue item nor as an expense item, the client claims the right to choose. This claim is in conflict with the right of users of the financial statements to receive information that is fairly presented and not misleading.

4 Specify the alternative actions and their consequences. Figure 1-2 identifies Ed Thick's choices.

5 Compare the alternatives with respect to ethical considerations;

   a. As they relate to principles, rules, norms, and values. Ed Thick's primary duty to the public and his duty to remain objective and act with integrity require him to disagree with the client's preferred accounting treatment. These duties outweigh his duties to enhance short-term profits for his firm and do not necessarily impede his long-term ability to provide for his family.

   The client's claim to the right to choose accounting treatments if not specifically prohibited by GAAP may be valid. However, it does not change the auditor's duty to exercise professional judgment when he reports his opinion of the "fairness" of the resulting financial statements. Thus, examination of the principles, rules, norms, and values would lead to the conclusion that Ed Thick should continue to disagree with his client and insist on the client recording the item as an expense reduction or, if the client refuses, reflecting the disagreement through the audit opinion process.

   b. As they relate to the consequences. Figure 1.2 seems to indicate that Ed Thick should agree with his client because the payoff is higher. However, keep in mind that Figure 1.2 represents only *one* decision tree, Ed Thick's, and thus takes into account only Ed's value system. If similar decision trees were constructed for the other stakeholders, the payoffs may change drastically. For example, users of the financial statements would have a different set of branches on Ed Thick's decision tree, with different value columns and different payoffs, as shown in Figure 1-3.

From the users' point of view, the payoff column clearly shows that Ed Thick should not agree with his client. If all the stakeholders' decision trees were constructed, weight would have to be given to each payoff column. Egoists, for example, would weight Ed's payoff "+1.0" and everyone else's "0." Utilitarians would weight each stakeholder equally. Mixed deontologists would probably give more weight to the users' payoff, since auditors owe their primary duty to that group.

Unless Ed Thick is an egoist, examination of alternatives and consequences would probably lead him to the same decision as above, to continue to disagree with the management of Benders.

6 Decide the best course of action and defend it. Although the author is tempted to give her own opinion at this point, she will refrain from doing so to allow the student to come to her or his own decision.

Cases and Questions

1. Maureen Turner's day was not going well. She had always been a good student in college and was used to positive feedback concerning her work. Now, six months after graduating and beginning her career in public accounting, she had received her third evaluation from the seniors in charge of the audits on

Figure 1-3. Ed Thick's Decision Tree with Users's Value Set.

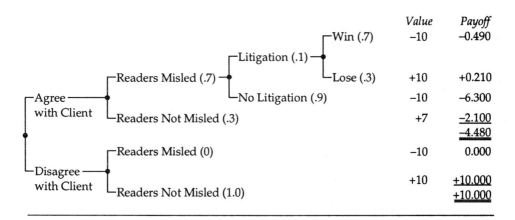

which she worked as a staff accountant. All three reviews praised her work but criticized the excessive time it took her to do it. Maureen had been trying hard to decrease the time she spent on each audit step, and was therefore discouraged to hear the same complaint from her third evaluator. To make matters worse, Maureen had just learned that Jim Lyon was to be the senior on her next audit assignment. Jim had a reputation among the staff accountants as being the hardest senior to please. His time budgets were very tight and he had an aggressive personality. He let everyone know when he was displeased, and Maureen feared that she would certainly be unable to meet his demanding expectations. She wanted very much to succeed at this firm, and now she was wondering if she could. She was also wondering about something another staff member had told her. That staff person, it seems, sometimes felt the need to take work home and not report the extra hours of time spent on it. Should Maureen take work home and donate some of her time for her next audit tasks, while omitting to count those extra hours? She was sure it would make Jim Lyon happier and result in a better work evaluation for herself.

a. If Maureen is a personal egoist, what course of action is she likely to take? An impersonal egoist?

b. Draw a simple decision tree for Maureen, assuming she is an act utilitarian. Assign probabilities and values to your decision tree. Which path has the highest payoff?

c. What other stakeholders are involved in Maureen's decision? How are they likely to view the consequences of her decision?

d. If Maureen is a rule utilitarian, she is likely to look to promulgated rules as a source of guidance. Where might she look to find rules covering her situation? If you were a rule maker for Maureen's firm, what rules would you make, if any, to guide staff members in Maureen's situation? Why?

e. If Maureen is a pure rule deontologist her thinking is likely to be governed by general principles. What principles should Maureen consider?

f. If Maureen is a mixed-rule deontologist, she will consider the principles named in Answer e, as well as the possible consequences of her available actions. Describe Maureen's thought processes if she is a mixed-rule deontologist.

g. What would you do in Maureen's situation?

2. Jack Tomlinson remembers when he finally found the woman of his dreams. He and Jill, then a medical intern on her way to becoming a Pediatrician, seemed to have so much in common. On the day he proposed marriage to her they had a heart-to-heart talk about all sorts of things and had come to a mutual under standing about most of them. Although Jill's career was extremely important to her, as Jack's was to him, they had both pledged to "put family first." "On my death bed," Jill joked, "I doubt that I will regret that I didn't spend more time at the office."

   Now Jack had recently received his CPA certificate and was mid-way through his third year at the CPA firm he joined after completing his MBA degree. Jill was having more success at keeping her pledge than was Jack. He felt torn between his career, which he really loved, and his family. He wanted to spend more time at home, but out-of-town assignments and an expanding workload at the office, coupled with several tight deadlines in a row, seemed to make it impossible. He felt compelled to work into the evening most weekdays, and to work at least one-half a day on Saturdays (more often it was the whole day). When he did have time to spend at home, he seemed drained of energy.

   What started Jack reminiscing was a brief conversation he had with a colleague, Bill Zumberg. Jack had asked Bill how his new daughter was getting along. "Fine, I think," Bill had replied, "But to tell you the truth, I haven't seen her for the last five days. When I go to work in the morning she is still sleeping, and by the time I get home late in the evening she has already been put to bed."

   Jack and Jill were recently discussing the fact that this was a good time in her career to begin planning their family. Jack wanted a baby, but also wanted to be an active parent in caring for and nurturing the child. He didn't know how he could balance the demands at work with his desire to spend more time with his family.

   a. Use the model of ethical decision making found in the Preface to analyze Jack's dilemma.

3. Geri was horror stricken! She had just spent several days performing a detailed review of cash for the Savings & Loan they were auditing. The S & L was going public, so her firm was auditing three years, not just one. This S & L must have had a kazillion checking accounts and because she was the newest staff auditor, Geri was assigned the detail work on cash. This morning she awoke from a nightmare in which she dreamed

she was in the S & L's vault and stacks of checks, filed from floor to ceiling, were tumbling down upon her and burying her alive. Now, as she was about to sign off on an audit step, she realized that she had not performed the step exactly as it was written. She was supposed to draw a random sample of checks from each account for each year and examine the cancelled checks while comparing their details to the cash payment journals. As she reread the step, before signing off, she realized that she had not examined the cancellation dates on the checks. She had examined the rest of the data: date, payee, amount, authorized signature, and endorsement. But she had forgotten about the cancellation date! She was already 15 percent over her assigned time budget, and she had already refiled all the checks. It would take hours for her to relocate them all and reexamine them for their cancellation dates. Her senior on the job had already yelled at her once for "blowing time" and she dared not risk spending much more time on this step. "Perhaps," she thought to herself, "I could just reexamine a few of those checks and then sign off."

   a. Use the model of ethical decision making found in the Preface to analyze Geri's dilemma.

Additional Readings

Bentham, J. "An Introduction to the Principles of Morals and Legislation." In *The Works of Jeremy Bentham*, J. Bowsing, ed., vol. 1. New York: Russell & Russell, 1979.

Kant, I. *The Fundamental Principles of the Metaphysics of Ethics*. New York: D. Appleton-Century Company, Inc., 1938.

Kant, I. *The Moral Law*. New York: Barnes & Noble, Inc., 1967.

Mill, J. S. (1965). "Mill's Journey." In *Mill's Ethical Writings*, J. B. Schneewind, ed., New York: Collier, 1965.

Ross, Sir W. D. *Foundations of Ethics*. Oxford: Clarendon Press, 1968.

Ross, Sir W. D. *The Right and the Good*. Oxford: Clarendon Press, 1965.

Smith, Adam. *The Wealth of Nations*. London: George Routledge & Sons, Ltd. 1913.

2
Developmental Psychology and Moral Maturation

Introduction

Philosophy is not the only discipline that examines moral decision making. During the twentieth century developmental psychologists have also studied the topic. Contrasting the two disciplines leads to a surprising, yet interesting, conclusion. Intuitively, one might assume that questions such as the one at the end of the last chapter regarding which philosophy is best would be answered by philosophers. Psychologists, however, would be expected to describe behavior, but not to delve into questions of value, such as naming a "better" philosophy. But what we find is just the opposite. At the end of the last chapter we saw that the study of moral philosophy alone is not sufficient to guide our moral decision making, as alternative, conflicting modes of thought are presented to us. Developmental psychologists, on the other hand, contend that individuals pass through levels and stages in their moral maturation process. Later stages are more advanced, or mature, than earlier stages and are therefore to be preferred. In short, more mature stages are better than less mature stages. Thus, by studying the work of developmental psychologists we can learn alternate methods of structuring moral thinking as well as which structures are best.

We will study Lawrence Kohlberg, a developmental psychologist, who works with adolescents and adults. However, the reader is encouraged also to read the works of Jean Piaget, who was the pioneer in studies of moral development, of James Rest, whose objective test in moral development has been utilized by hundreds of researchers, and of Carol Gilligan, whose research into women's moral reasoning adds another dimension to Kohlberg's work.

Lawrence Kohlberg

Before describing Kohlberg's stages of moral development, a few preliminary remarks are in order. First, a distinction must be made between the content and form of moral decision making. It is the maturation of the latter, the structures of reasoning, with which Kohlberg is concerned, not the content of his subjects' responses. For example, one might decide not to murder one's mother-in-law for several reasons, such as the following: "I might be caught and punished," "it is against the law," "human life is precious and all people have a right to its preservation." In each case the decision content is the same ("I should not murder my mother-in-law"), but the cognitive framework utilized to come to the decision is different.

Kohlberg's research methodology centered around story telling. His stories contained moral dilemmas. His most widely-quoted story was his Heinz dilemma, and it is reproduced here for illustrative purposes:

> In Europe, a woman is near death from a special kind of cancer. There is one drug that the doctors think might save her. It is a form of radium that a druggist in the same town has recently discovered. The drug is expensive to make, but the druggist is charging ten times what the drug cost him to make. He paid $200 for the radium and is charging $2000 for a small dose of the drug. The sick woman's husband, Heinz, goes to everyone he knows to borrow the money, but he can get together only about $1000, which is half of what it costs. He tells the druggist that his wife is dying and asks him to sell the drug cheaper or let him pay later. The druggist says, "No, I discovered the drug and I'm going to make money from it." Heinz is desperate and considers breaking into the man's store to steal the drug for his wife.

After reading the story to a subject, Kohlberg's researchers then asked a series of questions such as the following:

1. Should Heinz steal the drug?
2. If Heinz doesn't love his wife, should he steal the drug for her?
3. Suppose the person dying is not his wife but a stranger. Should Heinz steal the drug for a stranger?
4. (If you favor stealing the drug for a stranger): Suppose it's a pet animal he loves. Should Heinz steal to save the pet animal?
5. Is it important for people to do everything they can to save another's life?
6. It is against the law for Heinz to steal. Does that make it morally wrong?
7. Should people try to do everything they can to obey the law?
8. How does this apply to what Heinz should do?

The first question above was designed to elicit the respondent's initial thoughts on the subject. But the following questions, designed to probe his thinking further, were of primary interest to Kohlberg. They were designed to elicit the respondent's reasons for choosing one value over another. It was this reasoning process that Kohlberg categorized into levels and stages. Table 2-1 sets forth the three levels and six stages of moral reasoning developed by Kohlberg.

Level One

The three levels of moral maturity represent three possible perspectives that a person might use to relate to society's norms. The first, or preconventional level, has a focus on the self. That is, right and wrong, good actions and bad actions, are judged by their effect on the decision maker. If another's perspective is considered at all, it is only insofar as it impacts on the self's needs as well (for example, if reciprocity is involved).

Stage One
Stage one is a very primitive, childish stage. Most children grow out of it by preadolescence. The expressed wishes or orders of authority figures become laws for the child and if he breaks these laws he believes that punishment is sure and swift. Thus, the physical consequences of actions determine whether they are good or bad. Avoiding punishment and deference to power (because punishment is sure and swift for transgressions) are valued in their own right. Thus, stage one respondents would not steal the drug, in the Heinz example, because they fear the punishment which would surely follow.

Ed Thick It is difficult to apply stage one reasoning to Ed Thick's dilemma (presented in Chapter One) because the primitive nature of this stage makes it dysfunctional even among preadolescents. Therefore, we have to stretch our imagination a bit. Ed Thick's focus would be on the AICPA's Code of Professional Conduct and/or any rules promulgated by his state's Board of Accountancy. Ed knows that violation of the rules can lead to expulsion from the AICPA and perhaps even loss of his CPA license. There are no gray areas. Violators, if they are caught, are always punished. No mitigating circumstances exist. Ed also knows that one of the rules prohibits subordination of his judgment to his client. Therefore, Ed's decision really boils down to his estimate of the probability of getting caught. If he thinks the probability is low, he will give in to his client's wishes and reap the resulting benefits. If he thinks it is high, he will refuse to allow the client's preferred treatment of the rebate received, even though the consequences are painful, in order to avoid the more painful punishment meted out by the AICPA and his state's Board of Accountancy.

Stage Two
At stage two level of reasoning, the person still focuses on self-interest, but also recognizes that others also have needs and interests.

Table 2-1. The Six Stages of Moral Judgment

Level and Stage	Content of Stage		Social Perspective of Stage
	What Is Right	*Reasons for Doing Right*	
Level 1: Preconventional			
Stage 1: Heteronomous morality.	Sticking to rules backed by punishment; obedience for its own sake; avoiding physical damage to persons and property.	Avoidance of punishment; superior power of authorities.	**Egocentric point of view.** Doesn't consider the interests of others or recognize that they differ from the actor's; doesn't relate two points of view. Actions considered physically rather than in terms of psychological interests of others. Confusion of authority's perspective with one's own.
Stage 2: Individualism, instrumental purpose and exchange.	Following rules only when in one's immediate interest; acting to meet one's own interests and needs and letting others do the same. Right is also what is fair or what is an equal exchange, deal, agreement.	To serve one's own needs or interests in a world where one has to recognize that other people also have interests.	**Concrete individualistic perspective.** Aware that everybody has interests to pursue and that these can conflict; right is relative (in the concrete individualistic sense).
Level 2: Conventional			
Stage 3: Mutual interpersonal expectations, relationships, and interpersonal conformity.	Living up to what is expected by people close to you or what people generally expect of a good son, brother, friend, etc. "Being good" is important and means having good motives, showing concern for others. Being good also means keeping mutual relationships such as trust, loyalty, respect and gratitude.	The need to be a good person in your own eyes and those of others; caring for others; belief in the Golden Rule; desire to maintain rules and authority that support stereotypical good behavior.	**Perspective of the individual in relationships with other individuals.** Aware of shared feelings, agreements, and expectations that take primacy over individual interests. Relates points of view through the concrete Golden Rule, putting oneself in the other guy's shoes. Does not yet consider generalized system perspective.

Stage 4: Social system and conscience	Fulfilling duties to which you have agreed; laws to be upheld except in extreme cases where they conflict with other fixed social duties. Right is also contributing to the society, group, or institution.	To keep the institution going as a whole and avoid a breakdown in the system "if everyone did it"; imperative of conscience to meet one's defined obligations. (Easily confused with stage 3 belief in rules and authority.)	**Differentiates societal point of view from interpersonal agreement or motives.** Takes the point of view of the system that defines roles and rules; considers individual relations in terms of place in the system.
Level 3: **Postconventional or Principled** **Stage 5:** Social contract or utility and individual rights.	Being aware that people hold a variety of values and opinions and that most of their values and rules are relative to their group. Relative rules usually upheld in the interest of impartiality and because they are the social contract. Some nonrelative values and rights (e.g., life and liberty) must be upheld in any society and regardless of majority opinion.	A sense of obligation to law because of one's social contract to make and abide by laws for the welfare of all and for the protection of all people's rights. A feeling of contractual commitment, freely entered upon, to family, friendship, trust, and work obligations. Concern that laws and duties be based on rational calculation of overall utility, "the greatest good for the greatest number."	**Prior-to-society perspective.** Rational individual aware of values and rights prior to social attachments and contracts. Integrates perspectives by formal mechanisms of agreement, contract, objective impartiality, and due process. Considers moral and legal points of view; recognizes that they sometimes conflict and finds it difficult to integrate them.
Stage 6: Universal ethical principles	Following self-chosen ethical principles. Particular laws or social agreements usually valid because they rest on such principles; when laws violate these principles, one acts in accordance with principle. Principles are universal principles of justice: equality of human rights and respect for the dignity of human beings as individuals.	The belief as a rational person in the validity of universal moral principles and a sense of personal commitment to them.	**Perspective of a moral point of view from which social arrangements derive.** Perspective is that of a rational individual recognizing the nature of morality or the fact that persons are ends in themselves and must be treated as such.

Source: Lawrence Kohlberg. "Moral Stages and Moralization: The Cognitive-Developmental Approach." In *Moral Development and Behavior: Theory, Research and Social Issues*, Thomas Lickona, ed. (New York: Holt, Rinehart and Winston, 1976), 34–35.

Thus, the notion of fairness is first introduced. Another concept also makes its first appearance, that of extenuating circumstances. Rules can be broken, such as rules against stealing, if fairness seems to so dictate, as in the Heinz story. But a person at level two who concludes that stealing the drug is all right would do so at a concrete, not abstract, level. His reasoning might be as follows: "the druggist is causing me great harm because of his greed and because I love my wife and want to keep her. The druggist is not being fair. If I steal the drug the judge will not punish me because she or he will understand why I stole it. To save my wife's life is a good enough reason."

Ed Thick At stage two, Ed is less concerned with obedience to authority than he was at stage one. His guiding light is still self-interest, but his fear of punishment does not predominate his thinking. He would likely reason through the situation as follows, "If I don't do what Benders Department Store wants, they will cause me great harm. Why shouldn't I do it their way? Who is it hurting? Not Benders, not me, not even users of the financial statements, since classifying the item as revenue is a judgment call and some informed experts would probably report it that way anyway."

Level Two

At level two, the conventional level, focus shifts from the self to the group and its rules. The decision maker realizes that the group, or society, expects individuals to act in accordance with its moral norms. Thus, the person strives not only to avoid punishment, but to live up to the expectations of the group—in a positive way.

Stage Three

At stage three the decision maker is concerned with the views of significant others toward herself. The motivation for moral action becomes living up to whatever those others expect of her as a member of their group. Since the individual is aware that people in her group have expectations toward her, she is also aware of interpersonal relationships and the commitments they require. Where fairness was a dominant concept at stage two, trust and living up to one's commitments is the dominant concept at stage three. The relationships and commitments at this stage are among individuals. The decision maker has not yet expanded the notion to include the concept of systems and interrelations between groups. Where stage two respondents often agreed that Heinz had a right to steal the drug, they never saw it as his duty. Stage three respondents, on the other hand, believe that Heinz has a duty toward his wife because of his relationship with her. Whether or not that duty includes stealing the drug, respondents at stage three disagree.

Ed Thick At stage three, Ed Thick struggles to understand what significant others expect him to do in this situation. He knows what Benders expects—to report the item their way. But what would his partners expect him to do? What does his family expect from him? If Ed's firm has been consistently rewarding behavior entirely on its economic outcome while ignoring the development of professional attitudes among its members, then Ed has undoubtedly internalized the message that his firm wants whatever enhances the bottom line. Ed's decision then becomes an assessment of risks and financial payoffs. He will choose whatever pays the highest. If, however, Ed's firm has developed an *esprit de corps* among its partners where a sense of professionalism dominates and individuals are somehow rewarded for taking tough stands, then he will have received an entirely different message from his partners and will make his choice accordingly.

Stage Four

At stage four decision makers again look to external sources to define right from wrong. However, those sources are not confined to the significant others in one's immediate groups. Rather, the system as a whole is considered. How will one's actions affect the moral order of society? Law emerges for stage four decision makers as the central value that fairness was at stage two and trust was at stage three. Law is not primary for its own sake, but because the decision maker appreciates that societies can function smoothly only in the presence of certain agreements, many of which are codified into law. Thus, to break the law is to threaten the cohesion of the whole social system. Not all stage four decision makers believe that society's laws are inviolable. When they conflict with a higher set of laws (for example, the Ten Commandments, the teachings of Marx) the higher laws, as perceived by the decision maker, must take precedence.

Ed Thick Ed is a member of the AICPA. Accordingly, he has agreed to abide by their rules, which, he believes, in the long run benefit the profession, its members, and society as a whole. For guidance in his particular dilemma, Ed turns to the AICPA Code of Professional Conduct. There he encounters Rule 102, "Integrity and Objectivity." There Ed reads that CPAs must not subordinate their judgment to others. "After all," he reasons, "what would happen if all CPAs caved in to their clients when disagreements arose?" He knows that the profession's role in society would collapse. The public would no longer be served if financial statement attestors are not objective. Ed's decision is clear. The rule is too important and too central to the core of his profession to break. It is a good rule. He will stand firm with Benders Department Store and insist that the rebate be amortized over 10 years, or he will not render an unqualified opinion on their financial statements.

Level Three

Level three, the postconventional level, is a quantum leap from level two. The primary focus shifts away from the group and back to the individual. However, it does not shift back to a selfish or self-centered focus, as at level one. Rather the focus is on one's inner principles. One can look beyond the norms and laws of society and ask, "What are the principles upon which a good society should be based?" For example, in the Heinz dilemma, the perspective of a person at the postconventional level could be illustrated by the question, "Which should take precedence in a society—protection of property rights or protection of the right to life"?

Stage Five

Stage five reasoning is never reached by a number of people. Stage four usually emerges as a major stage only after age 18 or later. It remains adequate as long as one's society does a good job of preserving basic human rights with its set of norms and laws. However, if a person lives in a society in which the legal system denies some people their basic human rights, should that person try to preserve the unjust social order? Stage four respondents usually argue for working within the system to bring about needed change. But if the system itself is unjust, they may be forced to ascend to a new, higher level of reasoning. Stage five is rarely attained before a person reaches the mid-20s. Its central concept (similar to fairness, trust, and laws in earlier stages) is the principle of a social contract. It attempts to define where social obligations cease and individual rights dominate. Outside of democratically determined (just) laws, the right is a matter of personal values and opinions.

At stage five a person might ponder the Heinz dilemma as follows: "Societies should distribute scarce drugs in a fair and just manner. Heinz's society failed to do that, so he is under no obligation to obey the unjust distributive laws. Whether or not Heinz has a duty to steal for his wife is questionable. Some relationships are close enough that such a duty can be construed (for example, in the case of a marriage relationship). Certainly, however, Heinz would not have such a duty outside of a close relationship (for example, for a stranger)."

Ed Thick Ed begins his thought processes by reflecting on the different roles he is playing and the duties associated with each. His dilemma boils down to two contracts which seem to conflict with each other. As a CPA he has contracted with society to examine Benders' financial statements as an impartial, independent, objective expert and to attest to their fairness. To uphold his end of this contract will undoubtedly bring him harm in this case, and he has accepted the risk of that harm when he contracted with society to take on his particular role. Being fired by irate clients is simply part of the role. His other contract, however, is with his partners. This one makes him mad. While they give lip service to professionalism, the reward structure of his firm is such that client losses, even though justified, result in personal losses to individual partners. Ed perceives the expectations of his partners to be unjust. He refuses to be guided in this case by the pressures they put on him to expand his client base.

Stage Six

At stage six "right" is defined by the decision of conscience in accord with self-chosen ethical principles. The principles are abstract (not concrete rules) and center around justice and human dignity. In the case of Heinz, the stage six decision maker sees a duty to steal the drug in order to preserve the life of any human being, not just one in close relationship. Kohlberg argues that a decision maker must take certain steps in arriving at his or her decision:[1]

1. to imagine oneself in each person's position in that situation (including the self) and to consider all the claims he could make (or which the self could make in his position),

2. then to imagine that the individual does not know which person he is in the situation and to ask whether he would still uphold that claim,

3. then to act in accordance with these reversible claims in the situation.

Applying the above steps to the Heinz dilemma, we can imagine the druggist attempting to put himself in the wife's position and still maintain his claim to property rights. We can also imagine the wife putting herself in the druggist's position and still maintain her claim to the right to live. Intuitively, we feel the wife could maintain her claims, the druggist could not. The essence of the second step above is to imagine yourself about to draw straws for a role in a play. If you pull the long straw you are the druggist. If you pull the short straw you are the wife. Before you draw the straws, are you equally convinced of the "rightness" of each party's claim? Can you believe the part you are to play equally well, regardless of the straw you draw? Intuitively, one knows that the wife's claim is more believable. Thus, our actions must conform to our beliefs. We must act to uphold the wife's claims.

Ed Thick Ed knows that Harvey Ball, Benders' manager, is determined to recognize the net rebate received as income in the current

---

[1] Kohlberg, L. "The Claim to Moral Adequacy of a Higher Stage of Moral Judgment." *Journal of Philosophy* 40, (1973): 641–45.

year because he wants to enhance reported earnings for the year. Mr. Ball doesn't really care about the accounting principles involved. If the item were an expense to Benders, the man would be arguing just as adamantly to spread the item over the next 10 years. Thus, when Ed puts himself in Mr. Ball's shoes, his claim becomes something like the following: "I have a right to do whatever I have to do to report earnings as high as possible." His claim is one of self-interest only.

When Ed puts Mr. Ball in his (Ed's) shoes, he sees that Ed's claim is honestly based on the accounting issues involved. Ed is sincerely attempting to evaluate the net receipt in terms of generally accepted accounting principles, from the point of view of an impartial third party. His self-interest is served in agreeing with Benders, not in disagreeing. In fact, the disagreement comes with potentially great sacrifices. Ed's position is honestly the more believable of the two and he should act accordingly.

Conclusion

Even though developmental psychology appears to give more guidance in selecting "better" modes of thinking through ethical dilemmas than the field of philosophy, the reader should not conclude that philosophy is inadequate. Quite the contrary. Several developmental psychologists have reported studies in which they gave pre- and post-tests of moral reasoning to certain college classes. That is, they administered the test before the course began and again at its conclusion. Neutral subjects, such as mathematics, resulted in no significant changes in the pre- and post-test results. However, classes in philosophical ethical studies, as well as classes in moral development (psychology) resulted in significant improvement in moral reasoning test scores. Studying philosophical ethical reasoning helps one to mature in moral development.

The reader may have been aware of certain commonalities in the thinking processes described in Chapters One and Two. Indeed, they are not discrete categories. More will be said of the relationships between the philosophical and psychological categories at the end of Chapter Three.

Cases and Questions

1. Refer to Maureen Turner's case (Question One) at the end of Chapter One to answer a–d.

    a. Where will Maureen look for guidance if she is at level one of Kohlberg's model of moral development? Level two? Level three? (Be specific.)

b. According to Kohlberg's model, describe Maureen's reasoning process at each stage of moral development.

c. What is the likely choice Maureen will make at each stage?

d. Compare Maureen's choices at each stage with her choices as an egoist, utilitarian, and rule deontologist. Do you detect areas of similarity or overlap? Describe them.

2. Refer to Jack Tomlinson's case (Question Two) at the end of Chapter One to answer a–c.

a. Describe Jack's reasoning process at each stage of moral development.

b. What is his likely decision at each stage?

c. Compare those decisions with his decisions as an egoist, utilitarian, and rule deontologist. Are there any similarities or areas of overlap?

3. Refer to Geri's dilemma (Question Three) at the end of Chapter One to answer a–c.

a. Describe Geri's reasoning process at each stage of moral development.

b. What is her likely decision at each stage?

c. Compare those decisions with her decisions as an egoist, utilitarian, and rule deontologist. Are there any similarities or areas of overlap?

Additional Readings

Gilligan, C. "In a Different Voice: Women's Conceptions of Self and of Morality." *Harvard Educational Review* 47, (November 1977): 481–517.

Kohlberg, L. "Moral Stages and Moralization." In *Moral Development and Behavior*, T. Lickona, ed. New York: Holt, Rinehart, and Winston, 1976.

Rest, J. R. *Development in Judging Moral Issues.* Minneapolis: University of Minnesota Press, 1977.

Rest, J. R. *Moral Development Advances in Research and Theory.* New York: Praeger Publishers, 1986.

3
Professional Ethics

Introduction

The purpose of the first two chapters was to introduce the reader to philosophical and psychological theories of moral reasoning. A student of professional ethics needs such theories in order to reason properly and to appreciate the complexity of various ethical thought processes. Before examining ethical principles and rules in the accounting profession, it is necessary to consult one other discipline—sociology. Sociologists can help us understand the nature of professions and why ethical codes are at the heart of each profession.

Originally, the word "professional" meant "one who had professed," that is, one who had taken the vows of a religious order. By the seventeenth century, "profession" came to mean the occupation which one professed to be skilled in and the term was applied specifically to the three learned professions of divinity, law, and medicine. Today the term is used to refer to a vast number of occupations and no generally accepted definition of the term exists. Nevertheless, sociologists do distinguish between two types of professions, scholarly and consulting, and they also list characteristics of each type.

Scholarly professions, such as teaching and scientific research, usually are characterized by a large number of clients at the same time (teaching) or no personal clients (research). Thus, they do not have the same type of interaction with clients found in the consulting professions, such as physicians, lawyers, accountants, architects, and so on. It is this latter group, consulting professionals, to which the remainder of this book refers when it uses the terms "profession" and/or "professional."

Some sociologists employ a checklist approach to determine whether or not a particular occupation is a profession. The checklist can have as many as 15 characteristics. Other sociologists disagree concerning the necessity of all the items on the checklist. Usually, however, agreement can be found on at least 4 basic factors common to all consulting professions: expertise, monopoly, public service, and self-regulation.

Characteristics

Expertise implies special knowledge. Professionals acquire their special knowledge through extensive training. That training involves a significant intellectual component, as opposed to the physical training received by hair dressers or bricklayers. On-the-job training and experience enhance the expertise, but it is nonetheless grounded in its theoretical, academic nature. Thus, providing advice rather than things is often a characteristic of a professional.

Monopoly is achieved through certification. Because practice of the profession requires special knowledge, society enacts laws to restrict the practice to those so certified. But knowledge is power. Power and monopoly in the hands of a few can cause harm to the many. Therefore, in exchange for their monopoly, professions promise to use their expertise to benefit society.

Public service, or the promise by the profession to benefit society, is at the heart of all professions. It is usually embodied in a code of ethics. For example, in medicine the Hippocratic Oath is the service ideal around which the claim to professional status revolves.

Self-regulation is granted to the profession by society because of the intellectual training and judgment required for practice. Hence, society deems itself less capable of evaluating the conduct of professionals than the profession itself. It therefore grants the profession the privilege and duty to regulate its membership and conditions of practice, as well as to monitor and control the actions of its members.

To summarize: professionals are engaged in an exchange, or two-way street, with society. On the one hand, the profession offers expertise that benefits society and promises to regulate its own members. Society, on the other hand, offers monopoly to the profession and voluntarily limits its powers of public regulation in favor of self-regulation. These relationships are illustrated in Figure 3-1, and they point to an important concept: Legal monopoly and self-regulation are privileges granted by society. They are not rights to sound claims. These privileges are society's "permission" to perform certain acts if and only if specified conditions are fulfilled. With a privilege, the burden is on the group obtaining it to demonstrate that the conditions, in this case expertise, public service, and self-regulation, are being fulfilled.

Public Service

The concept of public service needs a closer look. The profession promises to use its expertise to benefit, not harm, society. A code of ethics is often the profession's way of expressing its public service ideal. However, codes of ethics also serve other functions as well. One needs to distinguish between efferent and afferent ethics. The former deals with

Figure 3-1. Characteristics of a Profession.

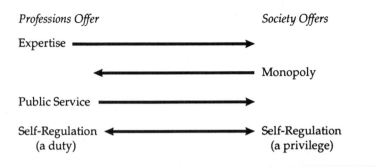

relationships between professionals and their clients or the general public. The latter promotes harmony within the profession by addressing relationships among the professionals themselves. An example of the latter is a rule prohibiting advertising. While some professionals have attempted to link afferent ethics to the public good, that link is questionable. Afferent ethics are, at best, etiquette, and, at worst, a restriction of free competition. For this reason, during the 1970s and 1980s the Federal Trade Commission pursued a policy of changing those professional codes of ethics which it deemed to be in restraint of trade and free competition. More will be said about this topic in Chapter Twelve.

It is efferent ethics that are at the heart of professionalism. Every profession must have a public service ideal which is expressed in, but not identical to, its written code of ethics. Written codes usually set forth obligations of the profession and its members. Those obligations can be expressed either as principles or rules. Principles state responsibilities and may be balanced or weighed against one another. Rules state duties that prescribe and proscribe specific conduct and do not allow for much discretion. More will be said about the AICPA Code of Professional Conduct in Part Two of this book.

The Accounting Profession

Now that we have examined the characteristics of professions in general, it is time to see how well they apply to the field of accounting. CPAs engage in a number of activities. Some work in industry for private enterprises as management accountants or internal auditors. Others work for governmental agencies or not-for-profit enterprises such as hospitals. CPAs in public accounting firms perform a variety of functions, primarily auditing (or the attest function), rendering tax advice and preparation, and offering management advisory services.

Another group of CPAs, academicians, will not be examined in the next sections, because their functions of teaching and research differ significantly from those of the other CPAs mentioned. Academia is classified as a scholarly, as opposed to a consulting, profession. In the next sections we will apply the characteristics of a profession to CPAs in industry, government, and public practice.

Expertise

The functions performed by *all* CPAs require expertise. The knowledge base, or foundation, is achieved at the baccalaureate level and includes course material covering accounting theory, authoritative pronouncements, and the functional areas of auditing, tax accounting, management accounting, and accounting for not-for-profit organizations. Advanced degrees are sometimes obtained by CPAs wishing to specialize in certain functional areas, for example, taxation or information systems. The academic foundation is enhanced by on-the-job training and professional staff training offered chiefly by CPA firms. In addition, continuing professional education is required by most state boards of accountancy for renewal of CPAs' licenses.

Monopoly

CPAs are licensed to practice public accounting by each state's board of accountancy. The licensing requirements differ from state to state, but most states require that a candidate pass all parts of the Uniform CPA Examination, have some experience (most often two years) working in public accounting under the supervision of another licensed CPA, and pass a written examination in professional ethics. Some states also require that the experience in public accounting contain a significant number of hours in auditing work.

Only the auditing, or attest, function requires licensing as a CPA. Non-CPAs can and do perform accounting services in industry and government, prepare tax returns, and offer consulting services to industry. Non-CPAs may *not* attest to the fairness of published financial statements.[1]

Practice before the Internal Revenue Service requires licensing as a CPA, an attorney, an enrolled agent, or enrolled actuary. Hence, that functional area, often performed by CPAs, also requires licensing, but is not restricted to the CPA license. This function will be discussed further in Chapter Seven.

It is clear that society regards the attest function as an extremely important function—important enough to grant a monopoly to those expert enough to perform it. Society does not regard the other func-

---

[1] A few states, called "title states" allow non-CPAs to perform audits.

tions CPAs perform as unique enough to grant monopoly status. This is not to say that the nonattest functions are not important, or even that they are not related to the expertise required of accountants. They are. For example, corporations often rely on the firm that audits their financial statements to advise them on tax matters and matters relating to their information systems *because* they are the auditors and have more knowledge of their company and its needs than any other CPA firm. Nevertheless, auditing services remain central to the concept of professionalism, while other services performed by CPAs are ancillary or secondary. Society does not deem it necessary to grant monopolies for the performance of those other services.

In recent years the primacy of the attest function, in terms of hours spent by CPAs and percentage of firms' revenues, has decreased dramatically relative to other services performed by CPA firms. As a result, society has begun to question the appropriateness of those other services when combined with the attest function. Part Four of this book looks at this issue in more detail.

Public Service

The public service ideal of the accounting profession is closely related to its monopoly. Since ours is a capitalistic society, we have chosen to allocate scarce resources via a free market system. In a socialistic system, central planning is utilized to allocate scarce resources. Debt and equity financing are scarce resources. Financial markets have been established in order to help allocate scarce financial resources. But free markets cannot function without information, and the quality of the information enhances or impedes the efficient working of markets. Thus, high quality financial information is required for the efficient allocation of scarce financial resources in a free market economy. The CPA profession benefits society as a whole when it aids in enhancing the quality of financial information. Therefore, it is again the attest function that benefits society. When auditors attest to the fairness of corporate financial statements, they enhance the believability, and hence the usefulness, of one primary source of financial information used by financial markets.

Other functions performed by CPAs also benefit society. For example, our tax system is so complex that without expertise the tax burden would be borne in unintended and unjust ways. That is, the tax burden would be borne more heavily by uninformed taxpayers than by informed taxpayers, and degree of information is an unjust measure for allocating society's tax burden. Nevertheless, society has not deemed it necessary to limit the selling of tax expertise to licensed CPAs, or to any particular group. Preparation of tax returns and giving tax advice does not generally require a license, only practicing before the IRS, and that privilege is extended to several separate licensee groups.

Self-Regulation

Self-regulation is both a privilege and a duty. Although state boards of accountancy issue CPA licenses, they are usually small bodies within state governmental units and do not have the resources to monitor and regulate the profession by themselves. Therefore, they have created alliances with state societies of CPAs, which are voluntary, fraternal organizations. It is the state societies, in conjunction with the AICPA (another voluntary, fraternal organization), that conduct organized programs of monitoring and rule enforcement. Chapter Six explores the issue of self-regulation further. In that chapter we will see that monitoring of CPAs is confined to those in public practice, and that the attest function is monitored more heavily than others.

Summary

Some CPAs are in public practice and others are not. Those in public practice perform a variety of functions. Nevertheless, only the attest function of CPAs in public practice enjoys the privilege of monopoly. Society recognizes that expertise is required by all CPAs, and that functions other than auditing benefit society, but only the attest function is really unique to CPAs. It is at the heart of the profession, and must be preserved above all other functions. Self-regulation, important for all functions performed by CPAs, is chiefly concerned with monitoring attest services.

An Integration

Chapter One discussed several ethical theories from the discipline of philosophy. Chapter Two reviewed the stages of moral development according to psychologists. Chapter Three has discussed the characteristics of professions as described by sociologists. These three disciplines touch concepts that are overlapping and important to the study of professional ethics. Although some of the concepts overlap, they are not necessarily identical. Rather, the concepts in one discipline relate to similar concepts in another discipline. The interrelationships among the disciplines studied in the first three chapters are depicted as overlapping areas in Figure 3-2.

Questions

1. Joe Marini is an enrolled agent. He performs bookkeeping services for clients, compiles some financial statements, gives tax advice, prepares tax returns, and sometimes represents clients before the IRS. Is Joe a "professional"? Why or why not?

Figure 3-2. Integration of Three Disciplines.

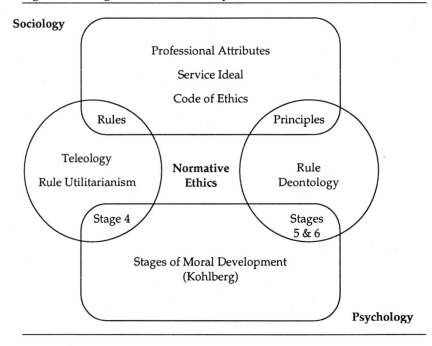

2. Marian Webster is a CPA and the controller for a Fortune 500 corporation. Is Marian a "professional"? Why or why not?

3. Michael Jordan is a professional basketball player. Describe the attributes that make him a "professional."

4. What is the difference between a "duty" and a "privilege"? Why is self-regulation both a duty and a privilege?

5. In 1985–1986, Price Waterhouse issued a White Paper, which suggested that a self-regulatory organization (SRO), similar to that used by the National Association of Security Dealers, be adopted by the accounting profession. The SRO would include mandatory participation by all CPA firms, credible disciplinary action, and direct public participation in the governing process. Several members of Congress have also suggested recently that the accounting profession should be regulated more strictly by the SEC than is now the case. If public regulation increases and self-regulation decreases, will CPAs still be professionals?

6. Some observers believe that the public service ideal of the accounting profession is its attestation to the fairness of financial information. Others believe that all services offered by CPAs, including tax advice and preparation, consulting, and so on,

constitute the profession's service ideal. What do you believe? Why?

Additional Readings

Bayles, M. D. *Professional Ethics*. Belmont, California: Wadsworth, 1981.

Buckley, J. W. "An Exploration of Professional Identity." In *Ethics in the Accounting Profession*, S. E. Loeb, ed. Santa Barbara: John Wiley & Sons, 1978.

PART TWO
The AICPA Code of Professional Conduct

4
Principles

Introduction

Chapters One, Two, and Three serve as an introduction to, or overview of, the philosophical, psychological, and sociological theories relating to professional ethics. Each discipline focuses on the need for and the importance of formal codes of conduct. Rule utilitarianism and rule deontology are both centered on the role of laws in moral decision making. Stages three, four, and even, to a limited degree, five of moral development focus on the rules of the group or of the larger society. And sociologists agree that professional ethics are at the core of each profession's reason for existence.

Because of the importance placed on codes of ethics for professionals, all CPAs need to be familiar with the codes promulgated by their states' Board of Accountancy and Society of CPAs. Those codes are often patterned after the Code of Professional Conduct of the AICPA. Hence, this text will discuss only the latter. The Code of Professional Conduct of the AICPA is divided into two sections: Principles and Rules. This chapter examines the Principles and Chapter Five discusses the Rules.

Recall from Chapters One and Two that rule deontologists and individuals at stages five and six of moral development organize their reasoning processes around broad principles, rather than detailed rules or proscriptions. The rules are the codification of the principles and should flow logically from them. For example, the Commandments, "Thou shalt not kill," "Thou shalt not steal," and so on, flow logically from the general principle, "Love thy neighbor as thyself." Thus, the Principles provide the framework for the Rules, which govern the performance of professional service by members of the Institute. CPAs who truly understand and internalize the Principles of the Code should find the Rules to be logical extensions of the Principles.

The Code lists six Articles (Principles), reproduced here[1] with permission of the AICPA, and discussed in the following sections of this chapter:

---

[1] Copyright © 1988 by American Institute of Certified Public Accountants, Inc. Reprinted by permission.

Responsibilities

The Public Interest

Integrity

Objectivity and Independence

Due Care

Scope and Nature of Services

Responsibilities

In carrying out their responsibilities as professionals, members should exercise sensitive professional and moral judgments in all their activities.

As professionals, certified public accountants perform an essential role in society. Consistent with that role, members of the American Institute of Certified Public Accountants have responsibilities to all those who use their professional services. Members also have a continuing responsibility to cooperate with each other to improve the art of accounting, maintain the public's confidence, and carry out the profession's special responsibilities for self-governance. The collective efforts of all members are required to maintain and enhance the traditions of the profession.

Article I of the Code stresses the importance of a sense of responsibility to users of CPAs' services, to other CPAs, and to the profession. Parents strive for years to teach their children to be responsible individuals. The word "responsible," according to Webster, means "accountable," or "trustworthy." It has its roots in the verb "to respond." Thus, a responsible individual sees needs and responds, or acts, to fulfill those needs. A responsible individual perceives the expectations of others, or of society, and responds to fulfill those expectations. A responsible person does not have to be told what to do or how to do it, but is self-motivated and responds to each situation in an appropriate manner, according to his or her perceptions and beliefs. A responsible citizen does more than refrain from breaking the laws. A responsible citizen keeps informed, votes, and works to improve society—in a positive manner. A lawful person will not litter; a responsible person will pick up and appropriately discard someone else's litter. The AICPA, first and foremost, wants its members to internalize a sense of responsibility toward users of CPAs' services and toward the profession itself.

Statisticians have developed a statistical tool, called multidimensional scaling, often used by marketing researchers, to uncover hidden relationships in data. The data are usually comparisons. For example, consumers are asked to compare several automobiles, two at a time, and rate them in terms of their similarity. The ratings are analyzed and the marketing researchers might conclude that the underlying constructs used by the consumers to rate the automobiles were "sportiness" and "luxury." Thus, in their advertising campaigns, marketers know what features to stress for best results.

Several years ago this author used multidimensional scaling on CPAs' ratings of ethical dilemmas encountered in public practice. The same CPAs took a test of moral maturity, patterned after Kohlberg's theory of moral development. Those CPAs who scored highest in terms of moral development were considered as a group. The other CPAs were considered the control group. The construct used by the control group of CPAs to rate the ethical dilemmas was the AICPA Code of Ethics. That is, the control group simply identified which dilemmas dealt with independence, with confidentiality, and so on. The CPAs who had scored high on the moral development test, however, used a sense of responsibility as their underlying construct. They categorized the dilemmas in terms of responsibility to the public, or to clients, or to colleagues. Thus, the research indicated that the CPAs who were the most advanced in moral maturity, according to Kohlberg's theory, had internalized a strong sense of responsibility.

The above research took place in 1984. The AICPA Code of Ethics at that time did not include "responsibility" as one of its Principles. In 1986, the Anderson Committee, which proposed extensive changes in professional standards, proposed that the first Principle be that of responsibility. The change was made effective January 12, 1988, when the Code of Conduct was revised. Chapter Eleven discusses other changes in professional standards that were adopted at the same time as a result of work by the Anderson Committee.

The Public Interest

Members should accept the obligation to act in a way that will serve the public interest, honor the public trust, and demonstrate commitment to professionalism.

A distinguishing mark of a profession is acceptance of its responsibility to the public. The accounting profession's public consists of clients, credit grantors, governments, employers, investors, the business and financial community, and others who rely on the objectivity and integrity of certified public accountants to maintain the orderly functioning of commerce. This reliance imposes a public interest responsibility on certified public accountants. The public interest is defined as the collective well-being of the community of people and institutions the profession serves.

In discharging their professional responsibilities, members may encounter conflicting pressures from among each of those groups. In resolving those conflicts, members should act with integrity, guided by the precept that when members fulfill their responsibility to the public, clients' and employers' interests are best served.

Those who rely on certified public accountants expect them to discharge their responsibilities with integrity, objectivity, due professional care, and a genuine interest in serving the public. They are expected to provide quality services, enter into fee arrangements, and offer a range of services—all in a manner that demonstrates a level of professionalism consistent with these Principles of the Code of Professional Conduct.

All who accept membership in the American Institute of Certified Public Accountants commit themselves to honor the public trust. In return for the faith that the public reposes in them, members should seek continually to demonstrate their dedication to professional excellence.

Chapter Three emphasized the importance of a public service ideal for all professions. Society will not grant monopoly and self-regulation to any group unless that group promises to benefit society. The "Public Interest" Principle was added to the AICPA Code on January 12, 1988, along with the other revisions in professional standards. The previous code acknowledged a responsibility to the public, but did not acknowledge its primacy. That is, the previous code discussed CPAs' responsibilities to the public, to clients, and to colleagues, but did not state, as an underlying principle, how to resolve conflicts among those responsibilities. The Code of Professional Conduct now explicitly states that such conflicts are to be resolved in favor of the public.

The United States Supreme Court voiced the same sentiments in *United States v. Arthur Young & Co.* when it stated that "the independent accountant has a public responsibility transcending any employment relationship with the client."[2] The court further stated that the accountants' responsibilities require him or her to "maintain total independence from the client at all times and complete fidelity to the public at large."[3]

The accounting profession does not stand alone in its attempt to reconcile conflicts between specific recipients of service and the general public. Physicians, psychiatrists and psychologists, and the clergy all recognize the importance of trust in their relationships with their clients. Nevertheless, confidentiality within those professions has limits. The limiting factors all have to do with protecting the public or individuals from harm. Thus, they are required to go public ("blow the whistle") in the case of a real threat of severe injury or death to others. In essence, the good of public trust can be outweighed by the good of preventing severe harm. For example, if an airline pilot were to complain of spells of dizziness and blacking-out to his physician, but refused to report these problems to his employer out of fear of losing his

---

[2] Saltzman, M. I. "The Arthur Young Decision and What it Means to Accountants." *The Practical Accountant* 17, (July 1984): 38.

[3] Ibid.

job, the physician would by required to report the medical problems in order to save future airline passengers from harm.

A very controversial topic within the accounting profession centers around the actions auditors should take when they discover irregularities and/or they disagree with their clients' accounting methods. Should they simply inform top management and the audit committees, and then resign the engagement if the items are not resolved to their satisfaction? Or should they inform regulatory authorities, such as the SEC? Traditionally, CPAs have been reluctant to resort to the latter, but public sentiment appears to be strongly in favor of such reporting. Lee Burton, a financial reporter for the *Wall Street Journal* and a former editor of the *Journal of Accountancy*, stated in 1984,

> U.S. accountants might have a bit more credibility with the public if they were more willing to discuss why they quit an auditing engagement. I do not consider such forthrightness as "kiss-and-tell" professionalism. For the life of me I do not know of any profession more qualified to enlighten the public in the mysteries and intricacies of business than the accounting profession. You hold the keys, but I think you worry that you may unleash a Pandora's Box of problems.
>
> But if you were willing to blow the whistle more, it might not be necessary to do it that often. The vast majority of American business people are ethical and, aware of your stiffer backbone, public companies might be more willing to tell it like it is. Increased independence on the part of the outside auditor would feed that ethical bent.[4]

Integrity

To maintain and broaden public confidence, members should perform all professional responsibilities with the highest sense of integrity.

Integrity is an element of character fundamental to professional recognition. It is the quality from which the public trust derives and the benchmark against which a member must ultimately test all decisions.

Integrity requires a member to be, among other things, honest and candid within the constraints of client confidentiality. Service and the public trust should not be subordinated to personal gain and advantage. Integrity can accommodate the inadvertent error and the honest difference of opinion; it cannot accommodate deceit or subordination of principle.

Integrity is measured in terms of what is right and just. In the absence of specific rules, standards, or guidance, or in the face of

---

[4] Burton, Lee. "Ethics—A Financial Journalist's Perspective." Proceedings of the Conference *Ethics in the Accounting Profession*, University of Southern California, (May 1984): 24.

conflicting opinions, a member should test decisions and deeds by asking: "Am I doing what a person of integrity would do? Have I retained my integrity?" Integrity requires a member to observe both the form and the spirit of technical and ethical standards; circumvention of those standards constitutes subordination of judgment.

Integrity also requires a member to observe the principles of objectivity and independence and of due care.

Integrity, a character trait, relates to honesty and uprightness. The root of the word, "integer," refers to wholeness. Thus, a person of integrity is a person of wholeness. Such a person looks beyond the letter of the law to its underlying spirit. To seek out loopholes and to adhere to the letter of law, while ignoring its spirit, violates the wholeness principle.

The accounting principle of substance over form is an example of professional integrity. CPAs are not limited to the legal form of a lease contract, for example, but analyze and record leases according to their underlying economic reality. The whole contract is examined, not just its form. Honesty requires that certain leases be recorded as if a sale/purchase has taken place because the economic reality is that the lease contract is a financing arrangement.

CPAs must apply the same honest, wholeness approach to the analysis of all technical issues and to ethical issues as well.

Objectivity and Independence

A member should maintain objectivity and be free of conflicts of interest in discharging professional responsibilities. A member in public practice should be independent in fact and appearance when providing auditing and other attestation services.

Objectivity is a state of mind, a quality that lends value to a member's services. It is a distinguishing feature of the profession. The principle of objectivity imposes the obligation to be impartial, intellectually honest, and free of conflicts of interest. Independence precludes relationships that may appear to impair a member's objectivity in rendering attestation services.

Members often serve multiple interests in many different capacities and must demonstrate their objectivity in varying circumstances. Members in public practice render attest, tax, and management advisory services. Other members prepare financial statements in the employment of others, perform internal auditing services, and serve in financial and management capacities in industry, education, and government. They also educate and train those who aspire to admission into the profession. Regardless of service or capacity, members should protect the integrity of their work, maintain objectivity, and avoid any subordination of their judgment.

For a member in public practice, the maintenance of objectivity and independence requires a continuing assessment of client relationships and public responsibility. Such a member who provides auditing and other attestation services should be independent in fact and appearance. In providing all other services, a member should maintain objectivity and avoid conflicts of interest.

Although members not in public practice cannot maintain the appearance of independence, they nevertheless have the responsibility to maintain objectivity in rendering professional services. Members employed by others to prepare financial statements or to perform auditing, tax, or consulting services are charged with the same responsibility for objectivity as members in public practice and must be scrupulous in their application of generally accepted accounting principles and candid in all their dealings with members in public practice.

Objectivity is a state of mind. An objective person is unbiased, open minded, and maintains an impartial attitude. Impartiality, or objectivity, is a key quality for judges. Since CPAs render judgment on the fairness of financial statements, it is absolutely essential for auditors to maintain their objectivity. But CPAs perform other functions, in addition to attestation, which require judgment. Tax practitioners; management consultants; and CPAs in industry, government, and education all make judgments relating to the art of accounting. If those CPAs are not objective, the fruit of their work is as tainted as the "guilty" or "innocent" judgments of biased courtroom judges.

Integrity and objectivity are both inner qualities. Essential as they are, their presence or absence is difficult to assess. Independence, on the other hand, refers to relationships. Independence has traditionally been defined by the profession as the ability to act with integrity and objectivity. That is, would a reasonable person, having knowledge of all the facts and taking into consideration normal strength of character and normal behavior under the circumstances, conclude that a specified relationship between a CPA and a client poses an unacceptable threat to the CPA's integrity or objectivity? For example, would a reasonable person believe in the integrity and objectivity of an auditor who owns 50 percent of the stock of a company she or he audits? If the answer is no, then the CPA is not independent, regardless of her or his honesty or impartiality. Thus, auditors must maintain the appearance of independence, as well as the inner qualities of integrity and objectivity.

Independence, in fact and in appearance, is required of CPAs who perform attestation services. Nonattestation engagements by CPAs in public practice, and all services by CPAs not in public practice, require integrity and objectivity, but not independence.

CPAs cannot avoid external pressures on their integrity and objectivity in the course of their professional work, but they are expected to resist these pressures. They must retain their integrity and objectivity in all phases of their practice and, when expressing opinions on financial statements, avoid involvement in situations that would impair the credibility of their independence in the minds of reasonable people familiar with the facts.

Due Care

A member should observe the profession's technical and ethical standards, strive continually to improve competence and the quality of services, and discharge professional responsibility to the best of the member's ability.

The quest for excellence is the essence of due care. Due care requires a member to discharge professional responsibilities with competence and diligence. It imposes the obligation to perform professional services to the best of a member's ability with concern for the best interest of those for whom the services are performed and consistent with the profession's responsibility to the public.

Competence is derived from a synthesis of education and experience. It begins with a mastery of the common body of knowledge required for designation as a certified public accountant. The maintenance of competence requires a commitment to learning and professional improvement that must continue throughout a member's professional life. It is a member's individual responsibility. In all engagements and in all responsibilities, each member should undertake to achieve a level of competence that will assure that the quality of the member's services meets the high level of professionalism required by these Principles.

Competence represents the attainment and maintenance of a level of understanding and knowledge that enables a member to render services with facility and acumen. It also establishes the limitations of a member's capabilities by dictating that consultation or referral may be required when a professional engagement exceeds the personal competence of a member or a member's firm. Each member is responsible for assessing his or her own competence—of evaluating whether education, experience, and judgment are adequate for the responsibility to be assumed.

Members should be diligent in discharging responsibilities to clients, employers, and the public. Diligence imposes the responsibility to render services promptly and carefully, to be thorough, and to observe applicable technical and ethical standards.

Due care requires a member to plan and supervise adequately any professional activity for which he or she is responsible.

Chapter Three pointed out that one of the characteristics of a profession is expertise. Society is willing to offer monopoly and self-regulation to professionals because of their expertise (and public service ideal and their agreement to regulate themselves). The principle of due care simply acknowledges that CPAs have a duty and responsibility to attain and maintain professional expertise or competence. Rule 201 (discussed further in Chapter Five) attempts to provide further guidance by enumerating four standards relating to professional expertise:

Professional Competence. Undertake only those professional services that the member or the member's firm can reasonably expect to be completed with professional competence.

Due Professional Care. Exercise due professional care in the performance of professional services.

Planning and Supervision. Adequately plan and supervise the performance of professional services.

Sufficient Relevant Data. Obtain sufficient relevant data to afford a reasonable basis for conclusions or recommendations in relation to any professional services performed.

Because the duty to provide expertise is a lifelong obligation, CPAs cannot consider their education complete when they have passed the CPA exam. The duty to maintain competence is just as important as acquiring enough proficiency to pass the exam in the first place. To ensure that CPAs maintain their expertise, the AICPA and most states require continuing professional education to renew membership and/or certification, and they also have established programs to monitor competence. Chapter 6 will discuss practice monitoring in more detail.

Scope and Nature of Services

A member in public practice should observe the Principles of the Code of Professional Conduct in determining the scope and nature of services to be provided.

The public interest aspect of certified public accountants' services requires that such services be consistent with acceptable professional behavior for certified public accountants. Integrity requires that service and the public trust not be subordinated to personal gain and advantage. Objectivity and independence require that members be free from conflicts of interest in discharging professional responsibilities. Due care requires that services be provided with competence and diligence.

Each of these Principles should be considered by members in determining whether or not to provide specific services in individual circumstances. In some instances, they may represent an overall constraint on the nonaudit services that might be offered to a specific client. No hard-and-fast rules can be developed to help members reach these judgments, but they must be satisfied that they are meeting the spirit of the Principles in this regard.

In order to accomplish this, members should

1. Practice in firms that have in place internal quality-control procedures to ensure that services are competently delivered and adequately supervised.
2. Determine, in their individual judgments, whether the scope and nature of other services provided to an audit client would

create a conflict of interest in the performance of the audit function for that client.
3. Assess, in their individual judgments, whether an activity is consistent with their role as professionals (for example, Is such activity a reasonable extension or variation of existing services offered by the member or others in the profession?).

Recall from Chapter Three that monopoly status has been granted to the profession because of its attestation function. Non-CPAs can provide tax and management consulting services. Non-CPAs cannot serve as independent, outside auditors. Not too many years ago fees from auditing services comprised the vast majority of large CPA firms' total revenues. Other services were clearly secondary, or ancillary, and were usually closely related to information systems or tax matters. During the 1970s and 1980s, however, the nature of professional services rendered by CPA firms changed dramatically. Tax and consulting rapidly lost their character as ancillary services as revenues from these services increased and revenues from auditing services decreased. The result has caused alarm for many, within and without the profession, who believe that the profession may lose the special status conferred upon it by law and public opinion. The original Anderson Committee report made the following observations (p. 43):

> Many observers are concerned ... that the long-term consequences for the profession of uncontrolled expansion of services will be a diminished faith in the auditor's independence. This issue cannot be left to the marketplace alone for resolution.
> Public concerns about the independence of the CPA must be a paramount concern for the profession, and the issues arising from the growth of nonattest services must be dealt with. If they are not, demands could arise for drastic actions, such as divestiture of the nonattest functions or loss of licensing. The profession must act before such a situation comes to pass.

To date, no specific rules have been promulgated by the profession to help control the expansion of nonattest services, especially for audit clients. Before 1988 the subject was not addressed in the AICPA's Code of Ethics at all. The inclusion of Article VI (Scope and Nature of Services) in the Principles section of the 1988 revision serves as a warning and a reminder that every CPA needs to be aware that a potential problem exists and every CPA has a responsibility to examine his or her own firm's activities in this area and come to some conclusion regarding their appropriateness.

Expansion of nonattest services is one of the most controversial topics in public accounting today. It is examined more thoroughly in Chapter Eight. Chapters Ten and Eleven examine Congressional and professional investigations of the problem, and Chapter Thirteen summarizes public opinion relating to the issue.

Cases and Questions

1. The CPA firm of Able, Baker, and Charlie are currently engaged in the examination of the financial statements of Toxigas, Inc., a large manufacturer of industrial chemicals. During their examination the auditors learn that Toxigas has been paying another company, Waste Management Co., to remove their toxic wastes. The auditors do not audit the financial statements of Waste Management Co., but the auditors become aware, by listening to Toxigas employees, that Waste Management Co. has been illegally dumping their toxic waste into a nearby river. The river is a source of irrigation water for many nearby farming communities, and a source of drinking water for a few small towns several miles down river.

   The auditors bring the matter to the attention of Toxigas management, who seems unconcerned. "We have not broken any laws," they responded. "If Waste Management has broken some laws, that is their concern, not ours."

   a. What philosophical ethical theory (or theories) is Toxigas' management utilizing? What level of moral maturity is indicated by their response? Explain your answers.

   b. What response are the auditors likely to make if they act as utilitarians? Mixed rule deontologists? Explain your answers.

   c. What guidance, if any, does the Principles section of the AICPA Code of Professional Conduct give to the auditors if they are deontologists? What guidance does it give to them if they are at stage four of moral maturity? Stage five? What other sources of guidance might a stage five auditor seek?

2. Art Freemont is a partner in a large, local CPA firm. One of his audit clients, Dixie Co., recently inquired if Art's firm could assist in the design of new systems and software for their company. The project is expected to take 18 months and Art's firm would earn considerably more than the amount of the annual audit fee. Art is aware that three of his firm's consulting personnel have some expertise in systems and software design, but not much expertise in Dixie Co.'s industry. Art believes, however, that the audit personnel could instruct the consulting personnel concerning peculiarities of the industry. Still, Art has two nagging concerns: Does his firm's consulting staff have enough expertise to handle the job; and would the consulting engagement impair the firm's independence in fact or in appearance?

   a. If Art is a pure rule deontologist, where is he likely to seek guidance (in addition to the AICPA Code of Professional Conduct)? What guidance will the Principles section of the Code give him? Suppose Art's partners are all rule utilitarians. What is their response likely to be? What will Art do? What would you do? Why?

    b. If Art is at stage five of moral development, what is a likely reasoning process for him? Suppose his partners are at stage four. What are they likely to conclude? Will there be conflicts? If so, how might they be resolved?

3. Phil Mendez, an audit supervisor with a large, regional CPA firm, was performing detail audit work for one of the firm's clients, Belco Chemical, just prior to the company's year-end audit. Phil suspected his client would be experiencing trouble this year, as the economy in general was in a slump and Belco's industry was one of the hardest hit. As Phil reviewed the company's interim financial statements, he realized that Belco's problems were even worse than he suspected. "The stockholders are not going to be happy with this year's results," Phil mused, "I wonder if the controller has suggested any accounting changes to the rest of the management team to soften the bad news."

    Phil considered talking to the controller himself. "If they converted their 10 LIFO pools to a couple of hundred LIFO puddles," he thought, "they could easily cause some LIFO liquidations, which would produce income and enhance the income statement without having to show the gains as a change in accounting principle. I'm sure there are a few other tricks I could show them as well."

    a. What guidance does the Principles section of the AICPA *Code of Professional Conduct* give to Phil?

    b. How will Phil likely respond to the guidance if he is an impersonal egoist? A rule utilitarian? A rule deontologist?

    c. How is Phil likely to respond to the guidance if he is at stage three of moral development? Stage four? Stage five?

Additional Readings

American Institute of Certified Public Accountants. *Restructuring Professional Standards to Achieve Professional Excellence in a Changing Environment.* New York: AICPA, 1986.

Anderson, G. D. "Fresh Look at Standards of Professional Conduct." *Journal of Accountancy* 160, (September 1985): 91–106.

5
Rules

Introduction

Rules of Conduct and Interpretations of the Rules are covered in this chapter. Two other forms of guidance, Ethics Rulings and the "Ethics Feature" section of the *Journal of Accountancy* also exist, and should be used as a reference source for practitioners who need additional guidance. The Ethics Rulings are formal rulings by the AICPA Professional Ethics Division Executive Committee after exposure to state societies and others for comments. These Rulings, in question-and-answer format, summarize the application of the Rules of Conduct and Interpretations to a particular set of facts and circumstances. The "Ethics Feature" section of the Journal of Accountancy consists of Ethics Division staff responses to inquiries from members. They follow the same format as Ethics Rulings, but have not been exposed to state societies for comment and are not formal rulings by the Executive Committee. Their status in ethics investigations is unclear. On the one hand, they do not appear to be official pronouncements. On the other hand, one would suspect that members who depart from these staff answers in similar circumstances would be requested to justify such departures.

The Rules of the Code of Professional Conduct,[1] reprinted herein with permission of the AICPA, are as follows:

Rule 101—Independence

Rule 102—Integrity and Objectivity

Rule 201—General Standards

Rule 202—Compliance with Standards

Rule 203—Accounting Principles

Rule 301—Confidential Client Information

Rule 302—Contingent Fees

Rule 501—Acts Discreditable

---

[1] Copyright © 1988 by American Institute of Certified Accountants, Inc. Reprinted by permission.

Rule 502—Advertising and Other Forms of Solicitation

Rule 503—Commissions

Rule 505—Form of Practice and Name

The numbering scheme may appear illogical to individuals who are unfamiliar with the predecessor code. Previously the Code of Ethics was divided into five sections, and rules were numbered according to section, as follows:

Rules 101–102 Independence, Integrity and Objectivity

Rules 201–204 General and Technical Standards

Rules 301–302 Responsibilities to Clients

Rules 401–402 Responsibilities to Colleagues

Rules 501–505 Other Responsibilities and Practices

Rule 204, "Other Technical Standards," was combined with Rule 202 in the 1988 revision of the Code. Rules 401 and 402, "Encroachment" and "Offers of Employment," were deleted in the late 1970s due to pressures by the Department of Justice and Federal Trade Commission to increase competition within the profession. Chapter Twelve examines this issue more closely. Rule 504, "Incompatible Occupations," was deleted in the 1988 revision because the Principles section offers guidance in this controversial area and because Rule 102 prohibits conflicts of interest.

Several Rules (101, 201, 202, and 203) make reference to "bodies designated by Council." Table 5-1 summarizes the officially designated bodies for each such Rule. To date no bodies have been designated to promulgate independence standards, although Interpretations of Independence made previous to the January 1988 Code revisions remain in effect.

Table 5-1. Bodies Designated by Council.

	Rule			
	101	201	202	203
Financial Accounting Standards Board (FASB)			X	X
Governmental Accounting Standards Board (GASB)			X	X
AICPA Accounting and Review Services Committee (ARSC)		X	X	
AICPA Audit Standards Board (ASB)		X	X	
AICPA Consulting Services Executive Committee (C)		X	X	

Because Interpretations of Independence (Rule 101) are numerous and sometimes quite lengthy, some of them are summarized in this chapter. Interpretations for the other Rules are reproduced in their entirety.

Rule 101 Independence

A member in public practice shall be independent in the performance of professional services as required by standards promulgated by bodies designated by Council.

Interpretations of Rule 101

101-1 Independence shall be considered to be impaired if, for example, a member had any of the following transactions, interests, or relationships:

A. During the period of a professional engagement or at the time of expressing an opinion, a member or a member's firm

1. Had or was committed to acquire any direct or material indirect financial interest in the enterprise.
2. Was a trustee of any trust or executor or administrator of any estate if such trust or estate had or was committed to acquire any direct or material indirect financial interest in the enterprise.
3. Had any joint, closely held business investment with the enterprise or with any officer, director, or principal stockholders thereof that was material in relation to the member's net worth or to the net worth of the member's firm.
4. Had any loan to or from the enterprise or any officer, director, or principal stockholder of the enterprise except as specifically permitted in Interpretation 101-5.

B. During the period covered by the financial statements, during the period of the professional engagement, or at the time of expressing an opinion, a member or a member's firm

1. Was connected with the enterprise as a promoter, underwriter or voting trustee, as a director or officer, or in any capacity equivalent to that of a member of management or of an employee.
2. Was a trustee for any pension or profit-sharing trust of the enterprise.

The above examples are not intended to be all inclusive.

101-2 Former practitioners and firm independence. For purposes of this interpretation, a former practitioner is defined as a proprietor, partner, shareholder, or equivalent who leaves by resignation, termination, retirement, or sale of all or part of the practice.

For purposes of determining a firm's compliance with Rule 101 and its interpretations, a former practitioner is not included in the term "a member or a member's firm" provided that

1. Payment of amounts due to the former practitioner ... do not cause substantial doubt about the firm's ability to continue as a going concern.... Such amounts should be fixed ... and may be adjusted only for inflation.
2. The former practitioner does not participate in the firm's business or professional activities....
3. The former practitioner does not appear to participate in the activities of ... the firm. [Such appearance might result from actions such as] including the former practitioner's name under the firm's name in an office building directory, inclusion of the former practitioner's name as a member of the firm in membership lists of business, professional or civic organizations, or inclusion of the former practitioner's name in the firm's internal directory without being designated as retired. The former practitioner will not be considered as participating or associating with his or her former firm solely because [s/he] is provided an office ... and related amenities. (See 4 below for restrictions ...).
4. A former practitioner in a position of significant influence with a client must no longer be provided with office space and related amenities by his or her former firm.

101–3 Accounting services. Members in public practice may be asked to provide manual or automated bookkeeping or data processing services to clients. Computer systems design and programming assistance may also be rendered by members either in conjunction with the data processing services or as a separate engagement. In addition, members may rent "block time" on their computers to their clients but are not involved in the processing of transactions or maintaining the clients' accounting records.

A member providing such services to a client must meet the following requirements to be considered independent:

1. The client must accept the responsibility for the financial statements as his own. The client must be sufficiently informed of the enterprise's activities and financial condition and the applicable accounting principles so that the client can reasonably accept such responsibility, including specifically fairness of "valuation and presentation" and adequacy of disclosure. When necessary, the member must discuss accounting matters with the client to assist the client in understanding such matters.
2. The member must not assume the role of employee or of management. For example, the member shall not consummate transactions, have custody of assets or exercise authority on behalf of the client. The client must prepare the source documents on all transactions in sufficient detail to identify clearly the nature and amount of such transactions. The member should not make changes in such basic data without the concurrence of the client.
3. When financial statements are prepared from books and records which the member has maintained, the member must comply with applicable standards for audits, reviews, or compilations.

101–4 Honorary directorships and trusteeships of not-for-profit organizations. Members may be asked to lend the prestige of their names to not-for-profit organizations that limit their activities to those of a charitable, religious, civic, or similar nature by being named as a director or a trustee. A member who permits his or her name to be used in this manner and who is associated with the financial statements of the organization would not be considered lacking in independence under Rule 101 so long as his or her position is clearly honorary, and he or she cannot vote or otherwise participate in board or management functions. If the member is named in letterheads and externally circulated materials, the member must be identified as an honorary director or honorary trustee.

101-5 Loans from financial institution clients and related terminology. Interpretation 101-1.A.4 provides that, except as permitted in this Interpretation, a member's independence shall be considered to be impaired if the member has any loan to or from the enterprise or any officer, director, or principal stockholder of the enterprise. This Interpretation does not consider independence to be impaired for certain grandfathered loans and other permitted loans from financial institution clients.

Grandfathered Loans:

This Interpretation grandfathers the following types of loans obtained from a financial institution under that institution's normal lending procedures, terms, and requirements, and existing as of January 1, 1992. However, independence will be considered to be impaired if, after January 1, 1992, a member obtains a loan of the type described in this paragraph from an entity that, at the time of obtaining the loan, is a client requiring independence...

1. Home mortgages.
2. Other secured loans. The collateral on such loans must equal or exceed the remaining balance of the loan at January 1, 1992 and at all times thereafter.
3. Loans not material to the member's net worth.

Other Permitted Loans:

This Interpretation permits the following types of personal loans obtained from a financial institution client for which independence is required under that institution's normal lending procedures, terms, and requirements. Such loans must, at all times, be kept current as to all terms.

1. Automobile loans and leases collateralized by the automobile.
2. Loans of the surrender value under terms of an insurance policy.
3. Borrowings fully collateralized by cash deposits at the same financial institution.
4. Credit cards and cash advances on checking accounts with an aggregate balance not paid currently of $5,000 or less.

Terminology:

For purposes of Interpretations 101-1.A.4 and 101-5 the following terms are defined: Loan; financial institution; normal lending procedures, terms, and requirements.

101-6 The effect of actual or threatened litigation on independence.... In some circumstances independence may be considered to be impaired as a result of litigation or the expressed intention to commence litigation. [If the litigation is between client and auditor, the following guidelines are offered]:

1. The commencement of litigation by the present management alleging deficiencies in audit work for the client would be considered to impair independence.
2. The commencement of litigation by the auditor against the present management alleging management fraud or deceit would be considered to impair independence.
3. An expressed intention by the present management to commence litigation against the auditor alleging deficiencies in audit work for the client is considered to impair independence if the auditor concludes that there is a strong possibility that such a claim will be filed.
4. Litigation not related to audit work for the client (whether threatened or actual) for an amount not material to the member's firm or to the client company would not usually be considered to affect the relationship in such a way as to impair independence....

If the litigation is by security holders, where the auditor and client are codefendants, independence would not ordinarily be impaired. However, a possibility of impairment may exist if cross-claims are filed against the auditor alleging that she or he is responsible for any deficiencies or if the auditor alleges fraud or deceit by the client as a defense.

If the litigation is by other third parties, such as lending institutions or insurance companies, who allege reliance on the audited financial statements as a basis for granting credit or insurance coverage, independence is not ordinarily impaired. However, independence may be impaired if the auditor alleges fraud or deceit by the client as a defense or if the plaintiff (the lending institution or insurance company) is also a client of the auditor.

101-8 Effects on independence of financial interests in nonclients having investor or investee relationships with a member's client. This interpretation deals with the effect on the appearance of independence of financial interests in nonclients that are related in various ways to a client. For purposes of this interpretation, "investor" means (a) a parent, (b) a general partner, or (c) a natural person or corporation that has the ability to exercise significant influence. "Investee" means (a) a subsidiary or (b) an entity that is subject to significant influence from an investor.

Most of this interpretation can be summed up in the following charts:

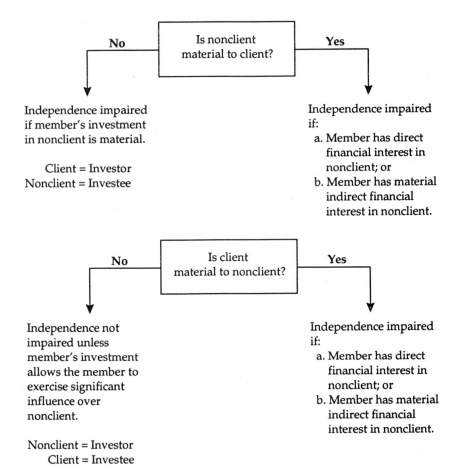

Other relationships, such as those involving brother–sister common control or client–nonclient joint ventures, may affect the appearance of independence.... In General, in brother–sister common control situations, an immaterial financial interest of a member in the nonclient investee would not impair the independence of a member with respect to the client investee, provided the member could not exercise significant influence over the nonclient investor. However, if a member's financial interest in a nonclient investee is material, the member could be influenced by the nonclient investor, thereby impairing the member's independence with respect to the client investee. In like manner, in a joint venture situation, an immaterial financial interest of a member in the nonclient investor would not impair the independence of the member with respect to the client investor, provided that the member could not exercise significant influence over the nonclient investor.

101-9 The meaning of certain independence terminology and the effect of family relationships on independence.

"Member or a member's firm"

A member (as used in Rule 101) and a member or a member's firm (as used in Interpretation 101–1) include

1. The member's firm and its proprietors, partners, or shareholders. A member's firm is defined as a proprietorship, partnership, or professional corporation or association engaged in the practice of public accounting.
2. All individuals participating in the engagement, except those who perform only routine clerical functions, such as typing and photocopying.
3. All individuals with a managerial position located in an office participating in a significant portion of the engagement.
4. Any entity (for example, partnership, corporation, trust, joint venture, or pool) whose operating, financial, or accounting policies can be controlled . . . by one or more of the persons described in (1) through (3) or by two or more such persons if they choose to act together.

A member or a member's firm does not include an individual solely because he or she was formerly associated with the client in any capacity described in Interpretation 101–1.B., if such individual has disassociated himself or herself from the client and does not participate in the engagement for the client covering any period of his or her association with the client.

A member or a member's firm includes individuals who provide services to clients and are associated with the client in any capacity described in Interpretation 101–1.B., if the individuals are located in an office participating in a significant portion of the engagement.

Managerial Position

The organizations of firms vary; therefore, whether an individual has a managerial position depends on the responsibilities and how he or she or the position itself is held out to clients and third parties. The following are some, but not necessarily all, of the responsibilities that suggest that an individual has a managerial position:

1. Continuing responsibility for the overall planning and supervision of engagements for specified clients.
2. Authority for determining that an engagement is complete, subject to final partner approval if required.
3. Responsibility for client relationships (for example, negotiating and collecting fees for engagements, marketing the firm's services).
4. Existence of profit sharing as a significant feature of total compensation.
5. Responsibility for overall management of the firm, development or establishment of firm policies on technical matters, and implementation of or compliance with the following nine elements of quality control:
    a. Independence
    b. Assigning personnel to engagements
    c. Consultation

  d. Supervision
  e. Hiring
  f. Professional development of personnel
  g. Advancement of personnel
  h. Acceptance and continuance of clients
  i. Inspection of compliance with policies and procedures

Significant Influence

A person or entity can exercise significant influence over the operating, financial, or accounting policies of another entity if, for example, the person or entity—

1. Is connected with the entity as a promoter, underwriter, voting trustee, general partner, or director.
2. Is connected with the entity in a policy-making position related to the entity's primary operating, financial, or accounting policies, such as chief executive officer, chief operating officer, chief financial officer, or chief accounting officer.
3. Meets the criteria established in APB Opinion No. 18, *The Equity Method of Accounting for Investments in Common Stock*, and its interpretations to determine the ability of an investor to exercise such influence with respect to an entity.

Office Participating in a Significant Portion of the Engagement

An office would be considered to be participating in a significant portion of an engagement if the office had primary client responsibility for a multioffice engagement. In addition, professional judgment must be exercised in deciding whether any other office participates in a significant portion of a multioffice engagement. . . .

Spouses and Dependent Persons

 The term member includes spouses (whether or not dependent) and dependent persons (whether or not related) for all purposes of complying with Rule 101, subject to the following exception.
 The exception is that the independence of the member and the member's firm will not normally be impaired solely because of employment of a spouse or dependent by a client if the employment is in a position that does not allow "significant influence" over the client's operating, financial, or accounting policies. However, if such employment is in a position where the person's activities are "audit sensitive," (even though not a position of significant influence), the member should not participate in the engagement.
 In general, a person's activities would be considered audit sensitive if such activities are normally an element of or subject to significant internal accounting controls (e.g., cashier, internal auditor, accounting supervisor, purchasing agent, inventory warehouse supervisor, etc.).

Nondependent Close Relative

The term "member or member's firm" excludes nondependent close relatives of the persons described in (1) through (3) of that definition. Nevertheless, in circumstances described below, the independence of a member or a firm can be impaired because of a nondependent close relative.

Close relatives are nondependent children, stepchildren, brothers, sisters, grandparents, parents, parents-in-law and their respective spouses. Close relatives do not include the brothers and sisters of the member's spouse.

The independence of a member's firm would be considered to be impaired with respect to an enterprise if—

1. During the period of the professional engagement or at the time of expressing an opinion, an individual participating in the engagement has a close relative with a financial interest in the enterprise that was material to the close relative and of which the individual participating in the engagement has knowledge.
2. During the period covered by the financial statements, during the period of the professional engagement, or at the time of expressing an opinion—
   a. An individual participating in the engagement has a close relative who could exercise significant influence over the operating, financial, or accounting policies of the enterprise or who is otherwise employed in a position where the person's activities are "audit sensitive," or—
   b. A proprietor, partner, shareholder, or [managerial employee], any of whom are located in an office participating in a significant portion of the engagement, has a close relative who can exercise significant influence over the operating, financial, or accounting policies of the enterprise.

Other Considerations

Members must be aware that it is impossible to enumerate all circumstances wherein the appearance of a member's independence might be questioned by third parties. For example, a member's relationship with a cohabitant may be equivalent to that of a spouse. In addition, in situations involving assessment of the association of any relative or dependent person with a client, members must consider whether the strength of personal and business relationships between the member and the relative or dependent person, considered in conjunction with the specified association with the client, would lead a reasonable person aware of all the facts and taking into consideration normal strength of character and normal behavior under the circumstances, to conclude that the situation poses an unacceptable threat to the member's objectivity and appearance of independence.

101–10 The effect on independence of relationships with entities included in the governmental financial statements. Under statements issued by the Governmental Accounting Standards Board, general-purpose financial statements may be issued for a governmental reporting entity, which consists of the financial statements of an oversight entity and one or more other entities (component units).

Because the oversight entity can exercise significant influence over the component units included in the reporting entity financial statements, Rule 101 is applicable and requires a member issuing a report on the general-purpose financial statements to be independent of the oversight entity and of each component unit that should be included therein.

A member who is the auditor of a material component unit but is not the auditor of the oversight entity should be independent of that component unit and the oversight entity.

A member who is the auditor of only an immaterial component unit is only required to be independent of that component because it is immaterial to the reporting entity. If this same member also audited other immaterial component units that, when aggregated, are material to the reporting entity, the member should be independent of the oversight entity and of the component units that the member audits.

Rule 102 Integrity and Objectivity

In the performance of any professional service, a member shall maintain objectivity and integrity, shall be free of conflicts of interest, and shall not knowingly misrepresent facts or subordinate his or her judgment to others.

Interpretations of Rule 102

102-1 Knowing misrepresentations in the preparation of financial statements or records. A member who knowingly makes, or permits or directs another to make, false and misleading entries in an entity's financial statements or records shall be considered to have knowingly misrepresented facts in violation of Rule 102.

102-2 Conflicts of interest. A conflict of interest may occur if a member performs a professional service for a client or employer and the member or his or her firm has a significant relationship with another person, entity, product, or service that could be viewed as impairing the member's objectivity. If this significant relationship is disclosed to and consent is obtained from such client, employer, or other appropriate parties, the rule shall not operate to prohibit the performance of the professional service. When making the disclosure, the member should consider Rule 301, "Confidential Client Information."

Certain professional engagements require independence. Independence impairments under Rule 101 and its interpretations cannot be eliminated by such disclosure and consent.

Rule 201 General Standards

A member shall comply with the following standards and with any interpretations thereof by bodies designated by Council.

- A. Professional Competence. Undertake only those professional services that the member or the member's firm can reasonably expect to be completed with professional competence.
- B. Due Professional Care. Exercise due professional care in the performance of professional services.

C. Planning and Supervision. Adequately plan and supervise the performance of professional services.
D. Sufficient Relevant Data. Obtain sufficient relevant data to afford a reasonable basis for conclusions or recommendations in relation to any professional services performed.

Interpretations of Rule 201

201-1 Competence. A member who accepts a professional engagement implies that he has the necessary competence to complete the engagement according to professional standards, applying his knowledge and skill with reasonable care and diligence, but he does not assume a responsibility for infallibility of knowledge or judgment.

Competence in the practice of public accounting involves both the technical qualifications of the member and his staff and his ability to supervise and evaluate the quality of the work performed. Competence relates both to knowledge of the profession's standards, techniques and the technical subject matter involved, and to the capability to exercise sound judgment in applying such knowledge to each engagement.

The member may have the knowledge required to complete an engagement professionally before undertaking it. In many cases, however, additional research or consultation with others may be necessary during the course of the engagement. This does not ordinarily represent a lack of competence, but rather is a normal part of the professional conduct of an engagement.

However, if a CPA is unable to gain sufficient competence through these means, he should suggest, in fairness to his client and the public, the engagement of someone competent to perform the needed service, either independently or as an associate.

Rule 202 Compliance with Standards

A member who performs auditing, review, compilation, management advisory, tax, or other professional services shall comply with standards promulgated by bodies designated by council.

The bodies designated by council and their related standards are shown in Table 5-2.

Rule 203 Accounting Principles

A member shall not (1) express an opinion or state affirmatively that the financial statements or other financial data of any entity are presented in conformity with generally accepted accounting principles or (2) state that he or she is not aware of any material modifications that should be made to such statements or data in order for them to be in conformity with generally accepted accounting principles, if such statements or data contain any departure from an accounting principle promulgated by bodies designated by Council to establish

Table 5-2. Bodies Designated by Council and Related Standards under Rule 202.

Body	Standards
Financial Accounting Standards Board	Statements of Financial Accounting Standards*
Governmental Accounting Standards Board	Statements of Governmental Accounting Standards
Accounting and Review Services Committee	Statements of Standards for Accounting and Review Services
Auditing Standards Board	Statements on Auditing Standards
Consulting Services Executive Committee	Statements of Standards for Consulting Services

such principles that has a material effect on the statements or data taken as a whole. If, however, the statements or data contain such a departure and the member can demonstrate that due to unusual circumstances the financial statements or data would otherwise have been misleading, the member can comply with the rule by describing the departure, its approximate effects, if practicable, and the reasons why compliance with the principle would result in a misleading statement.

Interpretations of Rule 203

203-1 Departures from established accounting principles. Rule 203 was adopted to require compliance with accounting principles promulgated by the body designated by Council to establish such principles. There is a strong presumption that adherence to officially established accounting principles would in nearly all instances result in financial statements that are not misleading.

However, in the establishment of accounting principles it is difficult to anticipate all of the circumstances to which such principles might be applied. This rule therefore recognizes that upon occasion there may be unusual circumstances where the literal application of pronouncements on accounting principles would have the effect of rendering financial statements misleading. In such cases, the proper accounting treatment is that which will render the financial statements not misleading.

The question of what constitutes unusual circumstances as referred to in Rule 203 is a matter of professional judgment involving the ability to support the position that adherence to a promulgated principle would be regarded generally by reasonable men as producing a misleading result.

Examples of events which may justify departures from a principle are new legislation or the evolution of a new form of business transaction. An unusual degree of materiality or the existence of conflicting industry practices are examples of circumstances which would not ordinarily be regarded as unusual in the context of Rule 203.

203-2 Status of FASB interpretations. Council is authorized under Rule 203 to designate a body to establish accounting principles and has designated the Financial Accounting Standards Board as such body. Council also has resolved that FASB Statements of Financial Accounting Standards, together with those Accounting Research Bulletins and APB Opinions which are not superseded by action of the FASB, constitute accounting principles as contemplated in Rule 203.

In determining the existence of a departure from an accounting principle established by a Statement of Financial Accounting Standards, Accounting Research Bulletin or APB Opinion encompassed by Rule 203, the division of professional ethics will construe such Statement, Bulletin or Opinion in the light of any interpretations thereof issued by the FASB.

Rule 301 Confidential Client Information

A member in public practice shall not disclose any confidential client information without the specific consent of the client.

This rule shall not be construed (1) to relieve a member of his or her professional obligations under Rules 202 and 203, (2) to affect in any way the member's obligation to comply with a validly issued and enforceable subpoena or summons, or to prohibit a member's compliance with applicable laws and government regulations, (3) to prohibit review of a member's professional practice under AICPA or state CPA society or Board of Accountancy authorization, or (4) to preclude a member from initiating a complaint with, or responding to any inquiry made by, the ethics division or trial board of the Institute or a duly constituted investigative or disciplinary body of a state CPA society or Board of Accountancy.

Members of any of the bodies identified in (4) above and members involved with professional practice reviews identified in (3) above shall not use to their own advantage or disclose any member's confidential client information that comes to their attention in carrying out those activities. This prohibition shall not restrict the members' exchange of information in connection with the investigative or disciplinary proceedings described in (4) above or the professional practice reviews described in (3) above.

Interpretation of Rule 301

301-2 Disclosure of confidential client information in certain circumstances. Rule 301 provides that "A member in public practice shall not disclose any confidential client information without the specific consent of the client." The rule provides four exemptions that permit AICPA members to disclose confidential client information without the client's specific consent.

Consistent with the AICPA's jurisdiction only over AICPA members, exemptions (1), (2), and (3) pertain to bodies designated by the AICPA to set standards or acknowledge the legal process to which members are subject.

Exemption (4) in Rule 301 provides that Rule 301 shall not be construed "to preclude a member from initiating a complaint with or responding to any inquiry from a recognized investigative or disciplinary body."

In keeping with the AICPA's jurisdiction solely over AICPA members and the other three exemptions in Rule 301, exemption (4) of the rule pertains to the disciplinary and investigative processes of the AICPA. Exemption (4) allows but does not require members to file complaints with the AICPA and other participants in the Joint Ethics Enforcement Program even though the complaint may necessitate disclosing confidential client information without the specific consent of the client. The concluding paragraph of the rule is evidence of this intent as it asserts that members of recognized investigative or disciplinary bodies and professional practice reviewers shall not use to their own advantage or disclose any member's confidential client information.

Consistent with this perceived intent of exemption (4), it is interpreted to state the following: Rule 301 shall not be construed to preclude a member from initiating a complaint with or responding to any inquiry made by a recognized investigative or disciplinary body of the AICPA or other participant in the Joint Ethics Enforcement Program.

In addition, the exemption (2) is interpreted to provide that Rule 301 should not be construed to prohibit or interfere with a member's compliance with applicable laws and government regulations.

301-3 Confidential Information and the purchase, sale, or merger of a practice. Rule 301 prohibits a member in public practice from disclosing any confidential client information without the specific consent of the client. The rule provides that it shall not be construed to prohibit the review of a member's professional practice under AICPA or state CPA society authorization.

For purposes of Rule 301, a review of a member's professional practice is hereby authorized to include a review in conjunction with a prospective purchase, sale, or merger of all or part of a member's practice. The member must take appropriate precautions (for example, through a written confidentiality agreement) so that the prospective purchaser does not disclose any information obtained in the course of the review, since such information is deemed to be confidential client information.

Members reviewing a practice in connection with a prospective purchase or merger shall not use to their advantage nor disclose any member's confidential client information that comes to their attention.

Rule 302 Contingent Fees

A member in public practice shall not

(1) Perform for a contingent fee any professional services for, or receive such a fee from, a client for whom the member or the member's firm performs
    (a) an audit or review of a financial statement; or

(b) a compilation of a financial statement when the member expects, or reasonably might expect, that a third party will use the financial statement and the member's compilation report does not disclose a lack of independence; or

(c) an examination of prospective financial information; or

(2) Prepare an original or amended tax return or claim for a tax refund for a contingent fee for any client.

The prohibition in (1) above applies during the period in which the member or the member's firm is engaged to perform any of the services listed above and the period covered by any historical financial statements involved in any such listed services.

Except as stated in the next sentence, a contingent fee is a fee established for the performance of any service pursuant to an arrangement in which no fee will be charged unless a specified finding or result is attained, or in which the amount of the fee is otherwise dependent upon the finding or result of such service. Solely for purposes of this rule, fees are not regarded as being contingent if fixed by courts or other public authorities, or, in tax matters, if determined based on the results of judicial proceedings or the findings of governmental agencies.

A member's fees may vary depending, for example, on the complexity of services rendered.

Interpretation of Rule 302

302–1 Contingent fees in tax matters. This interpretation defines certain terms in Rule 302 and provides examples of the application of the rule.

Definition of Terms

(a) Preparation of an original or amended tax return or claim for tax refund includes giving advice on events which have occurred at the time the advice is given if such advice is directly relevant to determining the existence, character, or amount of a schedule, entry, or other portion of a return or claim for refund.

(b) A fee is considered determined based on the findings of governmental agencies if the member can demonstrate a reasonable expectation, at the time of a fee arrangement, of substantive consideration by an agency with respect to the member's client. Such an expectation is deemed not reasonable in the case of preparation of original tax returns.

Examples

The following are examples, not all-inclusive, of circumstances where a contingent fee would be permitted:

1. Representing a client in an examination by a revenue agent of the client's federal or state income tax return.
2. Filing an amended federal or state income tax return claiming a tax refund based on a tax issue that is either the subject of a test case (involving a different taxpayer) or with respect to which the taxing authority is developing a position.

3. Filing an amended federal or state income tax return (or refund claim) claiming a tax refund in an amount greater than the threshold for review by the Joint Committee on Internal Revenue Taxation ($1 million at March 1991) or state taxing authority.
4. Requesting a refund of either overpayments of interest or penalties charged to a client's account or deposits of taxes improperly accounted for by the federal or state taxing authority in circumstances where the taxing authority has established procedures for the substantive review of such refund requests.
5. Requesting, by means of "protest" or similar document, consideration by the state or local taxing authority of a reduction in the "assessed value" of property under an established taxing authority review process for hearing all taxpayer arguments relating to assessed value.
6. Representing a client in connection with obtaining a private letter ruling or influencing the drafting of a regulation or statute.

The following is an example of a circumstance where a contingent fee would not be permitted:

1. Preparing an amended federal or state income tax return for a client claiming a refund of taxes because a deduction was inadvertently omitted from the return originally filed. There is no question as to the propriety of the deduction; rather the claim is filed to correct an omission.

Rule 501 Acts Discreditable

A member shall not commit an act discreditable to the profession.

Interpretations of Rule 501

501-1 Retention of client records. Retention of client records after a demand is made for them is an act discreditable to the profession in violation of Rule 501. The fact that the statutes of the state in which a member practices may specifically grant the member a lien on all client records in his or her possession does not change this ethical standard.

A client's records are any accounting or other records belonging to the client that were provided to the member by or on behalf of the client. If an engagement is terminated prior to completion, the member is required to return only client records.

A member's working papers—including, but not limited to, analyses and schedules prepared by the client at the request of the member—are the member's property and need not be made available.

In some instances a member's workpapers contain information that is not reflected in the client's books and records, with the result that the client's records are incomplete. This would include (1) adjusting, closing, combining or consolidating journal entries and (2) information normally contained in books of original entry and general ledgers or subsidiary ledgers. In those instances when an engagement has been completed, such information should also be made available to the client upon request. However, the member may require that fees due the member with respect to such completed engagements be paid before such information is provided.

Once the member has complied with the foregoing requirements, he or she need not comply with any subsequent requests to again provide such information.

501–2 Discrimination in employment practices. Discrimination based on race, color, religion, sex, age or national origin in hiring, promotion or salary practices is presumed to constitute an act discreditable to the profession in violation of Rule 501.

501–3 Failure to follow standards and/or procedures or other requirements in governmental audits. Engagements for audits of government grants, government units or other recipients of government monies typically require that such audits be in compliance with government audit standards, guides, procedures, statutes, rules, and regulations, in addition to generally accepted auditing standards. If a member has accepted such an engagement and undertakes an obligation to follow specified government audit standards, guides, procedures, statutes, rules and regulations, in addition to generally accepted auditing standards, he is obligated to follow such requirements. Failure to do so is an act discreditable to the profession in violation of Rule 501, unless the member discloses in his report the fact that such requirements were not followed and the reasons therefore.

501–4 Negligence in the preparation of financial statements or records. A member who, by virtue of his negligence, makes, or permits or directs another to make, false and misleading entries in the financial statements or records of an entity shall be considered to have committed an act discreditable to the profession in violation of Rule 501.

501–5 Failure to follow requirements of governmental bodies, commissions, or other regulatory agencies in performing attest or similar services. Many governmental bodies, commissions or other regulatory agencies have established requirements such as audit standards, guides, rules, and regulations that members are required to follow in performing attest or similar services for clients subject to their jurisdiction. When a member agrees to perform an attest or similar service for the purpose of reporting to such bodies, commissions, or regulatory agencies, the member should follow such requirements, in addition to generally accepted auditing standards (where applicable). Failure to substantially follow such requirements is an act discreditable to the profession, unless the member discloses in his or her report that such requirements were not followed and the reasons therefore.

If the agency requires additional disclosures of the auditor, they must be made in accordance with the disclosure requirements established by the governmental body, commission or other regulatory agency. Failure to substantially follow such requirements is an act discreditable to the profession.

The AICPA Bylaws give further guidance concerning acts discreditable. They provide, in Section 7.3, that a member shall be terminated without a hearing if a member is convicted of any one of the following:

1. A crime punishable by imprisonment for more than one year.
2. The willful failure to file any income tax return which he, as an individual taxpayer, is required by law to file.
3. The filing of a false or fraudulent income tax return on his or a client's behalf.
4. The willful aiding in the preparation and presentation of a false and fraudulent income tax return of a client.

Membership in the Institute shall also be suspended without a hearing should a member's certificate as a CPA be suspended as a disciplinary measure by any governmental authority. In addition to the above, Bylaw 7.4.3 adds conviction by a criminal court of an offense involving moral turpitude. The same Bylaw also provides for disciplinary actions to be taken (other than expulsion without a hearing) if a member has been convicted of a criminal offense which tends to discredit the profession.

Rule 502 Advertising and Other Forms of Solicitation

A member in public practice shall not seek to obtain clients by advertising or other forms of solicitation in a manner that is false, misleading, or deceptive. Solicitation by the use of coercion, over-reaching, or harassing conduct is prohibited.

Interpretations of Rule 502

502–2 False, misleading, or deceptive acts in advertising or solicitation. Advertising or other forms of solicitation that are false, misleading, or deceptive are not in the public interest and are prohibited. Such activities include those that—

1. Create false or unjustified expectations of favorable results.
2. Imply the ability to influence any court, tribunal, regulatory agency, or similar body or official.
3. Contain a representation that specific professional services in current or future periods will be performed for a stated fee, estimated fee or fee range when it was likely at the time of the representation that such fees would be substantially increased and the prospective client was not advised of that likelihood.
4. Contain any other representations that would be likely to cause a reasonable person to misunderstand or be deceived.

502–5 Engagements obtained through efforts of third parties. Members are often asked to render professional services to clients or customers of third parties. Such third parties may have obtained such clients or customers as the result of their advertising and solicitation efforts.

Members are permitted to enter into such engagements. The member has the responsibility to ascertain that all promotional efforts are within the bounds of the Rules of Conduct. Such action is required because the members will receive the benefits of such efforts by third parties, and members must not do through others what they are prohibited from doing themselves by the Rules of Conduct.

Rule 503 Commissions

A. Prohibited Commissions
A member in public practice shall not for a commission recommend or refer to a client any product or service, or for a commission recommend or refer any product or service to be supplied by a client, or receive a commission, when the member or the member's firm also performs for that client

(a) an audit or review of a financial statement; or
(b) a compilation of a financial statement when the member expects, or reasonably might expect, that a third party will use the financial statement and the member's compilation report does not disclose a lack of independence; or
(c) an examination of prospective financial information.

This prohibition applies during the period in which the member is engaged to perform any of the services listed above and the period covered by any historical financial statements involved in such listed services.

B. Disclosure of Permitted Commissions
A member in public practice who is not prohibited by this rule from performing services for or receiving a commission and who is paid or expects to be paid a commission shall disclose that fact to any person or entity to whom the member recommends or refers a product or service to which the commission relates.

C. Referral Fees
Any member who accepts a referral fee for recommending or referring any service of a CPA to any person or entity or who pays a referral fee to obtain a client shall disclose such acceptance or payment to the client.

Rule 505 Form of Practice and Name

A member may practice public accounting only in a form of organization permitted by state law or regulation whose characteristics conform to resolutions of Council.

A member shall not practice public accounting under a firm name that is misleading. Names of one or more past owners may be included in the firm name of a successor organization. Also, an owner surviving the death or withdrawal of all other owners may continue to practice under a name which includes the name of past owners for up to two years after becoming a sole practitioner.

A firm may not designate itself as "Members of the American Institute of Certified Public Accountants" unless all of its owners are members of the Institute.

Interpretations of Rule 505

505–1 Investment in commercial accounting corporation. A member in the practice of public accounting may have a financial interest in a commercial corporation which performs for the public services of a type performed by public accountants provided such interest is not material to the corporation's net worth, and the member's interest in and relation to the corporation is solely that of an investor.

505–2 Application of rules of conduct to members who operate a separate business. Members in public practice who participate in the operation of a separate business that offers to clients one or more types of services rendered by public accountants will be considered to be in the practice of public accounting in the conduct of that business. In such a case, members will be required to observe all of the Rules of Conduct in the operation of the separate business.

In addition, members who are not otherwise in public practice must observe the Rules of Conduct in the operation of their business if they hold out to the public as being a CPA or public accountant and at the same time offer to clients one or more types of services rendered by public accountants.

Cases and Questions

1. Compare the guidance given by the Principles (Chapter Four) and the Rules relating to Independence. If a member of the AICPA is a rule utilitarian, which source of guidance is more helpful? Which is more helpful for a rule deontologist? Is it likely that a CPA will consider both the Principles and the Rules when confronted with a dilemma relating to Independence? Explain your answer.

2. Susan Delgado is a CPA in public practice and is also on the board of directors of the local bank. One of her tax clients, Moritime, Inc., has a $100,000 90-day loan (due March 31) from this bank. In late February, Susan, while preparing Moritime's tax return, discovered that its earnings were down drastically. Any further deterioration of the business may force the client into bankruptcy. At a meeting of the bank's board of directors on March 15, Susan learned that Moritime has requested a renewal of the $100,000 note for another 90 days. From the comments of the other board members in discussing Moritime's request, Susan realizes that they are unaware of the current financial condition of Moritime. Just before voting on the issue of renewal, the chairman of the board, who knows that Moritime is a client of Susan's, asks Susan for her comments.

    a. What section of the Rules governs Susan's dilemma? What guidance does it give?

b. What section of the Principles governs Susan's dilemma? What guidance does it give?

c. If Susan's moral development is at stage four, what will be her response in all probability. At stage five?

3. Fred Thompson, a partner in a regional CPA firm, just emerged from a conference with a golf buddy, Trent O'Dell. Trent is the president of a fairly large manufacturing company in their city, and he had requested this meeting with Fred to discuss some accounting problems faced by his company. Trent's company was currently being audited by another CPA firm in the area. Trent had presented some rather unusual and complicated financing transactions to Fred and had asked Fred how he would advise recording them. Fred gave some generalized answers, told Trent that he would need to research the matter further, and requested that Trent make another appointment with him in about 10 days. Fred was torn between 2 emotions: he was delighted that his firm might be in a position to secure the audit of Trent's company, but he was also uneasy about Trent's characterizations of his company's transactions. Fred believed Trent already had his mind set on how he wanted to record them.

a. What section of the Rules governs Fred's situation? What guidance does it give?

b. What section (if any) of the Principles governs Fred's situation? What guidance does it give?

c. What will be a likely response if Fred is at stage four of moral development? Stage five?

4. A CPA in public practice has a 50% interest in an insurance agency. Her husband runs the agency and owns the other 50% interest. Whenever possible, the CPA refers her audit and tax clients to the insurance agency for their insurance needs. Since the agency's rates are competitive with other agencies, many of her clients purchase insurance from her and her husband's agency.

a. Has the CPA violated any ethics Rules? How?

b. What Principles apply to this situation?

5. Refer to Question Three in Chapter Four. If Phil Mendez suggests to the controller of Belco Chemical that the company enhance its reported earnings by converting their LIFO pools to LIFO puddles, will Phil be violating any of the Rules of the AICPA *Code of Professional Conduct* (assume such a change is not in violation of GAAP)?

6. Joe Denver, CPA, obtained as a new client, Becker Co., which had been in business for a year. Becker does not have a bookkeeper and their manager/owner, June Becker, brought Joe Denver the company's cash receipt, cash disbursement, and sales records. Using these records, bank statements, and so on, Joe prepared the necessary accounting records, financial statements, and income tax returns. After completing the engagement, Joe submitted to Ms. Becker a statement for his services. She told him that the amount was too high and that she would employ someone else next year. She demanded copies of the depreciation schedules and other schedules that support the figures shown in the financial statements and income tax returns. She adamantly refused to pay Joe's fee, not because of a shortage of funds by the company, but because she believed the amount was too high. He is tempted to refuse to give Ms. Denver anything until she pays his fees, as charged.

a. What guidance, if any, does the Rules section of the *Code of Professional Conduct* give to Joe? The Principles section? What else ought Joe to consider?

b. If you were Joe, what would you do?

6
Monitoring and Enforcement of the Rules

Introduction

Three groups are responsible for monitoring and enforcing ethics rules: the AICPA, state societies of CPAs, and state boards of accountancy. Because state boards have small numbers of personnel (compared to the AICPA or state societies) and because their funds are very limited, they often rely on state societies and the AICPA to monitor their memberships. Nevertheless, it is the state boards who have the authority to revoke a CPA's certificate for serious violations of the rules. The AICPA and state societies are limited to expulsion from their group, a sanction which may bear serious social repercussions, and to educational or remedial efforts to bring about changes in the conduct of members who may be unintentionally violating standards due to ignorance.

Some state boards have initiated programs in which a review of a sample of licensees' audit reports is conducted periodically. But most state boards rely on a complaint-based system to detect and correct poor quality audits and other attestation engagements.

The AICPA has developed a Joint Ethics Enforcement Program (JEEP) to make enforcement of the Rules more effective and consistent, and to reduce duplication of efforts. Most state societies participate with the AICPA in JEEP. This topic will be discussed in more detail later in the chapter.

For many years enforcement of the Rules was limited to a complaint-based system. Because of societal pressures, primarily by Congress in the mid-1970s (see Chapter 10 for a discussion of this topic), the AICPA created the Division for Firms in 1977. The primary purpose of this new division was to monitor the quality of member firms' audit engagements through its system of peer review. Not all CPA firms, however, submitted themselves to peer review because membership in the Division for Firms is voluntary. In 1988, the AICPA membership approved a mandatory quality review for firms not electing membership in the Division for Firms.

Peer review and quality review are important additions to the profession's efforts at self-regulation. Recall from Chapter 3 that society allows professions the privilege of self-regulation, but that privilege can and will be revoked if the profession does a poor job at self-regulation. By initiating peer review and quality review programs, the profession of public accounting has demonstrated its willingness to seek out and correct substandard practices, rather than sit back and wait for those practices to come to their attention, usually after someone has been seriously harmed. At the same time, the focus of both programs is educational, rather than punitive. That is, CPA firms found to have substandard practices are given opportunities to improve the quality of their work. Punishment is not the objective of the programs. Peer review is the topic of the next section.

Peer Review

The Division for Firms has two sections: the SEC Practice Section (SECPS) monitored by non-CPAs (the Public Oversight Board, or POB) and the Private Companies Practice Section (PCPS). To be a member in the SECPS a firm must follow rigid quality control standards and meet other requirements, summarized below. An Executive Committee oversees the Section's activities, and that committee can impose various sanctions such as additional continuing education requirements, special peer reviews, censures, fines, and expulsion from membership. The POB oversees the Executive Committee of the SECPS.

Another element of the SECPS is a Special Investigations Committee (SIC), which examines evidence of alleged audit failures and makes recommendations to the Executive Committee.

Membership in the SECPS involves compliance with 13 requirements (PCPS requirements are quite similar). Member firms must:[1]

1. Ensure that a majority of members of the firm are CPAs, and that the firm can legally engage in practice. Each partner of the firm resident in the United States and eligible for AICPA membership must be a member of AICPA.
2. Adhere to quality control standards established by the AICPA Quality Control Standards Committee.
3. Submit to peer review of their accounting and audit practice every three years. Those reviews must be conducted in accordance with standards established by the section's peer review committee.
4. Ensure that all professionals in the firm, CPAs and non-CPAs alike, take part in qualifying continuing professional education. That means participation in at least one hundred twenty hours every three years, but not less than twenty hours every year.

---

[1] Zick, John W. "Self-Regulation of the Accounting Profession: It Works." *Vital Speeches of the Day* 51, (July 15, 1985): 592.

5. Assign a different audit partner to be in charge of each SEC engagement where another audit partner has been in charge for a period of seven consecutive years. The incumbent partner may not return to in-charge status on the engagement for a minimum of two years.
6. Ensure that a concurring review by a second partner has been completed before issuance of an audit report on the financial statements of an SEC registrant.
7. File with the section each fiscal year certain information including
    — Form of business and number and location of offices.
    — Data concerning the number of CPAs, principals, professional staff and total personnel.
    — Number of SEC clients for which the firm is principal auditor-of-record.
    — A statement indicating that the firm has complied with AICPA and SEC independence requirements.
    — Disclosure regarding pending litigation indicating whether such litigation is expected to have a material effect on the firm's financial condition or its ability to serve clients.
    — Gross fees for accounting and auditing, tax, and MAS services, including data on fees for MAS and tax work performed for SEC audit clients.
    — Information on mergers.
8. Maintain minimum prescribed amounts and types of accountants' liability insurance.
9. Adhere to the AICPA Code of Professional Conduct and refrain from performing certain proscribed services for SEC registrant clients.
10. Report annually to the audit committee or board of directors of each SEC registrant client the total fees received from the client for MAS work during the year under audit, including a description of the types of such services rendered.
11. Report to the audit committee or board of directors of each SEC registrant client on the nature of disagreements with the management of the client on financial accounting and reporting matters and auditing procedures which, if not satisfactorily resolved, would have caused the issuance of a qualified opinion on the client's financial statements.
12. Report to the Special Investigations Committee any litigation (including criminal indictments) against the firm or its personnel, or any proceeding or investigation publicly announced by a regulatory agency that involves clients or former clients that are SEC registrants and that alleges deficiencies in the conduct of an audit or reporting thereon in connection with any required filing under the federal securities laws.
13. Pay dues.

The cornerstone of the Division for Firms is the mandatory peer review, which members of the PCPS must also undergo every three years. The purpose of the peer review is to evaluate a firm's quality control system and determine if there is a reasonable assurance that the firm is meeting professional standards. Before the review begins the firm being reviewed prepares a quality control document which describes their system. That system is then compared to nine established quality control standards, categorized as follows: independence, assigning personnel, consultation, supervision, hiring, professional development, advancement, acceptance and continuance of clients, and inspection. At the conclusion of the review a written report is presented at an exit conference.

Reports on peer review are placed in a public file at the AICPA, where copies are available upon request. An unqualified opinion is issued when the reviewer concludes that the firm's quality control system meets the objectives of the nine standards listed above. An unqualified opinion is usually accompanied by a letter of comments which may note deficiencies or lack of compliance with the firm's quality control system. If the system deficiencies are significant, a qualified or adverse report is issued.

Review teams may be provided by the AICPA, a state CPA society, or one firm may engage another. However, reciprocal reviews are not allowed. Members of the review team must be CPAs and be highly knowledgeable in the reviewed firm's specialty areas.

In the first five years of the peer review program, almost 1,600 peer reviews were conducted (614 in SECPS and 981 in PCPS).[2] Over 85 percent of the initial peer reviews and approximately 93 percent of subsequent peer reviews resulted in unqualified reports. The remainder were primarily qualified reports, as adverse reports were rarely issued, especially for subsequent reviews.[3] In a survey of member firms, DeFatta and Smith found that over half of the deficiencies issued related to supervision, and the majority of the supervision deficiencies related to working papers.[4] Usually, however, supervision deficiencies, unless excessive or major, do not result in modified reports.

Quality Review

Self-regulation in the public accounting profession contained a large flaw until 1988; namely, that membership in the Division for Firms, and hence peer review, was voluntary. In late 1987 and early 1988 the AICPA membership voted to extend the periodic review process by making it a membership requirement for all AICPA members in public practice to work for firms that belong to the Division for Firms

---

[2] Bremser, W. G. "Peer Review: What's Happening and What's to Come." *The Practical Accountant* 19, (July 1986): 89.

[3] Ibid.

[4] DeFatta, J. A., and Smith, J. D. "Peer Review Deficiencies Disclosed by Survey." *The Practical Accountant* 19, (July 1986): 96.

(and hence undergo peer review) or to belong to firms that undertake a periodic quality review (QR). In 1990 AICPA members voted to make membership in the SECPS mandatory for firms that audit *any* companies that are SEC registrants. Membership in the PCPS remains voluntary.

In 1988 the AICPA began establishing the QR program, designed after the Division for Firms' peer review program. The goal of quality is sought primarily through education and remedial or corrective actions. To enroll in the program, a firm is required to agree to the following:[5]

1. To adhere to the applicable quality control standards of the AICPA.
2. To require its proprietor, partners, or shareholders eligible for AICPA membership to be AICPA members.
3. To undergo a quality review of its accounting and auditing practice every three years or to declare that it has no accounting and auditing practice.
4. To file with the AICPA an annual information form containing certain specified information required in the administration of the program within ninety days of the end of the firm's fiscal year.
5. To allow the AICPA to disclose on request the following information:
   a. The firm's participation in the program
   b. The firm's name and address
   c. The date of, and the period covered by, the firm's last review and that the report on the review can be obtained from the firm
   d. If applicable, the termination of the firm from the program and the suspension or termination of a partner from the AICPA.
6. To comply with established rules and regulations, to cooperate with the committee responsible for administering the firm's reviews, and to accept final decisions on disciplinary matters.
7. To ensure that AICPA members in the firm meet their continuing professional education requirements.

Reviews are off-site report reviews, for firms that limit their accounting practice to review or compilation engagements, and on-site reviews for firms with audit engagements. Both types of reviews will result in a written report. The quality review committee administering the reviews evaluate the report and, where deficiencies are found, recommend action to improve the quality of practice. Such actions may include educational and corrective measures such as additional continuing professional education courses for firm members, changes in

---

[5] *Plan to Restructure Professional Standards*, p. 24. Copyright © 1987 by American Institute of Certified Public Accountants, Inc. Reprinted by permission.

the firm's quality control system, engaging another CPA to perform preissuance reviews of the firm's audit (or review or compilation) reports, or additional special quality reviews.

Unlike peer review, which is administered entirely by the AICPA, QR may be administered by state societies, utilizing AICPA procedures and under AICPA oversight, if the state societies so elect.

Joint Ethics Enforcement Program

The emphasis of peer review, or quality review, is to improve the quality of audit, review, and compilation reports *before* problems surface and cause harm to the users of the reports. Other mechanisms exist to investigate complaints that various ethical standards, including technical standards, have been violated. The Joint Ethics Enforcement Program, or JEEP, is such a mechanism.

Currently about 80 percent of state societies of CPAs have signed JEEP agreements with the AICPA in order to bring uniformity to ethics enforcement and to avoid unnecessary duplications when a complaint is brought against a CPA who is a member of both the AICPA and a state society.

The JEEP program was restructured in early 1988. Under the new arrangement all complaints are submitted to the professional ethics division of the AICPA, which in turn may refer the complaint for investigation and recommendation to an ethics committee (or its equivalent) of a state society that has signed a JEEP agreement. If the complaint is against a member in public practice for violation of technical or independence standards, a copy is sent to the AICPA or state CPA committee that administers the reviews of the member's firm under the practice monitoring program (SECPS, PCPS, or QR). This information is to aid the committee in its review of the firm, but the committee itself will not investigate the complaint.

The professional ethics division (or the state society's ethics committee) initiates an inquiry to ascertain the validity of the complaint. Depending on its findings, and the cooperation of the member, the complaint is disposed of in one of the following manners:[6]

1. The inquiry is terminated if no deficiencies in performance are found.
2. A complaint involving technical or independence standards may be resolved through referral to the appropriate committee administering peer or quality review to aid that committee in planning and conducting its review.
3. Educational and remedial or corrective actions are required when deficiencies in performance are found that are not suffi-

---

[6] Ibid., 34.

ciently serious to warrant referral to the Joint Trial Board (to be described below).
4. If a member refuses to cooperate or if the deficiencies are found to be sufficiently serious or to have resulted from actions undertaken knowingly with the intent to mislead, the matter is presented to the Joint Trial Board for disciplinary action.

The final outcome of the inquiry is sent to the appropriate review committee if the complaint involved technical or independence standards. When educational and corrective or remedial actions are required, the complete file is also sent to the appropriate review committee.

For disciplinary actions taken as a result of a decision of the Joint Trial Board, the professional ethics division maintains a record of, and discloses upon request, the information allowed by the bylaws (that is, the firm's participation in the peer review or quality review program, the date and period of the firm's latest review, and, if applicable, termination of membership). The information is also published in *The CPA Letter*, which is sent periodically to all AICPA members.

Joint Trial Board

The state societies of CPAs are divided into 12 regions. California, Illinois, New York, and Texas each comprise 1 region and the other states are divided into 8 more regions based on the number of CPAs in those regions and their geographical locations. Each state society submits enough qualified nominees (present or former Council members) to the AICPA Nominations Committee to permit selection of at least 3 nominees from each of the 12 regions. The structure, size, and operations of the Joint Trial Board are as follows:[7]

1. Hearings are conducted by subboards consisting of at least five board members appointed to maximize representation from the general area in which the member resides.
2. The trial board consists of at least thirty-six members selected by the AICPA Nominations Committee from present and former members of Council and are elected by Council. The Nominations Committee solicits nominations from the state societies in order to select at least three highly qualified nominees from each of the twelve existing regions.
3. Membership on the trial board is limited to two consecutive three-year terms and is staggered to permit orderly turnover.
4. The trial board is authorized to establish its own operating procedures, and the members of the trial board are authorized to elect a chairman and vice chairman.

---

[7] Ibid., 38.

Membership in the Institute shall be suspended without a hearing by the Joint Trial Board should there be filed with the secretary of the Institute a judgment of conviction imposed upon any member for any of the items described in Chapter Five, under the heading "Acts Discreditable."

Conclusion

Although the Joint Trial Board may discipline individual members who violate the profession's standards, such disciplinary actions have been limited to between one and two dozen per year. The real backbone of self-regulation is practice monitoring. The peer review programs of the SECPS and the PCPS have been effective vehicles for improving the quality of practice of participating firms, but they have been limited because membership in the Division for Firms is voluntary. Because of changes enacted in 1988, however, the 1990s should see an enormous expansion of report reviews among CPAs in public practice. The next steps in self-regulation will probably include reviews of other, nonattest activities such as tax practice and consulting services. Also, CPAs not in public practice may be subject to some sort of review process. For example, the Institute of Internal Auditors has undertaken a program of Quality Assurance Reviews designed to bring the benefits of peer review to internal auditors.

Cases and Questions

1. A CPA has been charged with bribing a revenue agent. At her trial in a federal court, the evidence clearly shows that she did offer to pay a bribe to the agent. However, the judge dismissed the case because, upon arrest, she had not been properly read her rights.

    a. In your opinion, is the CPA guilty of an "act discreditable"? Support your answer.

    b. If you were a member of the AICPA Ethics Division, would you proceed with an investigation of the matter and bring the CPA before the Joint Trial Board, or would you drop the matter because there was no criminal conviction?

2. Ed Tucker is a CPA in a small town. A new tax client brought Ed his current year's tax information as well as copies of his previous year's tax return, which had been prepared by another CPA in Ed's town. Upon review of the previous year's return, Ed noted some serious errors made by the previous CPA, and Ed

suggested to his new client that he ought to file an amended return (the client owed an additional sum to the IRS). Ed wondered if he should talk to the other CPA and inform him of his errors, or perhaps urge his client to initiate a complaint against the CPA with the state board of accountancy or state society of CPAs. Perhaps Ed should initiate such a complaint himself.

    a. If you were Ed Tucker, what would you do? What guidance does the Principles section of the AICPA *Code of Professional Conduct* offer? What guidance do the Rules offer?

    b. If Ed Tucker is a pure rule deontologist, what course of action is he likely to take? Explain your answer.

3. Every profession has a duty to regulate its members. List and describe all the various measures the profession of public accounting has taken to provide self-regulation. Do you believe these measures are adequate? Why or why not?

Additional Readings

American Institute of Certified Public Accountants. *Plan to Restructure Professional Standards*. New York: AICPA, 1987.

American Institute of Certified Public Accountants. *Code of Professional Conduct*. New York: AICPA, 1988.

Bremser, W. G. "Peer Review: What's Happening and What's to Come." *The Practical Accountant* 19, (July 1986): 87–98.

DeFatta, J. A. and Smith, J. D. "Peer Review Deficiencies Disclosed by Survey." *The Practical Accountant* 19, (July 1986): 96–98.

Zick, J. W. "Self-Regulation of the Accounting Profession: It Works." *Vital Speeches of the Day* 51, (July 15, 1985): 591–5.

PART THREE
Ethics in Tax Practice,
Consulting Services,
Industry and Government

7
Ethics in Tax Practice

Introduction

Chapter Three discussed the concept of a public service ideal and its centrality to all professions. Although the attest function is the service ideal for which CPAs are granted their monopoly, it is not the only public service performed by CPAs. Tax practitioners are also professionals, requiring expertise, licensing (as a CPA, attorney, enrolled agent, or enrolled actuary) and performing a public service. CPAs and attorneys have attempted to regulate their own tax professionals, and the Treasury Department has also issued regulations governing all who practice before the IRS.

The first sections of this chapter discuss governmental regulation of tax practice before the IRS, in particular Treasury Department Circular No. 230 and various penalty regulations. The latter half of the chapter discusses self-regulation by CPA tax practitioners, namely the *Statements on Responsibilities in Tax Practice* promulgated by the AICPA.

Public Service Ideal

Before discussing governmental regulation or self-regulation, however, it is important to take a closer look at tax professionals' public service ideal. Chapter Three pointed out that the complexity of the tax system, without availability of tax expertise, would result in an unjust basis for allocation of the tax burden. That is, the tax burden would be borne most heavily by uneducated and uninformed taxpayers. Degree of information is an unjust measure for allocating society's tax burden.

To help in the allocation of the tax burden can take many forms. Currently the exact nature of the tax professional's role is under debate because tax professionals have acknowledged duties to two parties—the tax system and their clients. In many situations, the duties to these two parties seem to conflict. The conflict is most apparent in areas of tax law that are unclear or in situations where the facts are subject to more than one legitimate interpretation. In those cases, the tax professional "cannot serve two masters." Decisions are made and advice is given which seems to benefit one party at the expense of the other. To whom does the tax professional owe his or her primary responsibility in such cases?

IRS View

The IRS argues that the tax practitioner's primary responsibility is to the tax system. In 1983 Roscoe Egger, IRS Commissioner, stated:

> ...a strong and equitable tax system does not consist of the tax administration entity alone—in this case IRS. It must also consist of the Congress, the administration, and the practitioner community. Not as separate segments of the community at large, but rather pulling together towards a common goal.[1]

In 1986 Leslie Shapiro, IRS Director of Practice, was even more emphatic:

> While it is generally agreed that a tax practitioner owes a client competence, loyalty and confidentiality, it also is recognized that the practitioner has responsibilities to the tax system as well. The latter responsibility is of pervasive importance.... In the normal practitioner–client relationship, both duties are recognized and carried out. However, there are situations in which this is difficult. In those situations, the practitioner is required to decide which obligation prevails and, in so doing, may correctly conclude that the obligation to the tax system is paramount.... The IRS relies on tax practitioners to assist it in administering the tax laws by being fair and honest in their dealings with the Service and by fostering confidence by their clients in the integrity of the tax system and in complying with it.[2]

Shapiro continues his argument by identifying three basic services a practitioner performs and by distinguishing different levels of responsibility among them. Tax practitioners offer tax advice, prepare tax returns, and represent taxpayers before the Service. In offering tax advice the practitioner "bears perhaps a heavier responsibility" because she or he is not dealing in past conduct nor taking the facts as they come. Therefore, giving tax advice is not an advocacy role and the tax adviser needs to proceed in an objective manner.

Other Views

Not all tax professionals agree with the IRS viewpoint. As early as 1966 William L. Raby argued that the tax system is biased in favor of the IRS whenever tax disputes arise. Therefore, the practitioner better serves the public by adopting an advocacy attitude. He argues:

> The fundamental ethical rule in tax practice at the level of personal ethics is that the tax practitioner must allow the client to make the final decision. The practitioner has no right to substitute his scale of values for that of the client.

---

[1] Ayres and Jackson. "Professional Tax Preparers: Problems and Responsibilities." *Federal Taxation* (October 1986): 80.

[2] Shapiro, L. "Professional Responsibilities in the Eyes of the IRS." *The Tax Advisor* (March 1986): 139.

Beyond that, the practitioner must recognize a positive responsibility not to provide false or misleading information to the government...

But within the framework of the Code [of Professional Ethics] and the Circular [230], it seems clear that the practitioner is concerned with protecting and advancing the interests of his client and not that of the Internal Revenue Service. If the client has a right... then the practitioner would be derelict in not advising him as to that right and assisting him in asserting it.... The public expects advocacy from the CPA in tax matters; no rule of professional conduct requires otherwise; and it would appear unethical to not offer the client a service primarily geared to protecting his interests.[3]

AICPA View

The AICPA appears to favor an approach somewhere between the two opinions given above. Before its 1988 revision, Rule 102 of the Code of Professional Ethics stated that "In tax practice, a member may resolve doubt in favor of his client as long as there is reasonable support for his position." That sentence has been deleted in the present Rule 102. To explain the deletion, the AICPA in its *Plan to Restructure Professional Standards*, stated (p. 14) "The provision allowing members to resolve doubts in favor of a client in tax practice has been deleted because resolving doubts in favor of a client in an advocacy engagement is not deemed, by itself, to impair integrity or objectivity." Thus, the AICPA acknowledges that tax professionals take on an advocacy role for their clients, but do not define its extent.

In February, 1987 the AICPA responded to proposed changes in Circular 230 with a letter that stated that all practitioners have the responsibility to be "fair and honest in their dealings with the IRS and should instill in their clients confidence in our tax system. However, it is well established that the taxpayer is under no obligation to pay more taxes than are legally owed and the CPA has a duty to the client to assist in achieving that result." In 1988 the AICPA revised their *Statements on Responsibility in Tax Practice* and redefined for their members the standard a CPA should use when giving advice to a tax client. This topic is discussed in more detail later in this chapter.

Summary

The public service ideal for tax professionals is not clear cut. Although the IRS would like to characterize the practitioner as being an extension of the government, and hence in the "same corner" as the IRS, the CPA profession disagrees. CPA tax practitioners see their role as akin to walking a tightrope. Their dual responsibilities require delicate bal-

---

[3] Raby, W. L. 1978. "Ethics in Tax Practice." In *Ethics in the Accounting Profession*, S. E. Loeb, ed. New York: John Wiley & Sons, (1978), 277.

ancing. The tax system is best served by professionals who act with integrity (basic honesty and fairness) and who do not subordinate their judgment to others. At the same time they best serve the public good by helping their clients determine their minimum tax liability under the law. To resolve honest doubts in favor of one's client does not, by itself, impair the CPA's integrity or objectivity. The standard required of a CPA when resolving those doubts has been evolving in recent years and will be discussed later in this chapter.

Treasury Department Circular 230

T.D. Circular 230 governs the conduct of anyone in practice before the IRS. "Practice before the IRS" does not include, however, the acts of preparing tax returns, rendering tax advice, or appearing as a witness for a taxpayer. Rather, the term refers to the representation of a client by a CPA, attorney, or enrollee before the IRS at conferences and meetings, corresponding with the IRS, and preparing or filing documents with the IRS on behalf of the client.

T.D. Circular 230 is composed of the following subparts:

A. Rules Governing Authority to Practice (Regs. Sec. 10.1–10.8)

B. Duties and Restrictions Relating to Practice Before the Internal Revenue Service (Regs. Sec. 10.20–10.33)

C. Rules Applicable to Disciplinary Proceedings (Regs. Sec. 10.50–10.76)

D. Rules Applicable to Disqualification of Appraisers (Regs. Sec. 10.77–10.97)

E. General Provisions (Regs. Sec. 10.98–10.101)

Duties and Restrictions

Of particular interest to tax professionals is subpart B—Duties and Restrictions Relating to Practice Before the Internal Revenue Service. Its main provisions are summarized next.

10.20 Information to be Furnished

a) To the Internal Revenue Service:

No [practitioner] shall neglect or refuse promptly to submit records or information ... upon proper and lawful request ... or shall interfere ... with any proper and lawful effort by the [IRS] to obtain such record or information, unless he believes in good faith and on reasonable grounds that such record or information is privileged or that the request ... is of doubtful legality.

"Prompt" does not necessarily mean "immediately." If a CPA believes she or he has a conflict between client confidentiality and an IRS request for information, she or he should seek legal counsel.

b) To the Director of Practice:

It shall be the duty of [a practitioner], when requested by the Director of Practice, to provide the Director with any information he may have concerning violation of the regulations in the past by any person, and to testify thereto in any proceeding instituted under this part for the disbarment or suspension of [a practitioner] unless he believes in good faith and on reasonable grounds that such information is privileged or that the request therefore is of doubtful legality.

This is not a "whistleblowing" provision, because it does not require one practitioner to inform on another unless the practitioner is requested by the Director of Practice to provide information or to testify. Thus, it is more like a subpoena provision.

10.21 Knowledge of Clients's Omission

A [practitioner] who knows that the client has not complied with the revenue laws... or has made an error in or omission from any return..., shall advise the client promptly of the fact.

Note that all errors seem to be included, not just material errors. Also note that the practitioner is *not* required to notify the IRS of the noncompliance.

10.22 Diligence as to Accuracy

[Practitioners] shall exercise due diligence... in preparing... and filing returns, documents [etc.]... in determining the correctness of oral or written representations made by him to the Department of the Treasury; and in determining the correctness of oral or written representations made by him to clients.

Due diligence refers to a standard of research. Practitioners are, in essence, required to research properly revenue laws, cases, facts, and so on, and not be lazy or sloppy in their tax practice.

10.23 Prompt Disposition of Pending Matters

No [practitioner] shall unreasonably delay the prompt disposition of any matter before the [IRS].

10.24 Assistance from Disbarred or Suspended Persons and Former Internal Revenue Service Employees

No [practitioner] shall knowingly and directly or indirectly:

(a) Employ or accept assistance from any person who is under disbarment or suspension from practice before the [IRS].

(b) Accept employment as associate, correspondent, or subagent from . . . any such person.

(c) Accept assistance from any former government employee where the provisions of Sec. 10.26 of these regulations or any Federal law would be violated.

10.25 Practice by Partners of Government Employees

No partner of an officer or employee [of certain governmental positions] shall represent anyone in any matter administered by the [IRS] in which such officer or employee of the Government participates . . . personally and substantially as a Government employee.

10.26 Practice by Former Government Employees, Their Partners and Associates

This section is quite lengthy. Its purpose is to exclude former governmental employees, and others related to them, from somehow influencing legislation, rulings, or other transactions to which they were a party during their governmental employment.

10.27 Notaries

This section prevents practitioners who are also notaries public from performing any official act before the IRS "in connection with matters in which he is employed as counsel, attorney, or agent."

10.28 Fees

No [practitioner] shall charge an unconscionable fee for representation of a client in any matter before the [IRS].

10.29 Conflicting Interests

No [practitioner] shall represent conflicting interests in his practice before the [IRS], except by express consent of all directly interested parties after full disclosure has been made.

10.30 Solicitation

Part (a) states that no practitioner shall "in any way use or participate in the use of any form of public communication containing a false, fraudulent, misleading, deceptive, unduly influencing, coercive or unfair statement or claim." It goes on to state:

No [practitioner] shall make, directly or indirectly, an uninvited solicitation of employment, in matters related to the [IRS]. . . . This restriction does not apply to: (i) seeking new business from an existing or former client in a related matter; (ii) solicitation by mailings, the contents of which are designed for the general public; or (iii) non-coercive in-person solicitation by those eligible to practice before the [IRS] while acting as an employee, member, or officer of an exempt organization.

Part (b) of this section describes Permissible Advertising. In short, it allows publication of factual information (for example, names of individuals associated with a firm, foreign language ability) and "customary biographical insertions in . . . professional journals and directories, as well as professional cards, letterheads and announcements: *Provided* . . . (ii) [CPAs] do not violate applicable standards of ethical conduct adopted by the [AICPA]."

Part (c) lists what Fee Information may be disseminated and states that practitioners are bound to charge the rates "published for a reasonable period of time, but no less than thirty days from the last publication of such [rates]."

Part (d) states that Communications, including fee information, shall be limited to professional lists, telephone directories, print media, permissible mailings, . . . radio and television."

Part (e) prohibits a practitioner from participating in an employment relationship with anyone who "obtains clients or otherwise practices in a manner forbidden under this section: *Provided*. That a practitioner does not . . . act or hold himself out as an [IRS] practitioner in connection with that relationship."

10.31 Negotiation of Taxpayer Refund Checks

> No [practitioner] who is an income tax preparer shall endorse or otherwise negotiate any check made in respect of income taxes which is issued to a taxpayer other than [him/her self].

10.32 Practice of Law

> Nothing in the regulations in this part shall be construed as authorizing persons not members of the bar to practice law.

10.33 Tax Shelter Opinions

This lengthy section was added in 1984 and imposes requirements on practitioners with respect to tax shelter opinions used in the marketing or sale of tax shelters.

> A [practitioner] must be satisfied that factual matters relevant to a tax shelter are accurately and completely described in the offering material. . . . [S/he must] ascertain that all material Federal tax issues have been considered and that all. . . . issues which involve the reasonable possibility of a challenge by the [IRS] have been fully and fairly addressed in the offering materials. . . . [If possible], the practitioner must provide an opinion whether it is more likely than not that an investor will prevail on the merits of each material tax issue [in] the offering. . . . [If possible], the practitioner must provide an overall evaluation whether the material tax benefits in the aggregate more likely than not will be realized. . . . [The reasons for any opinion that is not favorable must be fully described and] must be clearly and prominently disclosed in the offering materials. . . . [Finally], the practitioner must assure that the offering materials correctly and fairly represent the nature and extent of the tax shelter opinion.

Penalty Provisions

In addition to Circular 230, different pieces of legislation have been passed in recent years that impose penalties on taxpayers, and sometimes on tax preparers. For example, the Tax Reform Act of 1976 (TRA '76) added Code Sections 6694(a) and (b) which imposed two levels of penalties on preparers when client/taxpayers' tax deficiencies appeared to arise from a preparer's inadvertent or intentional departure from the existing income tax rules. The penalties under 6694(a) are $250 and are imposed if an understatement of liability is due to a position for which there is not a "realistic possibility of being sustained on its merits." This "realistic possibility" standard is further defined as follows: "A position will be considered to have a realistic possibility of being sustained on its merits if a reasonable and well-informed analysis by a person knowledgeable in the tax law would lead such a person to conclude that the position has approximately a one in three, or greater, likelihood of being sustained on its merits." (Notice 90–20, 1990–91 C.8. 328). A preparer is not subject to the penalty, even if there is not a realistic possibility of a position being sustained, if the position is not frivolous and is adequately disclosed or if the understatement was due to reasonable cause and the preparer acted in good faith.

The penalty under Section 6694(b) is $1,000 and is almost always the subject of a practice investigation that culminates in the withdrawal of the right to practice. This provision is applicable when the understatement is due to a willful attempt by a tax preparer to understate the tax liability and/or there is a "reckless disregard" of rules or regulations. This penalty can be avoided if proper disclosures are made and if the position is not frivolous.

Other penalty provisions in the tax code include the following:

Civil Penalties:

- Organizing or promoting abusive tax shelters (IRC Sec 6700)
- Aiding and abetting an understatement of tax liability (IRC Sec 6701)
- Improper disclosure or use of return data (IRC Sec 6713)

Criminal Penalties:

- Attempting to evade or defeat tax (IRC Sec 7201)
- Fraud and false statements (IRC Sec 7206 and 7207)
- Disclosure or use of information by preparer (IRC Sec 7616)

In addition to penalties against tax preparers, the Tax Code also assesses penalties against taxpayers for substantial underpayment. The chief section providing such penalties is Sec. 6661. In non-tax shelter cases, the penalty can be avoided if the filing position resulting in the understatement was supported by "substantial authority" or if the taxpayer disclosed all relevant facts on the return. In tax shelter cases, the penalty can be avoided only if there is "substantial authority" for the position taken *and* the taxpayer believed that the position taken was "more likely than not" the proper tax treatment. These "substantial authority" and "more likely than not" standards are greater than the "realistic possibility" standard imposed on tax preparers, and are much greater than the Code's previous guidance which required only a "reasonable basis" for a tax position.

AICPA Guidance

Self-regulation is an element of professionalism. The first part of this chapter discussed regulation of practitioners before the IRS by the Treasury Department, but that regulation is imposed by external sources. CPAs in tax practice are also guided by pronouncements made by the profession itself. The Committee on Responsibilities in Tax Practice, a committee of the AICPA's Division on Federal Taxation, has issued eight *Statements on Responsibilities in Tax Practice* [SRTP].

The statements are educational in nature. That is, they are advisory, not authoritative. They are not subject to enforcement proceedings, as are the rules of conduct of the Code of Professional Conduct. The principal objectives of the statements are threefold: (a) to identify and develop appropriate standards of responsibilities in tax practice and to promote their uniform application by CPAs; (b) to encourage increased understanding of the responsibilities of the CPA by the Treasury Department and IRS; and (c) to foster increased public compliance with and confidence in our tax system.

Statements on Responsibilities in Tax Practice

Each statement is divided into three sections: an introduction, a statement, and an explanation. The first two sections of each statement are reproduced in the chapter. The explanations are summarized, but readers engaged in tax practice should refer to the actual explanations in their entirety. Following is the 1988 revision.[4]

SRTP (1988 Rev.) No. 1: Tax Return Positions

I Introduction:

.01 This Statement sets forth the standards a CPA should follow in recommending tax return positions and in preparing or sign-

---

[4] Copyright © 1988 by American Institute of Certified Public Accountants, Inc. Reprinted with permission.

ing tax returns including claims for refunds. For this purpose, a "tax return position" is (1) a position reflected on the tax return as to which the client has been specifically advised by the CPA or (2) a position as to which the CPA has knowledge of all material facts and, on the basis of those facts, has concluded that the position is appropriate.

II Statement:

.02 With respect to the tax return positions, a CPA should comply with the following standards:

a. A CPA should not recommend to a client that a position be taken with respect to the tax treatment of any item on a return unless the CPA has a good faith belief that the position has a realistic possibility of being sustained administratively or judicially on its merits if challenged.

b. A CPA should not prepare or sign a return as an income tax return preparer if the CPA knows that the return takes a position that the CPA could not recommend under the standard expressed in paragraph .02a.

c. Notwithstanding paragraphs .02a and .02b, a CPA may recommend a position that the CPA concludes is not frivolous so long as the position is adequately disclosed on the return or claim for refund.

d. In recommending certain tax return positions and in signing a return on which a tax return position is taken, a CPA should, where relevant, advise the client as to the potential penalty consequences of the recommended tax return position and the opportunity, if any, to avoid such penalties through disclosure.

.03 The CPA should not recommend a tax return position that—

a. Exploits the Internal Revenue Service audit selection process; or

b. Serves as a mere "arguing" position advanced solely to obtain leverage in the bargaining process of settlement negotiation with the Internal Revenue Service.

.04 A CPA has both the right and responsibility to be an advocate for the client with respect to any positions satisfying the aforementioned standards.

III Explanation:

Our self-assessment tax system can only function effectively if taxpayers report their income on a tax return that is true, correct, and complete. A tax return is primarily a taxpayer's representation of facts, and the taxpayer has the final responsibility for positions taken on the return.

CPAs have a duty to the tax system as well as to their clients. However, it is well-established that the taxpayer has no obligation to pay more taxes than are legally owed, and the CPA has a duty to the client to assist in achieving that result. The aforementioned standards will guide the CPA in meeting responsibilities to the tax system and to clients.

The standards suggested herein require that a CPA in good faith believe that the position is warranted in existing law or can be supported by a good faith argument for an extension, modification, or reversal of existing law. For example, a CPA may reach such a conclusion on the basis of well-reasoned articles, treatises, IRS General Counsel Memoranda, a General Explanation of a Revenue Act prepared by the staff of the Joint Committee on Taxation, and Internal Revenue Service written determinations whether or not such sources are treated as "authority" under section 6661.

Where the CPA has a good faith belief that more than one position meets the standards suggested herein, the CPA's advice concerning alternative acceptable positions may include a discussion of the likelihood that each such position might or might not cause the client's tax return to be examined and whether the position would be challenged in an examination.

In some cases, a CPA may conclude that a position is not warranted under the standard set forth in paragraph .02a. A client may, however, still wish to take such a tax return position. Under such circumstances, the client should have the opportunity to make such an assertion, and the CPA should be able to prepare and sign the return provided the position is adequately disclosed on the return or claim for refund and the position is not frivolous. A "frivolous" position is one which is knowingly advanced in bad faith and is patently improper.

Where particular facts and circumstances lead the CPA to believe that a taxpayer penalty might by asserted, the CPA should so advise the client and should discuss with the client issues related to disclosure on the tax return. Disclosure should be considered when the CPA believes it would mitigate the likelihood of claims of taxpayer penalties under the Internal Revenue Code.

A 1990 interpretation of this standard (Interpretation 1–1) rejects the Treasury Department's "one in three" definition of realistic possibility when it makes the following statement:

> The realistic possibility standard cannot be expressed in terms of percentage odds. The realistic possibility standard is less stringent than the "substantial authority" and the "more likely than not" standards that apply under the Code to substantial understatements of liability by taxpayers. It is more strict than the "reasonable basis" standard that exists under regulations issued prior to the Revenue Reconciliation Act of 1989.

SRTP (1988 Rev.) No. 2: Answers to Questions on Returns

I Introduction:

.01 This statement considers whether a CPA may sign the preparer's declaration on a tax return where one or more questions on the return have not been answered. The term "questions" includes requests for information on the return, in the instructions, or in the regulations, whether or not stated in the form of a question.

II Statement:

.02 A CPA should make a reasonable effort to obtain from the client, and provide, appropriate answers to all questions on a tax return before signing as preparer.

III Explanation:

The explanation recognizes that not all questions on returns are of uniform importance, but two considerations dictate that reasonable efforts be made to answer all questions:

1. A question may be of importance in determining tax liability, and therefore the omission detracts from the quality of the return.

2. The CPA must sign the preparer's declaration stating that the return is true, correct, and complete.

Examples of reasonable grounds for omitting an answer are given:

1. The information is not readily available and the answer does not impact the tax liability on the return; or

2. The answer might prove to be significant but, either:

   a) genuine uncertainty exists regarding the meaning of the question in relation to the particular return; or

   b) the information obtainable is not sufficiently reliable.

3. The answer to the question is voluminous; however, assurance should be given that the data will be supplied to the revenue agent.

Where reasonable grounds exist for omission, a brief explanation of the reason should be provided on the return.

SRTP (1988 Rev.) No. 3: Certain Procedural Aspects of Preparing Returns

I Introduction:

.01 This statement considers the responsibility of the CPA to examine or verify certain supporting data or to consider information related to another client when preparing a client's tax return.

II Statement:

.02 In preparing or signing a return, the CPA may in good faith rely without verification upon information furnished by the client or by third parties. However, the CPA should not ignore the implications of information furnished and should make reasonable inquiries if the information furnished appears to be incorrect, incomplete, or inconsistent either on its face or on the basis of other facts known to the CPA. In this connection, the CPA should refer to the client's returns for prior years whenever feasible. Although the examination of supporting data is not required, the CPA should encourage his client to provide him with supporting data where appropriate.

.03 Where the Internal Revenue Code or income tax regulations impose a condition with respect to deductibility or other tax treatment of an item (such as taxpayer maintenance of books and records or substantiating documentation to support the reported deduction or tax treatment), the CPA should make appropriate inquiries to determine to his or her satisfaction whether such condition has been met.

.04 The individual CPA who is required to sign the return should consider information actually known to that CPA from the tax return of another client when preparing a tax return if the information is relevant to that tax return, its consideration is necessary to properly prepare that tax return, and use of such information does not violate any law or rule relating to confidentiality.

III Explanation:

The preparer's declaration on the income tax return states that the information contained therein is true, correct, and complete to the best of the preparer's knowledge and belief "based on all information of which the preparer has any knowledge." This reference should be understood to relate to information furnished by the client or by third parties to the CPA in connection with the preparation of the return.

The preparer's declaration does not require the CPA to examine or verify supporting data.... In fulfilling his or her obligation to exercise due diligence in preparing a return, the CPA ordinarily may rely on information furnished by the client unless it appears to be incorrect, incomplete, or inconsistent. Although the CPA has certain responsibilities in exercising due diligence in preparing a return, the client has ultimate responsibility for the contents of the return.

Even though there is no requirement to examine underlying documentation, the CPA should encourage the client to provide supporting data where appropriate.

A CPA may accept information provided by a pass-through entity, such as a limited partnership, without further inquiry unless there is reason to believe it is incorrect, incomplete, or inconsistent.

SRTP (1988 Rev.) No. 4: Use of Estimates

I Introduction:

.01 This statement considers the CPA's responsibility in connection with the CPA's use of the taxpayer's estimates in the preparation of a tax return. The CPA may advise on estimates used in the preparation of a tax return, but responsibility for estimated data is that of the client, who should provide the estimated data. Appraisals or valuations are not considered estimates for purposes of this statement.

II Statement:

.02 A CPA may prepare tax returns involving the use of the taxpayer's estimates if it is impracticable to obtain exact data and the estimated amounts are reasonable under the facts and circumstances known to the CPA. When the taxpayer's estimates are used, they should be presented in such a manner as to avoid the implication of greater accuracy than exists.

III Explanation:

In the case of transactions involving small expenditures, accuracy in recording some data may be difficult to achieve. Therefore, the use of estimates by the taxpayer in determining the amount to be deducted for such items may be appropriate.

In other cases where all of the facts relating to a transaction are not accurately known, estimates of the missing data may be made by the taxpayer.

Estimated amounts should not be presented in a manner which provides a misleading impression as to the degree of factual accuracy.

Although specific disclosure that an estimate is used for an item in the return is not required in most instances, there are unusual circumstances where such disclosure is needed to avoid misleading the IRS regarding the degree of accuracy of the return. Some examples of unusual circumstances include the following:

1. The taxpayer has died or is ill at the time the return must be filed.

2. The taxpayer has not received a K-1 for a flow-through entity at the time the tax return is to be filed.

3. There is litigation pending which bears on the return.

4. Fire or computer failure destroyed the relevant records.

SRTP (1988 Rev.) No. 5: Departure from a Position Previously Concluded in an Administrative Proceeding or Court Decision

I Introduction:

.01 This statement discusses whether a CPA may recommend a tax return position that departs from the treatment of an item as concluded in an administrative proceeding or a court decision with respect to a prior return of the taxpayer. For this purpose, a "tax return position" is (1) a position reflected on the tax return as to which the client has been specifically advised by the CPA, or (2) a position about which the CPA has knowledge of all material facts and, on the basis of those facts, has concluded that the position is appropriate.

.02 For purposes of this statement, "administrative proceeding" includes an examination by the Internal Revenue Service or an appeals conference relating to a return or a claim for refund.

.03 For purposes of this statement, "court decision" means a decision by any federal court having jurisdiction over tax matters.

II Statement:

.04 The recommendation of a position to be taken concerning the tax treatment of an item in the preparation or signing of a tax return should be based upon the facts and the law as they are evaluated at the time the return is prepared or signed by the CPA. Unless the taxpayer is bound to a specified treatment in the later year, such as by a formal closing agreement, the treatment of an item as part of concluding an administrative proceeding or as part of a court decision does not restrict the CPA from recommending a different tax treatment in a later year's return. Therefore, if the CPA follows the standards in SRTP (1988 Rev.) No. 1, the CPA may recommend a tax return position, prepare, or sign a tax return that departs from the treatment of an item as concluded in an administrative proceeding or a court decision with respect to a prior return of the taxpayer.

III Explanation:

The IRS usually acts consistently with regard to similar items, but maintains that it must look upon the examination of each return as a new matter. Similarly, a CPA usually will recommend a position consistent with the handling of similar items in previous years, but is not necessarily bound to do so. The CPA should consider the following:

1. An unfavorable court decision does not prevent a taxpayer from taking a position contrary to the earlier court decision in a subsequent year.

2. The consent in an earlier administrative proceeding and the existence of an unfavorable court decision are factors that the CPA should consider in evaluating whether the standards in SRTP (1988 Rev.) No. 1 are met.

3. The taxpayer's consent to the treatment in the administrative proceeding or the court's decision may have been caused by a lack of documentation, whereas supporting data for the later year is adequate.

4. The taxpayer may have yielded in the administrative proceeding for settlement purposes or not appealed the court decision even though the position met the standards in SRTP (1988 Rev.) No. 1.

5. Court decisions, rulings, or other authorities that are more favorable to the taxpayer's current position may have developed since the prior administrative proceeding was concluded or the prior court decision was rendered.

SRTP (1991 Rev.) No. 6: Knowledge of Error: Return Preparation

I Introduction:

.01 This statement considers the responsibility of a CPA who becomes aware of an error in a client's previously filed tax return or of the client's failure to file a required tax return. As used herein, the term "error" includes any position, omission, or method of accounting that, at the time the return is filed, fails to meet the standards set out in SRTP No. 1. The term "error" also includes a position taken on a prior year's return that no longer meets these standards due to legislation, judicial decisions, or administrative pronouncements having retroactive effect. However, an "error" does not include an item that has no more than an insignificant effect on the client's tax liability.

.02 This statement applies whether or not the CPA prepared or signed the return which contains the error.

II Statement:

.03 The CPA should inform the client promptly upon becoming aware of an error in a previously filed return or upon becoming aware of a client's failure to file a required return. The CPA should recommend the measures to be taken. Such recommendation may be given orally. The CPA is not obligated to inform the Internal Revenue Service, and the CPA may not do so without the client's permission, except where required by law.

.04 If the CPA is requested to prepare the current year's return and the client has not taken appropriate action to correct an error in a prior year's return, the CPA should consider whether to withdraw from preparing the return and whether to continue a professional relationship with the client. If the CPA does prepare such current year's return, the CPA should take reasonable steps to ensure that the error is not repeated.

III Explanation:

While performing services for a client, a CPA may become aware of an error in a previously filed return or may become aware that the client failed to file a required return. The CPA should advise the client of the error and the measures to be taken. It is the client's responsibility to decide whether to correct the error. In appropriate cases, particularly where it appears that the IRS might assert the charge of fraud or other criminal misconduct, the client should be advised to consult legal counsel before taking any action. In the event that the client does not correct an error, or agree to take the necessary steps to change from an erroneous method of accounting, the CPA should consider whether to continue a professional relationship with the client.

If the CPA decides to continue a professional relationship with the client and is requested to prepare a tax return for a year subsequent to that in which the error occurred, then the CPA should take reasonable steps to ensure that the error is not repeated. If a CPA learns the client is using an erroneous method of accounting, when it is past the due date to request IRS permission to change to a method meeting the standards of SRTP No. 1, the CPA may sign a return for the current year, providing the return includes appropriate disclosure of the use of the erroneous method.

Whether an error has no more than an insignificant effect on the client's tax liability is left to the judgment of the individual CPA based on all the facts and circumstances known to the CPA. In judging whether an erroneous method of accounting has more than an insignificant effect, the CPA should consider the method's cumulative effect and its effect on the current year's return.

Where the CPA becomes aware of the error during an engagement which does not involve tax return preparation, the responsibility of the CPA is to advise the client of the existence of the error and to recommend that the error be discussed with the client's tax return preparer.

SRTP (1991 Rev.) No. 7: Knowledge of Error: Administrative Proceedings

I Introduction:

.01 This statement considers the responsibility of a CPA who becomes aware of an error in a return that is the subject of an administrative proceeding, such as an examination by the IRS or an appeals conference relating to a return or a claim for refund. As used herein, the term "error" includes any position, omission or method of accounting, which, at the time the return is filed, fails to meet the standards set out in SRTP No. 1. The term "error" also includes a position taken on a prior year's return that no longer meets these standards due to legislation, judicial decisions or administrative pronouncements having retroactive effect. However, the term "error" does not include an item that has an insignificant effect on the client's tax liability.

.02 This statement applies whether or not the CPA prepared or signed the return which contains the error; it does not apply where a CPA has been engaged by legal counsel to provide assistance in a matter relating to the counsel's client.

II Statement:

.03 When the CPA is representing a client in an administrative proceeding with respect to a return which contains an error of which the CPA is aware, the CPA should inform the client promptly upon becoming aware of the error. The CPA should recommend the measures to be taken. Such recommendation may be given orally. The CPA is neither obligated to inform the IRS nor is he or she permitted to do so without the client's permission, except where required by law.

.04 The CPA should request the client's agreement to disclose the error to the IRS. Lacking such agreement, the CPA should consider whether to withdraw from representing the client in the administrative proceeding and whether to continue a professional relationship with the client.

III Explanation:

When the CPA is engaged to represent the client before the IRS in an administrative proceeding with respect to a return containing an error of which the CPA is aware, the CPA should advise the client to disclose the error to the IRS. It is the client's responsibility to decide whether to disclose the error. In appropriate cases, particularly where it appears that the IRS might assert the charge of fraud or other criminal misconduct, the client should be advised to consult legal counsel before taking any action. If the client refuses to disclose or permit disclosure of an error, the CPA should consider whether to withdraw from representing the client in the administrative proceeding and whether to continue a professional relationship with the client.

Once disclosure is agreed upon, it should not be delayed to such a degree that the client or CPA might be considered to have failed to act in good faith or to have, in effect, provided misleading information. In any event, disclosure should be made before the conclusion of the administrative proceeding.

Whether an error has an insignificant effect on the client's tax liability should be left to the judgment of the individual CPA based on all the facts and circumstances known to the CPA. In judging whether an erroneous method of accounting has more than an insignificant effect, the CPA should consider the method's cumulative effect and its effect on the return which is the subject of the administrative proceeding.

SRTP (1988 Rev.) No. 8: Form and Content of Advice to Clients

I Introduction:

.01 This statement discusses certain aspects of providing tax advice to a client and considers the circumstances in which the CPA has a responsibility to communicate with the client when subsequent developments affect advice previously provided. The statement does not, however, cover the CPA's responsibilities when it is expected that the advice rendered is likely to be relied upon by parties other than the CPA's client.

II Statement:

.02 In providing tax advice to a client, the CPA should use judgment to ensure that the advice given reflects professional competence and appropriately serves the client's needs. The CPA is not required to follow a standard format or guidelines in communicating written or oral advice to a client.

.03 In advising or consulting with a client on tax matters, the CPA should assume that the advice will affect the manner in which the matters or transactions considered ultimately will be reported on the client's tax returns. Thus, for all tax advice the CPA gives to a client, the CPA should follow the standards in SRTP (1988 Rev.) No. 1 relating to tax return positions.

.04 The CPA may choose to communicate with a client when subsequent developments affect advice previously provided with respect to significant matters. However, the CPA cannot be expected to have assumed responsibility for initiating such communication except while assisting a client in implementing procedures or plans associated with the advice provided or when the CPA undertakes this obligation by specific agreement with the client.

III Explanation:

Concerning the form and content of advice provided to clients, the CPA should consider the following:

1. Importance of the transaction and amounts involved.
2. The specific or general nature of the inquiry.
3. The time available for development and submission of the advice.
4. Technical complications presented.
5. Existence of authorities and precedents.
6. Tax sophistication of the client and the client's staff.
7. The need to seek legal advice.

The explanation recommends written communications in important, unusual or complicated transactions. It also recommends precautionary language to the effect that the advice is based on facts as stated and authorities which are subject to change.

Conclusion

In the beginning of this chapter we learned that the Tax Code imposes penalties against preparers when their client's return has understated the tax liability and there was not a "realistic possibility" that the tax position taken would be sustained if challenged. The IRS defined "realistic possibility" as a one in three chance (or greater). The AICPA promotes a standard that uses similar language. The CPA must have a "good faith belief" that the position advocated has a "realistic possibility" of being sustained if challenged. However, the AICPA rejects the quantification of that standard (one in three), presumably because such quantification is too rigid and does not allow the exercise of professional judgment. The AICPA's standard is essentially the same as that of the American Bar Association.

Cases and Questions

1. What is meant by the term "advocate"? The AICPA speaks of tax practice as an "advocacy engagement." At the same time, in

the Principles section of the *Code of Professional Conduct*, the AICPA stresses the primacy of the profession's responsibility to the public. Are these two concepts contradictory? Explain your answer.

2. The main provisions of subpart B of Circular 230 are summarized in this chapter. They are detailed rules. From what general principles are these rules derived?

3. Christine Schwartz, a CPA and tax practitioner, was not sure how to proceed. Her client had brought a complicated set of facts to her and pleaded that he be allowed to take a certain large deduction if at all possible. Christine carefully researched the Code, Regulations, Rulings, and all the applicable court cases she could locate. Nothing seemed to speak directly to her client's set of circumstances. However, five court cases came close, although each one had slightly different facts. In four of the five cases the taxpayer was denied the deduction. In one of the cases, the deduction was allowed. None of the cases were more (or less) applicable to her client's set of facts than any of the others. Christine summarized the applicable law and the five cases for her client, who barely listened to her. He simply said, "If it was allowed in one case, let's chance it and take the deduction on my tax return."

   a. What guidance (if any) does Circular 230 give to Christine? Does the AICPA *Code of Professional Conduct* offer her any guidance? Do the Statements?

   b. If Christine is a rule utilitarian, how will she likely proceed? If she is a pure rule deontologist?

   c. If Christine is at stage four of moral maturity, how is she likely to reason? At stage five?

4. The Statements are examples of detailed rules. From what general principles are these rules derived? Give examples of other rules which might logically flow from the same general principles.

5. Recall the controversy concerning tax practitioners' primary responsibility, whether it is to the IRS or to the tax client. Do the Statements give any guidance for the resolution of this controversy? Be specific.

6. Do the Statements give guidance over and above the requirements of Treasury Department Circular 230? Be specific. The provisions of Circular 230 are binding whereas the Statements are advisory in nature. For which of the following persons would

that distinction be most meaningful? Least meaningful? Explain your answers.

a. Rule utilitarians.

b. Pure rule deontologists.

c. Mixed rule deontologists.

d. Persons at stage four of moral development.

e. Persons at stage five of moral development.

f. Persons at stage six of moral development.

7. Juan Garcia, a sole practitioner in a local CPA firm, began reviewing the financial information given to him by a tax client whose returns Juan had prepared for several years. This year's information showed a 50 percent decrease in gross profits (from $400,000 to $200,000) without any decrease in net sales or inventory. Juan asked his client about the accuracy of the information he was given, and his client replied, "I've had nothing but trouble with bookkeepers this year. In March, I lost the one who worked for me for years, and since then I've had four replacements. None of them seem to understand how our books work. Finally I got fed up and decided to pull the numbers together myself. I'm sure I got most of the important stuff. Go ahead and use the numbers I gave you; I'm sick of looking at them."

a. What guidance (if any) do the Statements give to Juan? Does Circular 230 give him any guidance? The AICPA *Code of Professional Conduct*?

b. If Juan is a rule utilitarian, how will he likely proceed? If he is a mixed rule deontologist?

c. If Juan is at stage 4 of moral maturity, how is he likely to reason? At stage 5?

Additional Readings

Ayers, F. L., and Jackson, B. R. "Professional Tax Preparers: Problems and Responsibilities." *Federal Taxation* (October 1986): 80–82.

Cheifetz, A. J. "Practitioner Penalties and Circular 230." *The National Public Accountant* (September 1987): 44–46.

Gardner, J. C., and Broden, B. C. "AICPA Comments on Circular 230." *The Tax Advisor* (April 1987): 275–277.

Hutton, M. R., and Liao, W. M. "A CPA's Responsibility: Ethics and Tax Practice." *The CPA Journal* (October 1985): 26–34.

Podolin, L. "Treasury Raises the Stakes in Circular 230 Proposal." *Journal of Accountancy* 165, (April 1988): 60–68.

Raby, W. L. "Ethics in Tax Practice." In *Ethics in the Accounting Profession*, S. E. Loeb, ed. New York: John Wiley & Sons, 1978: 268–277.

Shapiro, L. "Professional Responsibilities in the Eyes of the IRS." *The Tax Advisor* (March 1986): 138–143.

8
Ethics in Consulting Services

Introduction

Chapter Four briefly described the controversy, both within and without the profession, concerning the scope and nature of services rendered by CPA firms. The topic is not new. It was debated in the pages of the *Journal of Accountancy* as early as 1925. But in the last two decades the debate has grown in intensity as a direct result of changes in the profession itself. Tables 8-1 and 8-2 indicate the nature of the changes in one 10-year period: 1974 to 1984.

Not only do audit fees account for less of large firms' revenues, but annual expenditures on auditing as a percentage of revenue of companies audited has been shrinking. In short, if auditing, tax, and consulting are considered product lines, the first appears to have reached its peak and is now decreasing, while the other two are still increasing. Thus, firms wishing to expand must do so by expanding tax and consulting.

The dilemma for the profession is that its monopoly has been granted because of its audit function. As auditing begins to decrease in importance and other services correspondingly increase, the public may begin to question the appropriateness of continuing to grant the monopoly. This is especially true if society believes that expanding

Table 8-1. Average Fee Distribution of Big Eight Accounting Firms.

	1977*	1984*	1989**
Audit	70%	62%	54%
Tax	18%	22%	24%
MAS	11%	16%	22%
Other	1%	0%	0%
	100%	100%	100%

* Source: Adapted from AICPA SEC Practice Section Annual Data and John C. Burton and Patricia Fairfield, "Auditing Evolution in a Changing Environment," *Auditing*, Winter 1982, p. 5.

** Source: Adapted from *Accounting Today* survey, 1989.

Table 8-2. Average Dollar Expenditure on External Audit Fees per Million Dollars of Revenue.

	1974	1984
Manufacturing	$630	$480
Oil/Mining	642	408
Financial	1,482	1,007
Insurance/Utility	306	243
Retail/Services	429	268
Average	698	481

Source: Adapted from R. Mautz, P. Tiessen, and R. Colson, *Internal Auditing: Directions and Opportunities*, Institute of Internal Auditors, 1984, Table C-5.

consulting services impair auditors' independence, the very essence of the profession's public service ideal. Fear that such an erosion of independence might be taking place has led to congressional investigations of the profession during the last two decades. Those investigations are discussed in more detail in Chapters Ten and Eleven.

Consulting and Auditor's Independence

Possible impairment of auditor independence is based on several arguments: those related to independence in fact and those related to independence in appearance.

Independence in Fact

Critics of expanding consulting by auditing firms argue that independence is too important to the profession and to the public to risk its impairment. They point out that consulting performed for an audit client has the potential to reduce independence in fact in a number of ways:

1. Auditors may end up auditing their own work. For example, if a firm advises management to select a certain configuration of computer hardware, then assists in developing appropriate software and information systems, can that firm be independent when auditing the output of those same systems? If a CPA firm assists with the merger of two companies, including the appraisals of assets and determination of goodwill, can it then be independent when auditing the goodwill account?

2. The size of fees received for nonattest services may impair independence. For example, if the annual audit of a company is $90,000 but that company has hired its auditors to perform a

$250,000 consulting engagement, can the CPA firm be independent during the audit?

3. A CPA firm that is expanding its nonattest services may put pressure on auditors to sell additional services to audit clients. The pressure to sell, sell, sell, may impair the auditor's judgment, and therefore his or her independence. For example, Jose Gomez, the partner in charge of the ESM audit, accepted bribes and subverted his firm's quality control procedures in order to cover previous years' audit errors which he had overlooked. In explaining his actions, Gomez told the *Wall Street Journal*,

> In 1977 it became apparent to me that those being promoted early were the business producers . . . they were the ones that were able to produce new clients. The salesmen. It became apparent to me . . . that my own promotion depended on my becoming more productive. That's when I began turning more sales-oriented. I think I would have been able to be more objective about my client relationships if I weren't so concerned about selling. . . . If I had not had the sales pressure, I would perhaps have caught it [the fraud] before it happened.[1]

Those disagreeing with the critics point to a number of empirical studies, two of which, the Cohen Commission report and the Treadway Commission report, are discussed in more detail in Chapters Ten and Eleven. The studies invariably point out that a potential for impairment of independence may exist, but actual impairment has not occurred, at least not on a widespread basis.

The vast majority of companies continue to be audited by CPAs who maintain their integrity and objectivity and independence whether their firms engage in nonattest services with the same clients or not. These same advocates for consulting argue that CPAs whose firms provide consulting for audit clients obtain a greater understanding of the clients' operations and therefore perform more effective audits.

Independence in Appearance

Critics also point out that, even if independence in fact is not impaired, certainly the appearance of independence has been negatively affected. Even if this negative effect cannot be identified with specific firms, the profession as a whole is suffering from the appearance of loss of independence. Why else would the subject continue to be raised by persons within and without the profession? Why else would congress continue to investigate the profession?

Those disagreeing with the critics point out that the appearance of independence, like beauty, is in the eye of the beholder. The public can

---

[1] Martha Brannigan. "Auditor's Downfall Shows a Man Caught in Trap of His Own Making." *Wall Street Journal* (March 4, 1987): 33.

be divided into the uninformed and the informed. To the uninformed, a much more serious impairment of independence than consulting services is the fact that auditors are paid by the very clients from whom they are supposed to be independent. This seems to be an inherent contradiction. Thus, to the uninformed masses, the consulting/audit connection is a minor problem, compared to other structural weaknesses in the system. More sophisticated observers, on the other hand, understand the auditor's function as an objective, third-party expert who examines financial information and attests to its fairness. They understand the term "independence," as used by the profession, to mean the ability to be objective and free from outside influence when making professional judgments. Their working relationships with CPAs reinforce their belief that auditors can be and are independent of their clients, even in those cases where the auditors' firm performs consulting engagements for their audit clients.

The opinions expressed above, concerning what significant groups of non-CPAs believe about auditors' independence and its impairment when combined with consulting, may or may not be valid. Public opinion surveys conducted by Louis Harris and the AICPA's Public Oversight Board (POB) shed more light on the beliefs of those outside the profession. Those surveys are examined in more detail in Chapter Thirteen.

Responsibilities of Profession vs. Firms

Because of the steady growth of nonattest services relative to attestation work, the profession as a whole is approaching a dilemma. It cannot allow auditing, for which the profession receives its monopoly, to become an ancillary service. To do so would be to risk the monopoly itself. Yet individual firms do not face the same threat. They can offer more tax or consulting services than auditing and still reap the benefits of the "CPA" designation. A similar dilemma faces other professions as well. For example, the medical profession acknowledges a responsibility, as a profession, to make medical services available. Yet no particular M.D. has a corresponding responsibility to practice medicine in, say, Appalachia. The only way to resolve such dilemmas is to somehow weave solutions into the structure of the profession itself. For example, the medical profession could mandate national service by each M.D. for a certain length of time. It could attract M.D.s to otherwise unattractive specialties or locations through professional or governmental subsidies. Private insurance mechanisms could be used to fund certain services or medical care could be socialized. The possible solutions are limited only to our collective imaginations.

The accounting profession has only begun, in a very limited way, to solve its scope of services dilemma through structural changes. The

AICPA has exhorted its members to be prudent in Article VI of the Principles section of its *Code of Professional Conduct* (see Chapter Four). In addition, it has offered some guidance in its *Statement on Standards for Consulting Services No. 1*, which is considered next.

Statements on Standards for Consulting Services

In 1975, the Management Advisory Services Executive Committee issued eight *MAS Practice Standards*. Much like the *Statements on Responsibilities in Tax Practice* (see Chapter Seven), these new MAS Standards were advisory in nature, not mandatory. In 1978, the consulting Executive Committee was officially designated by the AICPA Council to promulgate technical standards under Rule 204 of the Rules of Conduct ("Other Technical Standards"). In 1981, the MAS Executive Committee was again designated to promulgate technical standards, this time under Rule 201 ("General Standards"). As a result, the Executive Committee issued three mandatory Statements, the first of which became effective in 1982 and the next two in 1983. Much of the content of the three Statements was similar to their predecessor MAS Practice Standards.

In 1991, the MAS Executive Committee replaced the existing SSMASs with a new *Statement on Standards for Consulting Services No. 1* [SSCS], which is reproduced below.[2] The most significant difference in the new SSCS is its definition of the broad range of functions considered to be consulting services. Previously CPAs had been performing consulting services without always realizing that their services were covered by the guidance offered in the SSMASs. In addition, the Executive Committee directly addressed the issue if consulting services for audit clients by stating that such services do not, in themselves, impair independence. However, professional and governmental requirements may prohibit providing certain consulting services for attest clients.

Statement on Standards for Consulting Services No. 1

Introduction

1. Consulting services that CPAs provide to their clients have evolved from advice on accounting related matters to a wide range of services involving diverse technical disciplines, industry knowledge, and consulting skills. Most practitioners, including those who provide audit and tax services, also pro-

---

[2] Copyright © 1991 by American Institute of Certified Public Accountants, Inc. Reprinted with permission.

vide business and management consulting services to their clients.

2. Consulting services differ fundamentally from the CPA's function of attesting to the assertions of other parties. In an attest service, the practitioner expresses a conclusion about the reliability of a written assertion that is the responsibility of another party, the asserter. In a consulting service, the practitioner develops the findings, conclusions, and recommendations presented. The nature and scope of work is determined solely by the agreement between the practitioner and the client. Generally, the work is performed only for the use and benefit of the client.

3. Historically, CPA consulting services have been commonly referred to as management consulting services, management advisory services, business advisory services, or management services.

4. This SSCS and any subsequent SSCSs apply to any AICPA member holding out as a CPA while providing consulting services as defined herein.

Definitions

5. Terms established for the purpose of the SSCSs are as follows:

Consulting Services Practitioner. Any AICPA member holding out as a CPA while engaged in the performance of a consulting service for a client, or any other individual who is carrying out a consulting service for a client on behalf of any Institute member or member's firm holding out as a CPA.

Consulting Process. The analytical approach and process applied in a consulting service. It typically involves some combination of activities relating to determination of client objectives, fact-finding, definition of the problems or opportunities, evaluation of alternatives, formulation of proposed action, communication of results, implementation, and follow-up.

Consulting Services. Professional services that employ the practitioner's technical skills, education, observations, experiences, and knowledge of the consulting process. Consulting services may include one or more of the following:

a. Consultations, in which the practitioner's function is to provide counsel in a short time frame, based mostly, if not entirely, on existing personal knowledge about the client, the circumstances, the technical matters involved, client representations, and the mutual intent of the parties. Examples of consultations are reviewing and commenting on a client-prepared business plan and suggesting computer software for further client investigation.

b. Advisory services, in which the practitioner's function is to develop findings, conclusions, and recommendations for client consideration and decision making. Examples of advisory services are an operational review and improvement study, analysis of an accounting system, assisting with strategic planning, and defining requirements for an information system.

c. Implementation services, in which the practitioner's function is to put an action plan into effect. Client personnel and resources may be pooled with the practitioner's to accomplish the implementation objectives. The practitioner is responsible to the client for the conduct and management of engagement activities. Examples of implementation services are providing computer system installation and support, executing steps to improve productivity, and assisting with the merger of organizations.

d. Transaction services, in which the practitioner's function is to provide services related to a specific client transaction, generally with a third party. Examples of transaction services are insolvency services, valuation services, preparation of information for obtaining financing, analysis of a potential merger or acquisition, and litigation services.

e. Staff and other support services, in which the practitioner's function is to provide appropriate staff and possibly other support to perform tasks specified by the client. The staff provided will be directed by the client as circumstances require. Examples of staff and other support services are data processing facilities management, computer programming, bankruptcy trusteeship, and controllership activities.

f. Product services, in which the practitioner's function is to provide the client with a product and associated professional services in support of the installation, use, or maintenance of the product. Examples of product services are the sale and delivery of packaged training programs, the sale and implementation of computer software and the sale and installation of systems development methodologies.

Standards for Consulting Services

6. The general standards of the profession are contained in rule 201 of the AICPA Code of Professional Conduct and apply to all services performed by members. They are as follows:

Professional Competence. Undertake only those professional services that the member or the member's firm can reasonably expect to be completed with professional competence.

Due Professional Care. Exercise due professional care in the performance of professional services.

Planning and Supervision. Adequately plan and supervise the performance of professional services.

Sufficient Relevant Data. Obtain sufficient relevant data to afford a reasonable basis for conclusions or recommendations in relation to any professional services performed.

7. The following additional general standards for all Consulting Services are promulgated to address the distinctive nature of Consulting Services in which the understanding with the client may establish valid limitations on the practitioner's performance of services. These Standards are established under Rule 202 of the AICPA Code of Professional Conduct.

Client Interest. Serve the client interest by seeking to accomplish the objectives established by the understanding with the client while maintaining integrity and objectivity.

Understanding With Client. Establish with the client a written or oral understanding about the responsibilities of the parties and the nature, scope, and limitations of services to be performed, and modify the understanding if circumstances require a significant change during the engagement.

Communication With Client. Inform the client of (a) conflicts of interest that may occur pursuant to interpretations of Rule 102 of the Code of Professional Conduct, (b) significant reservations concerning the scope or benefits of the engagement, and (c) significant engagement findings or events.

8. Professional judgment must be used in applying Statements on Standards for Consulting Services in a specific instance since the oral or written understanding with the client may establish constraints within which services are to be provided. For example, the understanding with the client may limit the practitioner's effort with regard to gathering relevant data. The practitioner is not required to decline or withdraw from a consulting engagement when the agreed-upon scope of services includes such limitations.

Consulting Services for Attest Clients

9. The performance of Consulting Services for an attest client does not, in and of itself, impair independence. However, members and their firms performing attest services for a client should comply with applicable independence standards, rules and regulations issued by the AICPA, the state boards of accountancy, state CPA societies, and other regulatory agencies.

Cases and Questions

1. In your opinion, does the expansion of nonattest services by auditors affect the profession's public service ideal? If so, how?

2. What structural changes might the profession make to help solve the issue referred to in Question One?

3. What guidance does the Principles Section of the AICPA Code of Professional Conduct give to CPAs confronted with the issue referred to in Question One? Is this guidance likely to help a

CPA who is a rule or act utilitarian? Is it likely to help a CPA at stage four of moral development? Explain your answers.

4. Why do you think there are no Rules of Conduct governing the issue referred to in Question One?

5. John McGregor, CPA worked as a software and systems consultant for a large CPA firm. He had been working on a project for Diverse Inc. and had more questions than he had answers. While helping Diverse convert their accounts payable system, he noted that some, but not all, accounts under the responsibility of a certain manager had an invisible digit which apparently served as a flag. John asked several employees of Diverse, including the manager and his supervisor, what the purpose of the digit was. It did not print out on any of the company's computer runs. Either his question was not understood, or the answer John got was general and not too satisfying. He didn't know if he should pursue the matter further or not. The invisible digit really had no direct bearing on the work he was doing (in fact he had stumbled upon its existence by accident). Still, John thought it too much of a coincidence that every account payable bearing the digit belonged to some vendor who had a post office box as an address, and the P.O. boxes were all in towns within a 30-mile radius of Diverse's Los Angeles headquarters. John's firm does not perform the annual audit for Diverse, Inc.; a competitor CPA firm has had the audit for the last five years.

   a. Does the Statement on Standards for Consulting Services offer John any guidance in solving his dilemma? Be specific.

   b. Does the AICPA *Code of Professional Conduct* offer John any guidance?

   c. Since this is not an attest engagement, does John have a responsibility to the general public? Why or why not?

   d. What is likely to be John's response if he is a mixed rule deontologist? At stage five of moral development?

Additional Readings

Andresky, J. "But I'm Just the Piano Player." *Forbes* (May 4, 1987): 56–57.

Burton, J. C. "A Critical Look at Professionalism and Scope of Services." *Journal of Accountancy* (April 1980): 48–56.

Elliott, M. S., and Kuttner, M. S. "MAS: Coming of Age." *Journal of Accountancy* (December 1982): 66–72.

Kuffner, M. S. "CPA Consulting Services: A New Standard." *Journal of Accountancy* (November 1991): 38–41.

Murns, Roussey, and Whitner. "Practical Definitions of Six Consulting Functions." *Journal of Accountancy* (November 1991): 43–45.

Previts, G. J. 1985. *The Scope of CPA Services*. New York: John Wiley & Sons.

Stevens, M. "Is Your Accounting Firm Still an Accounting Firm?" *Financial Executive* 6 (July 1985): 24–29.

9
CPAs in Industry and Government

Introduction

In the last 20 years, the percent of AICPA members in public practice has decreased from 61.6 percent to 45.8 percent as shown in Figure 9-1. At the same time AICPA members in industry have increased. Thus, it is appropriate to examine professional guidance and ethical issues facing CPAs in industry and government.

CPAs in industry and government are guided by a number of standards, codes, and other forms of official guidance. For example, the AICPA *Code of Professional Conduct* is applicable to all members (except where explicitly stated otherwise). *Standards of Ethical Conduct for Management Accountants* apply to CPAs functioning as controllers or as accountants with a for-profit organization. Members of the Financial Executives Institute are governed by a *Code of Ethics*, while internal auditors have two sources of guidance, their *Statement of Responsibilities of Internal Auditing*, as well as by their *Standards for the Professional Practice of Internal Auditing*. Government accountants also have a *Code of Ethics* and *Government Auditing Standards*. Thus, one CPA might have

Figure 9-1. AICPA Membership, Selected Years 1970 to 1989*

	1970	1980	1985	1987	1989
Total	75,381	161,319	231,333	254,910	286,358
Public Practice	46,435	87,339	117,850	121,349	131,014
Percent of Total:					
Public Practice	61.6	54.1	51.0	47.6	45.8
Corporate Practice	31.3	35.5	38.8	39.5	39.9
Government Practice	3.8	3.3	3.3	3.4	3.7
Education	3.3	2.9	2.7	2.8	2.7
Misc./Retirement	N/A	4.2	4.2	6.7	7.9

* Magill and Previts. 1991. *Professional Responsibilities: An Introduction.* Cincinnati: South-Western Publishing Co., 28.

allegiance to more than one of the above sources of guidance, as well as his or her own company's code of ethics.

All of the codes and statements for accountants mentioned above share some common themes: objectivity, integrity, honesty, competence, and confidentiality. The role of all accountants, whether providers of information or attestors to information, requires adherence to those principles. Recall from Chapter 1 that deontologists are concerned with principles, and duties or responsibilities often dictate which principles ought to be considered. Thus, the role one plays determines one's duties and duties have related principles. Often, however, CPAs in industry are placed in conflicting roles. They are accountants, and must uphold the principles of integrity, objectivity, competence, and confidentiality, but they are also members of an organization and have the duty of loyalty to that organization. Some codes explicitly state how they expect members to resolve such conflicts, while others do not.

Accountants in industry are not the only professional group faced with the dual roles of loyalty to their professional standards vs. loyalty to their organization. Engineers who work for corporations face the same dilemma. A few excerpts from engineering codes of ethics might highlight the evolution of their thinking about the issues.[1]

In 1912 the American Institute of Electrical Engineers' *Code of Ethics* stated that the engineer should consider "the protection of a client's or employer's interests his first professional obligation." By 1947 the Engineers' Council for Professional Development (a model for many engineers' codes) called for the engineer to "discharge his duties with fidelity to the public, his employers, and clients, and with fairness and impartiality to all. It is his duty to interest himself in public welfare and to be ready to apply his special knowledge for the benefit of mankind." Notice that duties to more than one group are named, but not prioritized, as in the electrical engineers' code of 1912.

A 1974 revision of the Engineers' Council for Professional Development *Canons of Ethics* stated that "Engineers shall hold paramount the safety, health and welfare of the public in the performance of their professional duties." Thus, in 62 years the engineers' thinking on the issues had evolved from a primary duty to clients and employers to conflicting (and presumably equal) duties to clients, employers, and public, to a primary duty to the general public.

The remainder of this chapter is devoted to a discussion of ethical codes (for management accountants, financial executives, internal auditors, and government accountants), to an introduction to the Foreign Corrupt Practices Act, and to a discussion of whistle-blowing.

---

[1] Peterson and Farrell. *Whistle-blowing: Ethical and Legal Issues in Expressing Dissent.* (Dubuque, Iowa: Kendall/Hunt Publishing Co., 1986), 8.

Management Accountants and Financial Executives

As mentioned in Chapter Three, the allocation of scarce financial resources in a free market economy depends upon the market receiving reliable information. Although independent auditors attest to the fairness of financial statements, the primary responsibility for those statements rests with management, especially management accountants. In addition, the effectiveness and efficiency with which managers are able to run their corporations depend upon the quality and quantity of information they receive. Thus, the ethics of management accountants and financial executives are an integral part of our free enterprise system.

A common problem faced by internal accountants is the pressure to compromise their professional standards "for the good of the company." For example, internal accountants have been cited in *Fortune* magazine as employing the following "tricks" in order to obscure the financial position or operating results of their company:[2]

— Smoothing quality profits by setting up a special reserve rather than reporting a large one-time gain.

— Recording bad news in a single quarter to get it behind you or blame the bad news on the old management.

— Delaying recognition of expenses by recording them at a more opportune time.

— Reducing inventories when profits start to flatten by continuing to ship products even though customers have stockpiles.

— Accelerating or decelerating the write-down of assets to produce changes in depreciation expense levels.

— Combining substantial non-recurring transactions with normal operating results.

All of the above "tricks" have one thing in common: a violation of accounting principles in order to achieve an end desirable to management. They are examples of a narrow form of utilitarianism. Recall from Chapter One that Professor Norm Bowie believes that "accountants are deontologists in a utilitarian world." In other words, it is the *role* of the accountant to apply the deontological principles of objectivity, integrity, competence, truth telling, and so on in a world where tremendous pressures exist for the "ends to justify the means."

---

[2] Gary Hector. "Cute Tricks on the Bottom Line." *FORTUNE* (April 24, 1989): 193–200. © 1989 Time Inc. All rights reserved.

Standards of Ethical Conduct for Management Accountants[3]

Management accountants have an obligation to the organizations they serve, their profession, the public, and themselves to maintain the highest standards of ethical conduct. In recognition of this obligation, the National Association of Accountants has promulgated the following standards of ethical conduct for management accountants. Adherence to these standards is integral to achieving the *Objectives of Management Accounting*.[4] Management accountants shall not commit acts contrary to these standards nor shall they condone the commission of such acts by others within their organizations.

Competence

Management accountants have a responsibility to:

— Maintain an appropriate level of professional competence by ongoing development of their knowledge and skills.

— Perform their professional duties in accordance with relevant laws, regulations, and technical standards.

— Prepare complete and clear reports and recommendations after appropriate analyses of relevant and reliable information.

Confidentiality

Management accountants have a responsibility to:

— Refrain from disclosing confidential information acquired in the course of their work except when authorized, unless legally obligated to do so.

— Inform subordinates as appropriate regarding the confidentiality of information acquired in the course of their work and monitor their activities to assure the maintenance of that confidentiality.

— Refrain from using or appearing to use confidential information acquired in the course of their work for unethical or illegal advantages either personally or through third parties.

Integrity

Management accountants have a responsibility to:

— Avoid actual or apparent conflicts of interest and advise all appropriate parties of any potential conflict.

— Refrain from engaging in any activity that would prejudice their ability to carry out their duties ethically.

---

[3] Copyright 1983 by the National Association of Accountants, now the Institute of Management Accountants. Reprinted by permission.

[4] Copyright 1982 by the National Association of Accountants, now the Institute of Management Accountants. Reprinted by permission.

- Refuse any gift, favor, or hospitality that would influence or would appear to influence their actions.
- Refrain from either actively or passively subverting the attainment of the organization's legitimate and ethical objectives.
- Recognize and communicate professional limitations or other constraints that would preclude responsible judgment or successful performance of an activity.
- Communicate unfavorable as well as favorable information and professional judgments or opinions.
- Refrain from engaging in or supporting any activity that would discredit the profession.

Objectivity

Management accountants have a responsibility to:

- Communicate information fairly and objectively.
- Disclose fully all relevant information that could reasonably be expected to influence an intended user's understanding of the reports, comments, and recommendations presented.

Resolution of Ethical Conflict

In applying the standards of ethical conduct, management accountants may encounter problems in identifying unethical behavior or in resolving an ethical conflict. When faced with significant ethical issues, management accountants should follow the established policies of the organization bearing on the resolution of such conflict. If these policies do not resolve the ethical conflict, management accountants should consider the following courses of action:

- Discuss such problems with the immediate superior except when it appears that the superior is involved, in which case the problem would be presented initially to the next higher managerial level. If satisfactory resolution cannot be achieved when the problem is initially presented, submit the issues to the next higher managerial level.

    If the immediate superior is the chief executive officer, or equivalent, the acceptable reviewing authority may be a group such as the audit committee, executive committee, board of directors, board of trustees, or owners. Contact with levels above the immediate superior should be initiated only with the superior's knowledge, assuming the superior is not involved.

- Clarify relevant concepts by confidential discussion with an objective advisor to obtain an understanding of possible course of action.
- If the ethical conflict still exists after exhausting all levels of internal review, the management accountant may have no

other recourse on significant matters than to resign from the organization and to submit an informative memorandum to an appropriate representative of the organization.

Except where legally prescribed, communication of such problems to authorities or individuals not employed or engaged by the organization is not considered appropriate.

Note that the principles management accountants are expected to adhere to include four named in the AICPA *Code of Professional Conduct*: competence, confidentiality, integrity, and objectivity. A fifth standard, Resolution of Ethical Conflict, essentially focuses on loyalty to one's employer. If a management accountant is faced with an irreconcilable conflict between professional principles and behavior that violates those principles, she or he is called upon to resign rather than violate the principles *or* betray her or his loyalty to the corporation. This issue is discussed in more detail later in the chapter.

Code of Ethics of Financial Executives Institute[5]

To be eligible for active membership in Financial Executives Institute, applicants must possess those personal attributes such as character, personal integrity and business ability that will be an asset to the Institute. They must also meet pre-established criteria indicating a high degree of participation in the formulation of policies for the operation of the enterprises they represent and in the administration of the financial functions. Members of the Institute are expected to follow this Code of Ethics.

As a member of Financial Executives Institute, I will:

— Conduct my business and personal affairs at all times with honesty and integrity.

— Provide complete, appropriate and relevant information in an objective manner when reporting to management, stockholders, employees, government agencies, other institutions and the public.

— Comply with rules and regulations of federal, state, provincial, and local governments, and other appropriate private and public regulatory agencies.

— Discharge duties and responsibilities to my employer to the best of my ability, including complete communication on all matters within my jurisdiction.

— Maintain the confidentiality of information acquired in the course of my work except when authorized or otherwise

---

[5] Copyright 1992 by the Financial Executives Institute, 10 Madison Avenue, Morriston, NJ 07962-1938. Reprinted by permission.

legally obligated to disclose. Confidential information acquired in the course of my work will not be used for my personal advantage.

— Maintain an appropriate level of professional competence through continuing development of my knowledge and skills.

— Refrain from committing acts discreditable to myself, my employer, FEI or fellow members of the Institute.

Note that Financial Executive Institute members are those persons in an organization who participate, to a high degree, in the formulation of policies for their corporation and are the administrators of its financial functions. They tend to occupy a higher position in their companies than most management accountants. It is their responsibility to set the "tone at the top," referred to by the Treadway Commission.

Statement of Responsibilities of Internal Auditing[6]

The purpose of this statement is to provide in summary form a general understanding of the role and responsibilities of internal auditing. For more specific guidance, readers should refer to the *Standards for the Professional Practice of Internal Auditing*.

Objective and Scope

Internal auditing is an independent appraisal function established within an organization to examine and evaluate its activities as a service to the organization. The objective of internal auditing is to assist members of the organization in the effective discharge of their responsibilities. To this end, internal auditing furnishes them with analysis, appraisals, recommendations, counsel, and information concerning the activities reviewed. The audit objective includes promoting effective control at reasonable cost. The members of the organization assisted by internal auditing include those in management and the board of directors.

The scope of internal auditing should encompass the examination and evaluation of the adequacy and effectiveness of the organization's system of internal control and the quality of performance in carrying out assigned responsibilities. Internal auditors should:

— Review the reliability and integrity of financial and operating information and the means to identify, measure, classify, and report such information.

— Review the systems established to ensure compliance with those policies, plans, procedures, laws, and regulations which could have significant impact on operations and reports, and determining whether the organization is in compliance.

---

[6] From *Statement of Responsibilities* by The Institute of Internal Auditors. Copyright 1990 by the Institute of Internal Auditors, Inc., 249 Maitland Avenue, Altamonte Springs, Florida 32701 U.S.A. Reprinted with permission.

— Review the means of safeguarding assets and, as appropriate, verifying the existence of such assets.

— Appraise the economy and efficiency with which resources are employed.

— Review operations or programs to ascertain whether results are consistent with established objectives and goals and whether the operations or programs are being carried out as planned.

Responsibility and Authority

The internal auditing department is an integral part of the organization and functions under the policies established by senior management and the board. The purpose, authority and responsibility of the internal auditing department should be defined in a formal written document (charter). The director of internal auditing should seek approval of the charter by senior management as well as acceptance by the board. The charter should make clear the purposes of the internal auditing department, specify the unrestricted scope of its work, and declare that auditors are to have no authority or responsibility for the activities they audit.

Throughout the world internal auditing is performed in diverse environments and within organizations which vary in purpose, size, and structure. In addition, the laws and customs within various countries differ from one another. These differences may affect the practice of internal auditing in each environment. The implementation of the *Standards for the Professional Practice of Internal Auditing* therefore, will be governed by the environment in which the internal auditing department carries out its assigned responsibilities. Compliance with the concepts enunciated by the *Standards for the Professional Practice of Internal Auditing* is essential before the responsibilities of internal auditors can be met. As stated in the *Code of Ethics*, members of The Institute of Internal Auditors, Inc. and Certified Internal Auditors shall adopt suitable means to comply with the *Standards for the Professional Practice of Internal Auditing*.

Independence

Internal auditors should be independent of the activities they audit. Internal auditors are independent when they can carry out their work freely and objectively. Independence permits internal auditors to render the impartial and unbiased judgments essential to the proper conduct of audits. It is achieved through organizational status and objectivity.

The organizational status of the internal auditing department should be sufficient to permit the accomplishment of its audit responsibilities. The director of the internal auditing department should be responsible to an individual in the organization with sufficient authority to promote independence and to ensure a broad audit coverage, adequate consideration of audit reports, and appropriate action on audit recommendations.

Objectivity is an independent mental attitude which internal auditors should maintain in performing audits. Internal auditors are not to subordinate their judgment on audit matters to that of others. Designing, installing, and operating systems are not audit functions. Also, the drafting of procedures for systems is not an audit function. Performing such activities is presumed to impair audit objectivity.

Note that independence, for internal auditors, refers to organizational status and objectivity. Examples of weak and strong organizational structures, from an internal audit perspective, are shown in Figure 9-2.

The weak form of organizational structure is weak because the internal auditors are expected to audit the work of the controller, to whom they directly report. Independence is lost. When the internal

Figure 9-2. Organizational Structures.

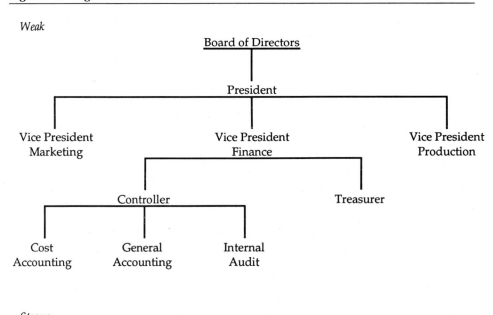

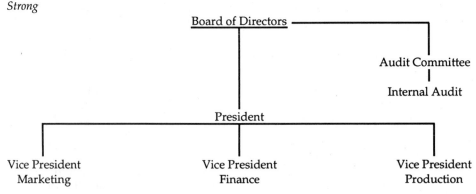

auditors report directly to the audit committee of the board of directors, however, they are much more independent from the managers whose work they audit.

Institute of Internal Auditors Code of Ethics[7]

Purpose

A distinguishing mark of a profession is acceptance by its members of responsibility to the interests of those it serves. Members of The Institute of Internal Auditors (Members) and Certified Internal Auditors (CIAs) must maintain high standards of conduct in order to effectively discharge this responsibility. The Institute of Internal Auditors (Institute) adopts this Code of Ethics for Members and CIAs.

Applicability

This Code of Ethics is applicable to all Members and CIAs. Membership in The Institute and acceptance of the "Certified Internal Auditor" designation are voluntary actions. By acceptance, Members and CIAs assume an obligation of self-discipline above and beyond the requirements of laws and regulations.

The standards of conduct set forth in this Code of Ethics provide basic principles in the practice of internal auditing. Members and CIAs should realize that their individual judgment is required in the application of these principles.

CIAs shall use the "Certified Internal Auditor" designation with discretion and in a dignified manner, fully aware of what the designation denotes. The designation shall also be used in a manner consistent with all statutory requirements.

Members who are judged by the Board of Directors of The Institute to be in violation of the standards of conduct of the Code of Ethics shall be subject to forfeiture of their membership in The Institute. CIAs who are similarly judged also shall be subject to forfeiture of the "Certified Internal Auditor" designation.

Standards of Conduct

    I. Members and CIAs shall exercise honesty, objectivity, and diligence in the performance of their duties and responsibilities.

   II. Members and CIAs shall exercise loyalty in all matters pertaining to the affairs of their organization or to whomever they may be rendering a service. However, Members and CIAs shall not knowingly be a party to any illegal or improper activity.

  III. Members and CIAs shall not knowingly engage in acts or activities which are discreditable to the profession of internal auditing or to their organization.

---

[7] From *Code of Ethics* by The Institute of Internal Auditors. Copyright 1988 by The Institute of Internal Auditors, Inc., 249 Maitland Avenue, Altamonte Springs, Florida 32701 U.S.A. Reprinted with permission.

IV. Members and CIAs shall refrain from entering into any activity which may be in conflict with the interest of their organization or which would prejudice their ability to carry out objectively their duties and responsibilities.

V. Members and CIAs shall not accept anything of value from an employee, client, customer, supplier, or business associate of their organization which would impair or be presumed to impair their professional judgment.

VI. Members and CIAs shall undertake only those services which they can reasonably expect to complete with professional competence.

VII. Members and CIAs shall adopt suitable means to comply with the *Standards for the Professional Practice of Internal Auditing*.

VIII. Members and CIAs shall be prudent in the use of information acquired in the course of their duties. They shall not use confidential information for any personal gain nor in any manner which would be contrary to law or detrimental to the welfare of their organization.

IX. Members and CIAs, when reporting on the results of their work, shall reveal all material facts known to them which, if not revealed, could either distort reports of operations under review or conceal unlawful practices.

X. Members and CIAs shall continually strive for improvement in their proficiency, and in the effectiveness and quality of their service.

XI. Members and CIAs, in the practice of their profession, shall be ever mindful of their obligation to maintain the high standards of competence, morality and dignity promulgated by The Institute. Members shall abide by the Bylaws and uphold the objectives of The Institute.

The role of internal auditors is located somewhere between that of external auditors and management accountants. Although they perform audits of controls and financial information, they do so as employees of the organization they audit. A strong organizational structure with effective internal auditors is one of the most effective internal control mechanisms open to modern corporations.

Association of Government Accountants Code of Ethics[8]

Introduction

The Association of Government Accountants is a national professional organization devoted to excellence in financial management at

---

[8] *Bylaws*, Article I, Section 3. Association of Government Accountants. 2200 Mount Vernon Avenue, Alexandria, VA 22301. Reprinted by permission.

all levels of government. It has 13,000 members in 85 chapters located in 39 states, the District of Columbia and several U.S. territories. Individually, members are dedicated financial managers, accountants, auditors, budget analysts or financial planners at the federal, state and municipal levels. Together, the members proudly serve government and its people with vitality and, above all, an unswerving commitment to quality.

The Association of Government Accountants' major program objectives are to:

- Unite professional financial managers in government service to perform more efficiently for their own development and thereby for the benefit of the government and society.

- Encourage and provide an effective means for interchange of work-related and professional ideas.

- Aid in improving financial management and accounting and auditing techniques and concepts.

- Improve financial management education in all levels of government and universities.

Purpose

To foster the highest professional standards and behavior, and to provide exemplary service to the government, this Code of Ethics has been developed to guide members of the Association of Government Accountants and for the information of their employers.

Definitions

When reference is made to a member, it is intended to include all classes of membership. Reference made to employer applies to a government agency as an entity and to a nongovernment organization to the extent the principle is considered applicable.

Explanations

To better define each ethical principle, an explanation is included.

ETHICAL PRINCIPLES

Personal Behavior

1. A member shall not engage in acts or be associated with activities which are contrary to the public interest or bring discredit to the Association of Government Accountants.

    This principle cautions members to avoid actions which adversely affect the public interest and the professional image of the association.

2. A member shall not engage in private employment or act as an independent practitioner for remuneration except with the employer's consent.

This principle identifies a restriction against private earnings which result from the use of a member's professional qualifications without the employer's expressed approval.

3. A member shall not purposefully transmit or use confidential information obtained in professional work for personal gain or other advantage.

This principle prohibits the improper use of official position or office for strictly personal purposes, monetary or otherwise.

4. A member shall adhere to all employer-generated Standards of Conduct. This principle endorses the commitment of employees to recognize the Standards of Conduct prescribed by their employers.

Professional Competence and Performance

5. A member shall strive to fulfill all work-related responsibilities and supervise the work of subordinates with the highest degree of professional care. This principle emphasizes the requirement that a member give special attention to the professional aspects of work and not condone substandard performance at any level.

6. A member shall continually seek to increase professional knowledge and skills and to improve service to employers, associates and fellow members.

This principle stresses the importance of professional development and skills in contributing to the profession as a whole.

7. A member shall render opinions, observations or conclusions for official purposes only after appropriate professional consideration of the pertinent facts.

This principle underscores the importance of avoiding unsupported opinions involving professional judgments which would cause inappropriate official actions.

8. A member shall exercise diligence, objectivity and honesty in professional activities and be aware of the responsibility to disclose any and all improprieties that may arise.

This principle places the responsibility upon a member to exercise moral and independent judgment and to disclose to appropriate authorities those illegal, improper or unethical practices noted in the course of work.

9. A member shall be aware of and strive to apply work-related requirements and standards prescribed by employers.

This principle recognizes that special professional criteria may be required by employers in certain assignments.

Responsibility to Others

10. In the performance of any assignment, a member shall consider the public interest to be paramount.

This principle stresses that a member's foremost concern must be the public interest in any work situation involving competing interest.

11. A member shall not engage in any activity or establish any relationship which creates or gives the appearance of a conflict with employer-related responsibilities.

   This principle cautions against becoming involved in situations in which a member's official or personal activities appear to be inconsistent with prescribed employer responsibilities.

12. In speaking engagements or writings for publications, a member shall identify personal opinions which may differ from official, employer-related positions.

   This principle underscores the need to avoid inappropriate interpretations by the public from speeches or articles by members which reflect their personal viewpoints rather than the official positions of their employers.

Note that the government accountants' code covers functions analogous to those of management accountants *and* internal auditors. While issues relating to personal behavior and competence are addressed, the code explicitly states the paramount status of the public interest. This is similar to the AICPA code, but differs from the codes of management accountants and internal auditors, neither one of which explicitly address nor prioritize their public service ideal.

Foreign Corrupt Practices Act of 1977

While the Treadway Commission emphasized the "tone at the top," a decade earlier Congress passed the Foreign Corrupt Practices Act (FCPA) to emphasize the importance of strong internal accounting controls. The FCPA amended the Securities Exchange Act of 1934 to require that:

Every issuer which has a class of securities registered pursuant to section 12 of this title and every issuer which is required to file reports pursuant to section 15(d) of this title shall—

(A) make and keep books, records, and accounts, which, in reasonable detail, accurately and fairly reflect the transactions and dispositions of the assets of the issuer; and

(B) devise and maintain a system of internal accounting controls sufficient to provide reasonable assurances that—

   (i) transactions are executed in accordance with management's general or specific authorization;

   (ii) transactions are recorded as necessary (1) to permit preparation of financial statements in conformity with generally accepted accounting principles or any other criteria applicable to such statements, and (2) to maintain accountability for assets;

(iii) access to assets is permitted only in accordance with management's general or specific authorization; and

(iv) the recorded accountability for assets is compared with the existing assets at reasonable intervals and appropriate action is taken with respect to any differences.

The task of implementing the FCPA falls primarily on accountants internal to the organization. To knowingly fail to comply with its provisions subjects management to possible fines and imprisonment.

Whistle-Blowing

What is a CPA to do when, in spite of the FCPA, the organization's formal structure and written policies (including its Code of Conduct), and the presence of external auditors, he or she is aware of wrong doing, which constitutes a serious threat of harm to the public interest? If that CPA has exhausted all internal channels of recourse to no avail, is there no other recourse than to resign? Is it ever appropriate to make authorities outside the organization aware of the problem? In other words, is it ever appropriate to "blow the whistle?"

Whistleblowing is a special form of dissent in which a member or former member of an organization goes outside the organization or outside normal organizational channels to reveal organizational wrong-doing, illegality, or actions that threaten the public. The term is reserved for revelations of significant misbehavior with consequences for a number of people.[9]

In a 1981 article titled, "What Is Business Ethics?" Peter Drucker stated that whistle-blowing is just another word for informing and "the only societies in Western history that encouraged informers were bloody and infamous tyrannies." In Drucker's view, "under 'whistleblowing,' under the regime of the 'informer' no mutual trust, no interdependence, and no ethics are possible."[10]

Others see whistle-blowers as courageous citizens, upholders of professional standards, and protectors of the public interest. For example, Ralph Nader has stated that employees "should have the right to go public, and the corporation should expect them to do so when internal channels of communication are exhausted and the problem

---

[9] Peterson and Farrell, op. cit., 4–5.

[10] Drucker, Peter. "What Is Business Ethics?" *The Public Interest* 63 (1981): 33.

remains uncorrected. In this way whistleblowing becomes a powerful lever for organizational responsibility and accountability."[11]

Currently, the *Standards of Ethical Conduct for Management Accountants* state clearly that "Except where legally prescribed, communication of such problems [that is, serious corporate misconduct] to authorities or individuals not employed or engaged by the organization is not considered appropriate."

For a management accountant at stage four of moral development, whistle-blowing is thus not an option. At stage five, however, a management accountant would ask "what *should* the rules be?" And not all management accountants at stage five would agree on the answer to that question.

If one believes that whistle-blowing should be an option, then other questions must first be answered. For example:[12]

> What takes precedence when professional judgment and organizational authority clash?
>
> When should one's responsibility to the public be placed before loyalty to one's employer?
>
> Does one ever have an *obligation* [as opposed to a *right*] to be a whistle-blower?
>
> Does one have to go public when revealing wrongdoing, or can this be done anonymously?

Codes of conduct change over time to reflect changes in society. Issues relating to confidentiality and whistle-blowing are being re-examined by several professional groups, including the professions of medicine, and engineering. These re-examinations reflect changes in society's expectations, particularly as reflected in case law. As more and more court cases reject confidentiality as a defense, professional organizations are beginning to grapple with questions such as those listed above. It is not unreasonable to expect that professional accountants will soon do the same.

Cases and Questions

1. Josephine Ruiz, controller of Q-Tech, felt uncomfortable about a conversation she had just had with Thomas Gates, president of Q-Tech. Up until now she had been pleased with their working relationship. Q-Tech was an independently run, wholly owned

---

[11] Peterson and Farrell, op. cit., 7.

[12] Ibid., 7.

U.S. subsidiary of an international corporation based in Japan. Mr. Gates had taken over as president just one year ago and had been responsible for a positive increase in revenues and earnings in that time.

The troubling conversation concerned Mr. Gates' expense reimbursement vouchers. Josephine knew that large entertainment expenditures were common in this Japanese firm, but some of Mr. Gates' expenditures appeared to be of a personal nature. When she asked him for details (for proper classification for tax purposes), Mr. Gates seemed defensive and annoyed. He responded, "The Home Office expects me to do a lot of entertaining. And I have an agreement with them about personal items. They are a part of my compensation package."

    a. Analyze Josephine's dilemma using the model of ethical decision making found in the Preface.

    b. What internal control structures or mechanisms might prevent dilemmas like this one for controllers?

2. Define "independence" as the term is employed by internal auditors. Contrast it to the concept of independence in the AICPA *Code of Professional Conduct*.

3. The American Association of Engineering Societies, an umbrella organization comprised of 22 engineering societies, states the following: "Engineers perceiving a consequence of their professional duties to adversely affect the present or future public health and safety shall formally advise their employers or clients and, if warranted, consider further disclosure."[13] Contrast that statement with the guidance given by the Institute of Management Accountants for its members. What do you think accounts for the differences?

4. Lee Jackson, an Associate Inspector General for the Department of Consumer Affairs, had made a lot of enemies in his day—it was his job. His audits and investigations often resulted in fines and bad publicity for large and well-known corporations. Lee was proud of his work and believed that he was truly a watchdog for the interests of consumers. He didn't understand, therefore, why a change in the political climate in his state should result in so much personal grief. He had heard a rumor that some executives at the corporations he had investigated were out to "get his scalp." Those same executives were now in favor

---

[13] Gorlin, Rena, ed., *Codes of Professional Responsibility.* (Washington, D.C.: Bureau of National Affairs, 1970), 64.

with the new "probusiness" administration and might be in a position to do just that.

Lee was completely bewildered and taken off guard when he arrived at work one morning and found that a subordinate, whom he had fired for incompetence over a month ago, was now filing charges against him for "recriminating" and was seeking protection under the state's Whistle-blowers Protection Act. It seems the subordinate claimed Lee, who had made some purely editorial changes (as he often did) on one of the subordinate's reports, had falsified the report and fired him for whistle-blowing about it. The fact that the firing preceded the whistle-blowing by a month would not deter the investigation.

Lee was advised by the investigator that he had two choices: he could fight the charges, but the publicity of the investigation would be personally damaging and would also hurt his family and legal fees would run upwards of $200,000 (which Lee did not have), or he could admit the charges and receive a "reprimand." The item would not be publicized and Lee could keep his job, although he probably would never be promoted. In the meantime, Lee was being transferred to another office until the item was settled. He would be given no assignments and was to discontinue all work on his present assignments.

a. Analyze Lee's dilemma using the model of ethical decision making found in the Preface.

Additional Readings

Albrecht, Steve. *Ethical Issues in the Practice of Accounting*. Cincinnati: South-Western Publishing Co, 1992, 115–124.

Bok, S. "Whistleblowing and Leaks." *Secrets: On the Ethics of Concealment and Revelation*. New York: Pantheon Books, 1982, 210–310.

Hector, Gray. "Cute Tricks on the Bottom Line," *Fortune* (April 24, 1989): 193–200.

Peterson and Farrell. *Whistle-blowing: Ethical and Legal Issues in Expressing Dissent*. Dubuque, Iowa: Kendall/Hunt Publishing Co., 1986.

PART FOUR
Congressional and Professional Investigations

10
Investigations During the 1970s

Introduction

By the mid-1970s, several events had occurred that alarmed the general public and, in turn, their elected representatives in Washington, D.C. The bankruptcy of several large publicly owned companies, such as Equity Funding, Penn Central, Four Seasons Nursing Homes, and National Student Marketing, turned everyone's attention to the auditors. Why weren't investors warned? Another, perhaps even larger factor causing scrutiny of the profession was the disclosure of illegal and improper payments by some large and prestigious corporations. After Watergate, the nation was in no mood to tolerate bribery, illegal political contributions, kickbacks, slush funds, or secret bank accounts. Again came the cry, "Where were the auditors?"

Congressman Moss

In 1976, the House of Representatives' Subcommittee on Oversight and Investigations issued a report calling for regulatory reform. The subcommittee was chaired by John E. Moss (D-Calif.), and hence the report is often referred to as the "Moss Report." It covered six independent regulatory commissions and three executive branch regulatory agencies. Although the report placed the SEC at the top of its list in rating the effectiveness of the nine federal agencies it studied, the chapter on the SEC was extremely critical of its role in overseeing the accounting profession. The report made the following suggestions:[1]

1. Uniform accounting principles should be prescribed by the SEC.

2. The "fairness" standard applied by auditors in the attest function is deficient.

---

[1] *Journal of Accountancy* (December 1976): 26. Copyright © 1976 by American Institute of Public Accountants, Inc. Reprinted with permission.

3. Auditors should attest to the quality of internal controls and the enforcement of those controls.

4. Corporate boards of directors should have a majority of members who are unrelated to management.

5. The SEC should prescribe and enforce auditing standards.

6. The SEC should prescribe and enforce a code of conduct for independent auditors.

7. Section 10(b) of the Securities Act should be amended so that negligence [of auditors] is a criminal act.

Clearly the above recommendations were tantamount to declaring that the public accounting profession should be regulated by government instead of being allowed to regulate itself.

Senator Metcalf

The Accounting Establishment

Accountants were still reeling from what they considered to be the "attack" by the Moss Report when another report was issued in January, 1977. This report, which contained 1,760 pages and weighed about 4 $\frac{1}{2}$ pounds, was titled "The Accounting Establishment: A Staff Study."

This report was issued by the staff of the Senate's Subcommittee on Reports, Accounting, and Management, which was chaired by Senator Lee Metcalf (D-Mont.). The extremely critical tone of this new report could be seen from the following excerpt, which comes from page four of its summary:

> The "Big Eight" are often called "public accounting firms" or "independent public accounting firms." This study finds little evidence that they serve the public or that they are independent in fact from the interests of their corporate clients. For that reason, this study refers to the "Big Eight" simply as accounting firms.

The main thesis of the staff report, that the accounting profession is dominated by the Big Eight firms, is depicted on page three of its summary and is reproduced in Figure 10-1.

The Metcalf staff report concluded with 16 recommendations which, taken together, amounted to a complete Federal takeover of the accounting profession:

1. Congress should exercise stronger oversight of accounting practices.

2. Congress should establish comprehensive accounting objectives.

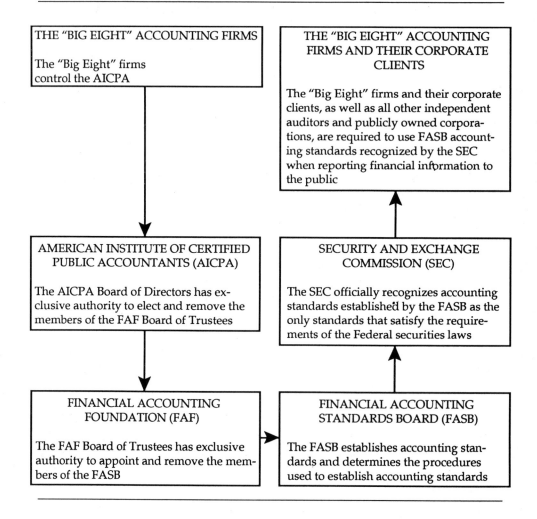

Figure 10-1. Control of the "Big Eight" Accounting Firms and the AICPA over Accounting Standards Approved by the SEC.

3. Congress should amend the Federal securities laws to allow individuals to sue auditors for negligence without having to prove "scienter" or intent to deceive.

4. Congress should consider methods of increasing competition among accounting firms.

5. The Federal Government should directly establish financial accounting standards for publicly-owned corporations.

6. The Federal Government should establish auditing standards used by independent auditors to certify the accuracy of corporate financial statements and supporting records.

7. The Federal Government should itself periodically inspect the work of independent auditors for publicly-owned corporations.

8. The Federal Government should promulgate and enforce strict standards of conduct for auditors. Those standards should specifically prohibit direct or indirect representation of clients' interests and performance of non-accounting management advisory services for public or private clients.

9. The Federal Government should require the nation's 15 largest accounting firms to report basic operational and financial data annually.

10. The Federal Government should define the responsibilities of independent auditors so that they clearly meet the expectations of Congress, the public, and courts of law. The independent auditor's certification should be understood by all auditors to mean that financial information is presented fairly and that corporate records are complete and accurate.

11. The Federal Government should establish financial accounting standards, cost accounting standards, auditing standards, and other accounting practices in meetings open to the public.

12. The Federal Government should act to relieve excessive concentration in the supply of auditing and accounting services to major publicly-owned corporations.

13. The Federal Government should retain accounting firms which act as independent auditors only to perform auditing and accounting services.

14. The SEC should treat all independent auditors equally in disciplinary and enforcement proceedings.

15. The membership of the Cost Accounting Standards Board should not be dominated by representatives of industry and accounting firms which may have a vested interest in the standards established.

16. Federal employees should not serve on committees of the AICPA or similar organizations.

Final Recommendations

After publication of the staff report, Senator Metcalf's Subcommittee conducted eight days of congressional hearings concerning the accounting profession. In November, 1977, the Subcommittee issued its final report, which was considerably toned down from its earlier staff report. Nevertheless, it continued to call for sweeping changes. Some of the recommendations were as follows:

1. Companies should reveal the effect of adopting one generally accepted accounting principle over others, and auditors should

give an opinion concerning the appropriateness of the chosen alternative.

2. Accounting firms should form an organization to oversee mandatory quality reviews of all auditing firms. The organization should be governed by an executive board that includes non-accountants, and results of reviews should be forwarded to the SEC and made public.

3. Non-accounting management services, such as executive recruitment, marketing analysis, plant layout, product analysis, and actuarial services are incompatible with the public responsibilities of independent auditors and should be discontinued. Management services related to accounting are confined to the limited area of providing certain computer and systems analyses that are necessary for improving internal control procedures.

4. There must be an immediate end to artificial professional restrictions against advertising and solicitation of other firms' clients or staff.

5. Independent auditors should be liable for their negligence to private parties who suffer damages as a result.

AICPA Response

In January, 1978, and again later that year, Congressman Moss held another series of hearings to determine what, if any, response the profession was making to all of the public scrutiny and congressional recommendations.

Institutional Changes

In testimony before the Subcommittee on Oversight and Investigations, AICPA officials cited the establishment of a new Division for CPA Firms. Prior to the Division for Firms, AICPA jurisdiction, in the form of its *Code of Professional Ethics*, extended only to individual CPAs. Now CPA firms would be monitored as well if they elected to join the voluntary Division for Firms. The division included two sections, one for firms with SEC practice and one for firms with private companies practice. Under the SEC practice section, self-regulation would be accomplished by mandatory peer review, sanctions of firms for failure to meet requirements, mandatory rotation of audit-engagement partners, public reporting of certain firm information, and monitoring of all section activities by a Public Oversight Board (POB).

The POB would consist of five "prominent individuals of high integrity and reputation" appointed by the SEC Practice Section's Executive Committee. The POB was given the following responsibilities and functions:

1. Monitor and evaluate the regulatory and sanction activities of the Peer Review and Executive Committees.

2. Determine that the Peer Review Committee is ascertaining that firms are taking appropriate action as a result of peer reviews.

3. Conduct continuing oversight of all other activities of the section.

4. Make recommendations to the Executive Committee for improvements in the operations of the section.

5. Publish periodic reports on results of its oversight activities.

6. Engage staff to assist in carrying out its functions.

7. Have the right for any or all of its members to attend any meetings of the Executive Committee.

In testimony before the Subcommittee, the SEC Chairman recommended that the profession be allowed more time to implement its new structural changes before Congress consider the imposition of other forms of regulation. The SEC also recommended that the profession be allowed more time to respond to the final recommendations of the Commission on Auditors' Responsibilities, which was about to be released.

Cohen Commission Report

The Commission on Auditors' Responsibilities (referred to as the "Cohen Commission" because its chair was Manual F. Cohen) was an independent commission funded by the AICPA. It issued its *Report, Conclusions, and Recommendations* in early 1978. Some observers believed that the Cohen Commission report was in response to congressional hearings during 1976–1978. The Commission, however, began its work in 1974, made two interim progress reports to the AICPA Council during this same period, and issued a *Report of Tentative Conclusions* in March, 1977. Thus, the work of the Cohen Commission really paralleled the congressional hearings and was undoubtedly in response to the same factors that triggered those hearings.

Manual Cohen was an attorney and was previously chairman of the SEC. Other members of the Commission included a professor of accounting; a chairman of the board and CEO of a large financial corporation; a former president of the Financial Analysts Federation; a retired managing partner of a large CPA firm, who was also a former president of the AICPA and a former chairman of the Accounting Principles Board; a senior technical partner of a Big Eight accounting firm; and a managing partner of a smaller CPA firm.

The main charge of the Commission was to determine whether or not a gap exists (an "expectations gap") between what the public expects and what auditors can and should reasonably expect to accomplish. If such a gap was determined to exist, the Commission was to offer recommendations to aid the profession in bridging the gap.

The Commission did indeed determine that there was an expectations gap, and offered widespread recommendations covering a range of topics, including the following:

1. Management should report to users the condition and effectiveness of controls over the accounting system and management's response to the suggestions of the auditor for correction of weaknesses.

2. The auditor should report on whether s/he agrees with management's description of the company's controls and should describe material uncorrected weaknesses not disclosed in that report.

3. The auditor's report should be revised to consist of a series of paragraphs, each describing a major element of the audit function. The audit function should be more clearly described as well as the findings of the auditor, and management's responsibilities. Reference to consistency and the phrase "presents fairly" should be deleted.

4. Corporations should be required to adopt codes of conduct. The auditor should review the company's code of conduct and the procedures adopted to monitor compliance with it. The auditor should determine whether there are material weaknesses in the related monitoring procedures and report on these matters.

5. An audit should be designed to provide reasonable assurance that the financial statements are not affected by material fraud and also to provide reasonable assurance on the accountability of management for material amounts of corporate assets.

The Commission's report discussed the concern of "a significant minority of users" who believe that the performance of management advisory services by auditors might impair their independence. The report discussed several empirical studies and concluded that, "Except in the Westec case, the Commission's research has not found instances in which an auditor's independence appears to have been compromised by providing other services." (p. xxviii).

Nevertheless, the Commission acknowledged that, "If the views of the minority were supported by empirical evidence of loss of independence, prohibition of management services would be essential." (p. xxviii).

Conclusion

The decade of the 1970s concluded without the passage of any of the legislation that appeared so threatening during 1976–1977. The lack of legislation was due partly to the structural changes in the profession, in particular the creation of the Division for CPA Firms within the AICPA and the creation of the Public Oversight Board. The Cohen Commission Report also influenced Congress to wait and see whether the profession would seriously attempt to correct its own problems by adopting some or all of the Commission's recommendations. By the end of the decade, the Watergate era had come to a close, Ronald Reagan had been elected to the White House, and the mood in Washington, D.C. had changed considerably. For a time, at least, the "heat" appeared to be off the profession.

Questions

1. Summarize, in your own words, the recommendations of the Moss report which would have been most radical to the profession. Do the same for the Metcalf staff report and Metcalf's final recommendations.

2. If the above recommendations had been mandated by Congress, would public accounting still be a profession? Why or why not?

3. Which of the above recommendations were substantially carried out by the creation of the Division for Firms? The POB? Which of the congressional recommendations were substantially repeated by the Cohen Commission recommendations? Which congressional recommendations were left unaddressed?

4. Do you agree with the Cohen Commission's report that, in the absence of empirical evidence of actual impairment of independence, auditors should be allowed to perform consulting services for their audit clients? Why or why not?

5. The profession's primary responsibility is to the general public. Do you believe the public's elected representatives (members of Congress) are a good surrogate for the general public (that is, should Congress' recommendations be equated with the public's recommendations)? Why or why not?

Additional Readings

Dixon, A. J. "Commentary on the Metcalf Committee Report." *The CPA Journal* (June 1977): 11–18.

Hagerman, R. L. "The Metcalf Report: Selling Some Assumptions." *Management Accounting* (January 1978): 13–16.

Moss, J. E. "Federal Regulatory Proposals Affecting the Profession." *California CPA Quarterly* (September 1977): 6–10.

11
Investigations During the 1980s

Introduction

Although no legislation was enacted during the 1970s, and although the 1980s appeared to dawn with a more favorable political climate, the calm before the storm was short lived. The early part of the decade brought deregulation of financial institutions and hence increased competition among institutions such as commercial banks and savings and loan associations and others. New, innovative investment vehicles began to emerge whose risks were not well understood. Combine those financial industry changes with the recession experienced by the economy in the early 1980s, and the results were predictable: a rash of financial institutions facing bankruptcy. ESM Government Securities, Penn Square Bank, Continental Illinois, Drysdale Government Securities, Beverly Hills Savings and Loan, Home State Savings Bank of Ohio, and American Savings and Loan of Florida were names becoming more and more common in the financial press. A disturbing feature of this new rash of bankruptcies was the fact that financial fraud was often a key element leading to the business failure. Public and congressional reaction was similar to the reactions a decade earlier: "Where were the auditors?" A new round of congressional hearings began in 1985.

Congressman Dingell

Representative John D. Dingell (D-Mich.) was chair of both the House Committee on Energy and Commerce and its Subcommittee on Oversight and Investigations (the same subcommittee chaired by Congressman Moss in the 1970s). He called for a series of investigative hearings that continued into 1988. He characterized the hearings, when they first began, as "a fact-finding mission concerning a rules-making and regulatory process." "It is becoming rather clear to us," he said "that the regulatory process is not being well served in many instances by the work being performed by auditors and accountants."[1]

The hearings began to focus on specific corporations and industries. One day of hearings was held "regarding the auditing, accounting, business and regulatory practices which led to the financial failure of ESM Government Securities, Inc.," and two weeks later the focus of a day of hearings was "the responsibilities of the independent audit firms which were involved in verifying the transactions of ESM." Next the Subcommittee directed its attention to the failure of Beverly Hills Savings and Loan Association, followed by a close scrutiny of the role of the Federal Home Loan Bank Board. Thus, by the end of 1985, the Subcommittee had shifted its attention away from the accounting profession, per se, to an examination of the savings and loan industry and its federal regulator.

In 1986 the Subcommittee continued investigating regulatory accounting principles used by thrift institutions and then began a similar inquiry into the accuracy of bank financial reporting. By June, 1986, the Subcommittee shifted its focus back to the accounting profession when it held hearings on "proposals for improving the performance of independent auditors under the federal securities laws, especially in the area of detecting and disclosing financial fraud." These hearings were in response to H.R. 4886, a bill titled "Financial Fraud Detection and Disclosure Act of 1986," introduced by Representative Ron Wyden (D-Ore.), a member of the Subcommittee. Congressman Wyden's bills will be discussed further in the next section of this chapter.

The year 1987 was rather quiet, compared to the two previous years. In July, the AICPA, as well as other sponsoring organizations of the "Treadway Commission" (to be discussed later in this chapter), testified before the Subcommittee concerning the work of the National Commission of Fraudulent Financial Reporting, chaired by James C. Treadway. Early in 1988 Congressman Dingell sent a letter to the SEC inquiring about implementing the Treadway Commission's recommendations. Specifically, the letter asked whether the SEC, using its existing authority, could require the following:

1. That independent audit firms report known or suspicious fraudulent activity by client companies directly to the SEC, either confidentially or publicly.

2. That independent audit firms report directly to a company's audit committee and require that audit committees have sole authority to hire, fire and set fees for independent audit firms.

---

[1] "Accountants Must Clean Up Their Act." *Management Accounting* (May 1985): 22.

3. That trading in a company's securities be temporarily suspended or otherwise restricted pending an SEC inquiry into reasons for an audit firm's resignation.

4. That independent audit firms annually review a client company's system of internal controls and issue a public report on the adequacy of such controls.

In January and February, 1988, the Subcommittee held two hearings concerning the failure of ZZZZ Best Co., a corporation described as "a Ponzi scheme" by committee Chairman Dingell, who also stated the following:[2]

The fact that auditors and attorneys repeatedly visited make-believe job sites and came away satisfied does not speak well for the present regulatory system. The fact that the audit firm discovering the fraud resigned the engagement without telling enforcement authorities is even more disturbing.... Cases such as ZZZZ Best demonstrate vividly that we cannot afford to tolerate a system that fails to meet the public's legitimate expectations in this regard.

Later in 1988, Congressman Dingell's attitude toward the profession began to soften in response to professional changes described later in this chapter. In April, 1988, Chairman Dingell commended the profession for adopting nine new Statements on Auditing Standards and for sponsoring the Treadway Commission. In May, 1988, SEC Chairman David Ruder testified before the Dingell subcommittee regarding the recommendations of the Treadway Commission. In his opening statement, Congressman Dingell stated, "The accounting profession—through the AICPA—has made substantial improvements in their audit standards to meet the Treadway Commission's recommendations. Their decisive and timely action, as well as their willingness to work with the subcommittee on further improvements, is commendable."[3]

Congressman Wyden

In May, 1986, Representative Wyden, a member of John Dingell's Subcommittee, introduced H.R. 4886 to force auditors to expand the scope of their audits to include the detection of fraud. The June, 1986, hearings of the Subcommittee were a response to this proposed legislation. Because of criticisms by the AICPA and the SEC during the June hearings, Wyden changed his proposed legislation and reintroduced it as H.R. 5439 in August, 1986. At the time of its reintroduction Congressman Wyden made the following remarks:

---

[2] "Hearings focus on ZZZZ Best." *Journal of Accountancy* (April 1988): 80.

[3] AICPA. *Digest of Washington Issues* vol. 1, no. 13 (Dec 1988): 14.

In sixteen hearings conducted by the Subcommittee on Oversight and Investigations during 1985 and 1986, the subcommittee compiled an overwhelming record of devastating financial frauds. Again and again, the subcommittee found that independent auditors have failed to detect or to report fraudulent activities at a number of major corporations and financial institutions in this country.

Contrary to the views of Mr. Shad [Chairman of the SEC] who believes the system is "working well," many other government regulators are calling for significant changes to protect the public from major financial fraud. The former and present chairmen of the FDIC testified before the subcommittee that 50 percent of the 120 bank failures that occurred last year were due to fraud and insider abuse. Both testified that increased measures are needed to combat the serious problem of financial fraud, and that independent auditors should be doing more in the area of detecting and reporting fraud and illegal activities.

Among other things, the new version of Wyden's bill called for the following:

1. Companies would be required to devise and maintain a system of internal control sufficient to ensure compliance with applicable law, and to periodically evaluate the controls in the annual report. Management would also be required to identify any material weaknesses identified in the system, describe plans to correct them, and report on progress made since the previous year's report.

2. Auditors would be required to include, in their audit plans, specific and substantive procedures that reasonably ensure the detection of any material illegality or irregularity.

3. Auditors would be required to evaluate the system of internal control as well as management's evaluation of the system.

4. Auditors would be required to issue a report that:

    a. Gives the auditor's opinion on the system of internal control and management's evaluation of it.

    b. States that procedures were performed to reasonably ensure detection of all material illegalities and irregularities.

    c. Is signed personally by the auditor principally responsible for the audit and by the firm conducting the audit.

5. When the auditor becomes aware of information that an illegal or irregular act has, or may have, occurred, the auditor must:

    a. Extend audit steps to determine the possible effect.

    b. Inform management and the audit committee.

    c. Review management's response, and if not satisfied, within 90 days report the incident to the proper authorities.

6. Auditors who perform their duties under the bill would be protected legally.

Congress did not take any action on Representative Wyden's new bill and it was not reintroduced in the following session. However, in 1991, Representative Wyden, together with Representative Edward Markey (D-Mass.) introduced legislation [H.R. 3159] that would require the SEC to prescribe methods for auditors to use to detect and report illegal activities to the client's Audit Committee or Board of Directors. The Board would have one day to inform the SEC and furnish the auditor with a copy of the notice. If the Board failed to do so, the auditors would then be required to resign from the engagement or furnish the SEC with a copy of its report within one day of the client's failure to notify the SEC.

H.R. 3159, titled the "Financial Fraud Detection and Disclosure Act," also would require the SEC to prescribe methods for auditors to use to detect illegal acts, and to conduct a study to determine if compliance would be improved by a requirement for annual public reports by management and a report by the auditors on the adequacy of internal controls. H.R. 3159 did not pass in 1991 and Congressman Wyden reintroduced another version (H.R. 4313) in 1992.

The 1992 version was very similar to the 1991 bill, except the latter no longer called for the SEC to require auditors to file internal control reports. The bill passed in the House of Representatives, but failed to pass in the Senate before the close of the Congressional year. Congressman Wyden promised to reintroduce it, or a close version, in 1993.

Congressman Brooks

In October, 1986, the Legislation and National Security Subcommittee of the House Government Operations Committee, chaired by Jack Brooks (D-Tex.), issued a report titled, *Substandard CPA Audits of Federal Financial Assistance Funds: The Public Accounting Profession is Failing the Taxpayers*. The report summarized a U.S. General Accounting Office (GAO) study of CPA audits of Federal grants funds and two days of public hearings.

The GAO study consisted of an examination of desk reviews and quality control reviews performed by the Inspector General's office, as well as a review by the GAO of a statistically selected sample of 120 CPA audits. The IG's desk reviews in 1984 had resulted in problem reporting in 84 percent of the cases. The IG's quality control reviews revealed problems with 45 percent of the audits under investigation. And finally, the GAO study indicated that 34 percent of the statistically selected audits failed to meet generally accepted government auditing standards (GAGAS). Of the audits performed by large firms, 14.5 percent failed to comply with GAGAS, while the corresponding figure for medium and small firms was 25.8 percent and 64.7 percent, respectively.

At the Subcommittee's second hearing Chairman Brooks stated:

The public accounting profession is facing a crisis situation. Congress simply will not tolerate continued sloppy, unprofessional, substandard CPA audits of Federal grant funds . . .

Decisive corrective actions are needed to dramatically improve the quality of these audits. Failure to achieve such improvements would force the Federal Government to reconsider its policy of relying on audits performed by CPA firms.

The subcommittee recommended the following:

1. The public accounting profession, GAO, and IG should take appropriate actions to assure that CPAs auditing Federal financial assistance funds are properly trained in governmental auditing.

2. The state boards of accountancy and the AICPA should impose strict sanctions on CPAs who perform substandard audits. In addition, the state boards and the Institute should make public the results of all cases in which disciplinary action is taken. They should also provide the GAO and IG with status reports on cases under investigation.

3. The IG of all agencies that receive CPA audits of Federal financial assistance funds should strengthen their quality review systems for monitoring such audits.

4. The GAO should revise "Standards for Audit of Governmental Organizations, Programs, Activities, and Functions" to include:

    a. A standard that CPAs involved in auditing Federal financial assistance funds must complete a specified amount of continuing professional education in governmental auditing; and

    b. A standard that CPA firms auditing Federal financial assistance funds must undergo periodic peer reviews.

Professional Responses

Once again the profession was shaken by the strength of public and congressional outcry, as well as by the revelations of fraudulent activities in a number of failed corporations and financial institutions and by mounting lawsuits against CPA firms. In response, the profession instituted a number of changes in professional standards, and in auditing standards. It also participated in the formation of an independent commission, chaired by James Treadway, to investigate fraudulent financial reporting.

Changes in Professional Standards

In 1983, the AICPA appointed a Special Committee on Standards of Professional Conduct for CPAs, referred to as the "Anderson Committee" because it was chaired by George D. Anderson. The committee deliberated for three years, then, in 1986, issued its report. The report called for a number of changes in the profession's code of ethics and other professional standards. CPAs around the nation met in membership forums to discuss the proposed changes and to inform the AICPA of their views. Two of the proposed changes were particularly controversial.

The existing Rule 302, banning contingent fee arrangements, would have been changed to the following: "A member in public practice who performs engagements for a contingent fee would be considered to have lost independence with regard to that client because a common financial interest has been established." Thus, members would have been allowed to work for contingent fees as long as it was for nonattest clients.

The existing Rule 503, banning commissions, would have been changed to the following: "The acceptance of a payment for referral of products or services of others by a member in public practice is considered to create a conflict of interest that results in a loss of objectivity and independence except under those circumstances where bodies designated by Council have determined that such conflicts of interest do not arise." Thus, the door would be left open for future rulings that would allow fee arrangements presently banned under the heading "commissions."

Many CPAs objected to those two proposed changes as violating the nature of the profession's service ideal. In California, a poll of the state's Society of CPAs revealed that 84 percent of the respondents believed that accepting commissions should be prohibited and 66 percent believed that allowing contingent fees for nonaudit clients would violate the objectivity standard. The items were so controversial that the AICPA decided to have its Council vote on whether or not the two recommendations should be sent to the general membership as ballot items. Just before Council was to vote, however, Lou Harris spoke on the results of a survey his firm had taken concerning public opinion of CPAs (see Chapter Thirteen for more details). He made an impassioned plea to the Council members:

> I tell you your reputation is in jeopardy if you seek out either commissions or contingent fees . . . If you have to choose between your professionalism and making more money, to put it in the bluntest terms I know, if you want your reputation as a professional to remain high, then you must opt for professional standards. There is a real

moral imperative at stake here. You, as individuals, hold the future of your profession within your grasp.[4]

When the question was put to a vote, it was defeated by one vote. Thus, these two controversial changes proposed by the Anderson Committee were never included in the final ballot questions, which summarized the remainder of the Committee's proposals. Those ballot questions were sent to all AICPA members in November, 1987, and all were accepted by the membership. A summary of the professional reforms follows:

1. The Code of Ethics was revised to modernize the language, make it more goal-oriented, and increase its applicability to all AICPA members, not just those in public practice.

2. All AICPA members in public practice must participate in a quality review program every three years.

3. The former 12 regional trial boards were consolidated into a centralized Joint Trial Board.

4. AICPA members in public practice must complete 120 hours of continuing professional education every three years.

5. AICPA members not in public practice must complete 90 hours of continuing professional education every three years (the first 3-year phase beginning in 1989 carries a 60 hour requirement only).

6. Beginning in the year 2000, new AICPA members must have 150 semester hours of education including a bachelor's degree.

Changes in Auditing Standards

In 1985, the AICPA's Auditing Standards Board (ASB) began a project to attempt to narrow the "expectation gap" between public expectations concerning audits and what, in fact, auditors do. In early 1987, the ASB issued 10 exposure drafts for public comment. In 1988, after reviewing nearly 1,200 comment letters, the ASB approved issuance of nine new Statements on Auditing Standards (SASs), as follows:

I. Detection of fraud and illegal acts:

SAS No. 53, *The Auditor's Responsibility to Detect and Report Errors and Irregularities.*

SAS No. 54, *Illegal Acts by Clients.*

II. More effective audits:

---

[4] Walters, R. "Why No Commissions?" *Monthly Statement* vol. 41, no. 6 (October 1987): 6.

SAS No. 55, *Consideration of the Internal Control Structure in a Financial Statement Audit.*

SAS No. 56, *Analytical Procedures.*

SAS No. 57, *Auditing Accounting Estimates.*

III. Improved external communications:

SAS No. 58, *Reports on Audited Financial Statements.*

SAS No. 59, *The Auditor's Consideration of an Entity's Ability to Continue as a Going Concern.*

IV. Improved internal communication:

SAS No. 60, *Communication of Internal Control Structure Related Matters Noted in an Audit.*

SAS No. 61, *Communication with Audit Committees.*

SAS No. 53 increases responsibility by obligating the audit or to design the audit to provide reasonable assurance of detection of material errors and irregularities, and it requires the auditor to inform the audit committee about all such irregularities.

SAS No. 54 extends the above requirements to violations of laws or governmental regulations that have a direct and material effect on line items in financial statements.

SAS No. 55 requires that a sufficient understanding of internal control structure is to be obtained to adequately plan the audit. Internal control structure has three major elements: control environment, accounting system, and control procedures. An understanding of each of the three is necessary for proper audit planning.

SAS No. 56 requires the use of analytical procedures in the planning and the final review stages of all audits. It also gives new guidance on designing, applying, and evaluating analytical procedures as substantive tests.

SAS No. 57 provides guidance on obtaining and evaluating evidence to support significant accounting estimates.

SAS No. 58 revises the auditor's standard report to include clearer descriptions of the auditor's responsibility, management's responsibility, the work the auditor does, and the assurance the auditor gives. It acknowledges that an audit provides reasonable assurance that the financial statements are free of material misstatements. The new report also deletes reference to consistency. Inconsistencies and uncertainties are to be discussed in an explanatory paragraph following the opinion paragraph.

SAS No. 59 obligates the auditor, in every audit, to evaluate whether there is substantial doubt about the client's ability to continue as a going concern. If such doubt exists, it must be included in an explanatory paragraph, similar to inconsistencies and uncertainties.

SAS No. 60 requires the auditor to report significant deficiencies in the control environment, accounting system, and control procedures. It also changes the wording of the auditor's report on internal control structure. Previously required discussions of the inherent limitations of internal control and the disclaimer of opinion on control are now deleted.

SAS No. 61 places a new responsibility on the auditor to make sure that the matters listed below are communicated to those responsible for oversight of the financial reporting process:

1. The auditor's responsibility in an audit and the nature of the assurance provided.

2. The initial selection of and changes in significant accounting policies or their applications.

3. The process that management uses in formulating sensitive accounting estimates and the basis for the auditor's conclusions about the reasonableness of those estimates.

4. Any audit adjustments, whether recorded or not, that could have a significant effect on the financial reporting process.

5. The auditor's responsibility for other information in documents containing audited financial statements.

6. Any disagreements with management, whether satisfactorily resolved or not, about matters that could be significant to the entity's financial statements or the auditor's report.

7. The auditor's view on significant matters that were the subject of consultation with other accountants.

8. The major issues that were discussed with management in connection with the initial or recurring retention of the auditor.

9. Any serious difficulties encountered with management in performing the audit (e.g., unreasonable timetable set by management).

Treadway Commission

In mid-1985 the AICPA spearheaded the formation of an independent commission (the "National Commission on Fraudulent Financial Reporting") to examine the extent to which management fraud undermines financial reporting and the forces and pressures that result in such acts, as well as the extent to which such fraud can be prevented or detected, and the role of the independent auditor relative to the detection of financial fraud. Joining the AICPA in financing the commission, chaired by James C. Treadway, were the Financial Executives Institute, the National Association of Accountants, the Institute of Internal Auditors, and the American Accounting Association. Treadway was a former commissioner of the SEC. The commission also included a past chairman of the New York Stock Exchange, the chairman of a Big Eight accounting firm, a chairman of the Institute of Internal Auditors, a retired bank chairman and the board chairman of a Fortune 500 corporation.

The commission began its charge by studying the results of many research projects, both internal and external. They learned, for example, the following items:

1. In an analysis of 456 lawsuits against auditors from 1960-1985, about one-half contained management fraud.

2. Only about 20 percent of the bankruptcies studied resulted in litigation against the auditor (and over one-half of those involved management fraud). Thus the claim that business failure automatically leads to an allegation of audit failure is not true.

3. A study of 119 actions brought by the SEC against public companies disclosed that most alleged frauds were perpetrated by upper-level management by using improper accounting methods to overstate revenue and assets. Corporate assets were seldom diverted. The majority of these alleged frauds occurred because of a breakdown in internal controls. About 31 percent of the companies involved did not have audit committees.

4. A study sponsored by the NAA found no concrete instances where the independence of the public auditor was compromised by the performance by the firm of non-audit services.

5. A study sponsored by the FEI found that many frauds do not begin with an overt, intentional act to deceive or mislead. The fraud is often a combination of Board apathy, unrealistic profit pressures, weak controls, and bonus-heavy compensation plans.

The final report was issued in late 1987 and included approximately 50 recommendations categorized as follows:

Chapter 2: Recommendations for the Public Company

Chapter 3: Recommendations for the Independent Public Accountant

Chapter 4: Recommendations for the SEC and Others to Improve the Regulatory and Legal Environment

Chapter 5: Recommendations for Education

Some of the more important recommendations follow.

Audit Committees:

1. Audit committees should be required for all publicly-owned corporations or those that accept public funds.

2. Audit committees should be provided adequate resources and authority to discharge their responsibilities.

3. The chairman of the audit committee should include in the Annual Report to Stockholders his own letter describing the activities of the committee.

4. The independence of the public accountant should be regularly evaluated by the audit committee and the level of audit fees to non-audit fees should be a required disclosure.

Management

5. All companies should adopt, publicize, and enforce written codes of conduct.

6. Management should be required to express an opinion on the adequacy of internal controls.

7. Management should advise the audit committee when it seeks a second opinion on a significant accounting issue.

8. Management should disclose any material accounting issues discussed with their old and new auditors during the three-year period preceding a change in auditors.

Auditors

9. Auditing standards should be revised to include some affirmative obligation of the auditors to detect fraudulent financial reporting.

10. The Auditing Standards Board should include public representation and participation.

11. The auditor's standard report should better describe the auditor's role and responsibilities, including the responsibility to detect material errors and fraud.

12. The auditor's report should describe the extent to which the auditor reviewed and evaluated the system of internal controls.

13. The SEC should require auditors of publicly-held corporations to undergo peer review and oversight functions approved by the SEC.

As mentioned earlier in the chapter, Congressman Dingell inquired of the SEC the scope of its present authority to implement several of the Treadway Commission's recommendations. Dingell also indicated his intention to propose legislation, to the extent it is necessary, to implement portions of the commission's recommendations. In early 1989, Representative Dingell introduced legislation (H.R. 975) to permit assessment of new civil monetary penalties and to allow the SEC to ask a court to suspend or bar violators from serving as directors or officers of public companies. In addition, a five-member committee of the sponsoring organizations of the Treadway Commission was formed in early 1988 to monitor progress in the implementation of the recommendations and to report periodically on such progress. After 18 months of study, in 1991, the Committee of Sponsoring Organizations [COSO] released an exposure draft, titled *Internal Control—Integrated Framework*. It provided a framework to serve as a guide for judging the effectiveness of internal control systems and for improving them. The COSO did not express an opinion on the merits of public reporting on internal control, but did provide guidance to those companies that do report externally on their internal control systems.

Representative Dingell also requested a GAO report concerning implementation of the commission's recommendations. In releasing the report, Dingell said, "The GAO found that the accounting profession has made substantial progress in addressing the Treadway Commission's proposals, and the profession deserves credit for that."[5]

Thus, as the 1980s drew to a close, some of the congressional heat felt earlier in the decade appeared to be diminished, much to the relief of the profession itself. As one leader in the profession quipped, "We can't afford to be investigated *every* decade."

Questions

1. Summarize, in your own words, the most radical recommendations of Congressman Dingell's Subcommittee, Congressman Wyden's bill H.R. 5439, and the Treadway Commission.

2. Which of the above recommendations were substantially carried out by the changes in professional standards or the changes in auditing standards? Which of the recommendations have not been addressed by the accounting profession?

3. The congressional investigations of the 1970s and the 1980s were triggered by a rash of bankruptcies and by high incidents of management fraud. Do you believe that the professional and auditing changes enacted in the late 1970s and 1980s are sufficient to prevent another rash of bankruptcies involving management fraud, and hence another series of congressional investigations? Why or why not?

4. What, if any, additional measures do you think the profession should take to further protect the public from losses due to management fraud?

---

[5] AICPA. *Digest of Washington Issues* vol. 2, no. 3 (June 1989): 18.

5. What, if any, additional measures do you think the profession should take to further protect the public from the types of inadequate audits described by Congressman Brooks?

Additional Readings

—"Accountants Must Clean Up Their Act." *Management Accounting* (May 1985): 21–56.

—"Fraud Commission Issues Final Report." *Journal of Accountancy* (November 1987): 39–48.

McGee, R. W. "The Financial Fraud Detection and Disclosure Act." *The CPA Journal* (January 1987): 86–87.

12
Governmental Actions to Increase Competition

Introduction

During the 1970s and 1980s, Congress and the SEC were not the only governmental bodies interested in the accounting profession. Both the Antitrust Division of the Department of Justice (DOJ) and the Federal Trade Commission (FTC) conducted investigations concerning the anticompetitive nature of some of the AICPA's Rules of Conduct. Prior to the mid-1960s most professionals, and some judges, considered the learned professions to be immune from antitrust laws. This immunity is based on three reasons: one, professional activities are not "trade or commerce" within the intent of the Sherman Antitrust Act. Two, professional activities are local, not interstate, and therefore do not fall within the Sherman Act. Three, professional activities are already regulated by the states, thereby superseding federal antitrust laws under the constitutional concepts of federalism and state sovereignty. The first two reasons would not apply to the accounting profession of today. Many activities of CPAs, such as personal financial planning, tax advising, and management advisory services, are performed by unlicensed practitioners as well as by CPAs. Thus, the distinction between professional activities and commercial activities is quite fuzzy. And certainly the audits of multinational firms, whose activities span most, if not all, of the 50 states, by international accounting firms with offices in all 50 states is "interstate." The third reason, known as the "state action doctrine," is still being used, successfully, in some court cases today. This topic will be discussed in more detail later in the chapter.

Department of Justice

In 1966, the DOJ warned the AICPA that [then existing] Rule 3.03 of the Code of Ethics, prohibiting competitive bidding, would probably be judged to be a restraint of trade. Therefore, the AICPA adopted a policy of not enforcing the rule. The DOJ, however, was not satisfied with that response, and began a full-fledged investigation of the Institute which culminated in a civil antitrust suit. In July, 1972, Rule 3.03

was declared null and void by the U.S. District Court for the District of Columbia in a consent judgment entered into between the DOJ and the AICPA. In a consent judgment, the accused (AICPA) does not contest any charges brought by the accuser (DOJ), and the result is not the same as a guilty plea, for purposes of other suits which might be brought (for example, some company injured by the AICPA's actions would still have to prove the Institute's guilt in court).

In response to Representative Moss' report (1976) and to Senator Metcalf's Staff Study (Jan. 1977), the DOJ, in 1977, reopened its investigation of the AICPA Code of Ethics. In particular, the DOJ attacked the Code's prohibition of advertising, solicitation, and encroachment by members on private practices of other members.

During the mid-1970s the DOJ had been actively pursuing other professions' codes of ethics as well, and the AICPA had been monitoring those events. In June, 1977, the U.S. Supreme Court held that a total ban on lawyers' advertising is unconstitutional. As a result of that decision and of continued pressure by the DOJ, the AICPA amended (then existing) Rule 502 to permit truthful advertising. The rule still prohibited direct, uninvited solicitation, however. In 1978, two U.S. Supreme Court decisions relating to lawyers' direct solicitations eroded their defensibility even further. Once again the Institute went through the process of changing Rule 502, such that both solicitation and advertising would be allowed as long as they are not false, misleading, or deceptive. At the same time, in response to continued DOJ pressure, the AICPA abolished its rule against "encroachment" for similar reasons.

Federal Trade Commission

Investigations by the FTC focused on the professions's prohibition of advertising and solicitation in the 1970s and commissions and contingent fees in the 1980s.

Advertising and Solicitation

Also in response to Congressmen Moss and Metcalf, the FTC's Bureau of Consumer Protection announced an investigation of the profession in March, 1977. Their investigation, however, was to be much more extensive than that of the DOJ, which had limited its inquiry to the AICPA Code of Ethics. The FTC also investigated state licensing boards and private accounting associations, such as state societies of CPAs and the AICPA. Among issues explored by the FTC were:

1. Educational, age, residency, citizenship, and character requirements of licensing boards and associations.

2. Code of ethics' prohibitions against solicitations, advertising, competitive bidding, and other practices.

3. Accounting/auditing standards.

4. The role and dominance of accounting firms within the profession.

Because of the AICPA's changes in its Code of Ethics and because of their cooperative spirit, the FTC closed its inquiry in September, 1980, without taking specific actions. It did, however, warn that Interpretation 502–4 "Self designation as an expert or specialist," may come under future investigation.

Commissions and Contingent Fees

In January, 1985, the FTC began an investigation of approximately 13 rules and interpretations banning the acceptance of commissions and contingent fees by AICPA members. The Commission obtained approximately 30,000 pages of documentation from AICPA files and warned Institute officials to expect a lawsuit if the profession did not remove its prohibitions against commissions and contingent fees. Recall from Chapter Eleven that the Anderson Committee was formulating proposed changes to the AICPA Code of Ethics during this same time. Partly in response to FTC pressures, in 1986 the Anderson Committee recommended modification of the rules prohibiting contingent fees and a possibility of future changes relating to commissions. The profession was sharply divided over those two Anderson Committee proposals. At the same Council meeting in which Lou Harris gave his impassioned speech (Oct. 1986), AICPA officials warned the Council members that FTC action was imminent if the two Anderson Committee proposals were not passed. Council voted 98 to 97 to defeat the two recommendations.

Part of the reason for the Council's rejection of Anderson's proposals was the belief that, even if passed, the FTC would probably have objected to them as being too lenient. In an August, 1986 letter by FTC attorney Anthony Joseph to AICPA legal counsel, Philip Corsi, Mr. Joseph expressed the opinion that proposed changes to Rule 302 (contingent fees) may be unacceptable to the FTC. Recall from Chapter Eleven that the Anderson Committee had proposed that contingent-fee arrangements would be acceptable for nonaudit clients only. Mr. Joseph enumerated three anticompetitive effects of the proposed Rule 302:

1. Loss of efficiencies available to a client if that client had to use two different CPA firms for two different types of services (audit and, e.g., a contingency-based Medicare reimbursement engagement).

2. A diminution in rivalry among CPA firms because one firm could not perform attest and contingency fee nonattest services for the same client. Thus CPAs would refrain from com-

peting for nonattest services for potential or existing audit clients, while CPAs providing contingent fee services would refrain from competing for audit services.

3. Lower quality CPA services because the contingent fee arrangement, which may motivate CPAs to perform better work, would be unavailable for all types of services performed for audit clients.

In mid-1987 the FTC proposed a consent order that would require the AICPA to change its code to permit members to accept commissions and contingent fees, use trade names, pay for referrals, engage in unrestricted advertising, and vouch for the achievability of forecasts. The order would also repeal the rule that requires accounting firms to operate only as partnerships, proprietorships or professional corporations. The AICPA declined to accept the proposed consent order and decided to fight the battle further in court. At the same time, they chose to suspend enforcement of the effected rules and interpretations until the matter was resolved. In August, 1988, the AICPA and FTC came to a compromise whereby the FTC amended their consent decree such that commissions and contingent fees would be allowed for nonattest clients only. On August 31, 1988, Council voted to accept that consent decree.

Efferent Vs. Afferent Ethics

In Chapter Three the distinction was made between efferent and afferent ethics. Efferent ethics deal with relationships between professionals and others outside the profession, such as clients and/or the general public. Afferent ethics deal with relationships among professionals themselves. At one time professional codes of ethics were heavily weighted with rules prohibiting conduct that might harm other professionals. For example, rules prohibiting advertising, solicitation of clients away from their present CPAs, solicitation of staff members away from their present CPA firms, and encroachment on the existing practice of other CPAs, were all prohibited before the DOJ began challenging these prohibitions. Chapter Three also pointed out that efferent, not afferent, ethics are at the heart of professionalism. Thus, although CPAs were not happy with governmental interference with their code of ethics, they nevertheless chose to bend to the pressures of the DOJ, since the rules being challenged concerned afferent ethics only.

Many CPAs, including the leadership of the AICPA, considered the recent challenge by the FTC to be a different matter, altogether, than the pressures exerted in the late 1970s. The profession has consistently banned contingent fee arrangements and commissions because of their incompatibility with the concepts of independence and objectivity, two cornerstones of the profession's efferent ethics. Attestation, the primary public service offered by CPAs, must be rendered by independent, objective professionals to be believable and to benefit society. If a CPA's fee is contingent on the outcome of his or her findings, how believable are those findings? For example, could society believe an audit opinion if a "clean" opinion brings more revenue to a firm than an adverse opinion? Hence, the profession was prepared to go to court, rather than risk impairment of their efferent ethics by allowing auditors to accept commissions or contingent fees from their audit clients.

Do contingent fees or commissions impair the service ideal of CPAs who are performing nonattest services? CPAs remain divided on this issue, despite the AICPA's recent decision to agree with the FTC's consent decree. The FTC viewed the prohibitions against commissions and contingent fees as additional examples of afferent ethics, restricting free competition among CPAs and thus denying the general public the possibility of receiving certain services at the lowest possible price. Many CPAs, on the other hand, viewed these fee arrangements as threats to the profession's efferent ethics, and hence to its basic service ideal and reason for being. Those CPAs argued that the public is better served by CPAs who are always objective. Nevertheless, based on advice from legal council who believed that the ban for nonaudit clients would not be upheld in court, AICPA Council voted to accept the consent decree, thus allowing for the first time, the acceptance of commissions and contingent fees by CPAs, except from clients for whom the CPAs' firm performs audit, review, or compilation services.

State Action Doctrine

Although one of the characteristics of a profession is self-regulation, CPAs in some states have chosen to compromise some degree of self-regulation at the state level in order to avoid the threat of increased loss of self-regulation due to DOJ and FTC actions. To understand the development of the concept of the state action doctrine as it applies to the regulation of professions, one must have some appreciation for the evolution of the concept. Accordingly, a review of pertinent court decisions is presented next.[1]

In *Parker v. Brown* [317 U.S. 341 (1943)] the Supreme Court ruled on the substance and scope of the Sherman Antitrust Act by declaring that "state action" was exempt from the Act. Many professionals believed that professional activities, regulated as they are by the states, would be included in this ruling. However, this case specifically addressed

---

[1] The following material has been excerpted from an unpublished manuscript by Cunningham, Tondkar, and Coffman, titled "Trust or Antitrust for the Profession of Accountancy?," *Research in Accounting Regulation*, Vol. 4, 1990, Greenwich, Connecticut: JAI Press, 111–127. Reprinted with permission.

the regulatory actions of state legislatures, not actions of state courts, agencies, or regulatory bodies such as state boards of accountancy.

In 1975, the Supreme Court ruled, in *Goldfarb v. Virginia State Bar* (421 U.S. 773), that rules of professional organizations governing commercial activities, such as fee setting, were not immune from federal antitrust laws. In order for the activity in question to be protected by the state action doctrine, it must be "required by the State acting as sovereign."

In *Cantor v. Detroit Edison Co.* [428 U.S. 579 (1976)] further guidance was given. State "authorization, approval, encouragement, or participation in restrictive private conduct confers no antitrust immunity." Rather, the state must clearly identify, regulate, and enforce the action of the agency in question.

According to the decision in *California Liquor Dealers Association v. Midcal Aluminum, Inc.* [445 U.S. 97 (1980)], two criteria must be met in order for an action to be protected under the state action exemption:

1. The action must be clearly articulated and affirmatively expressed as state policy.

2. The policy must be actively supervised by the state.

In 1987, a U.S. District Court dismissed a suit by the U.S. Justice Department against the State Board of CPAs of Louisiana because the state board's rules on advertising and solicitation were authorized, reviewed, and approved by the state legislature.

To summarize these and other pertinent rulings, the state action doctrine, as it is interpreted today, can be briefly stated. "Actions by a state legislature, measures adopted by a state supreme court, and some activities of a state's executive branch will be accorded state action immunity. State regulatory boards will be immune if it can be shown that they acted according to a clearly articulated state policy to displace competition. If the regulatory board members come from private interests, the board must also be subject to active state supervision."[2]

Recent actions by California CPAs illustrate how the state action doctrine might be used to achieve the profession's goals. In 1987, the California Society of CPAs and the State Board of Accountancy met with representatives of the state's administration and proposed legislation to prohibit the acceptance of commissions by CPAs. The legislation, A.B. 941, was signed into law in late 1987 and became effective January 1, 1988. As of that date, in California it is a violation of the law for those engaged in the practice of public accountancy to accept or pay commissions for the referral of clients, products, or services. CPAs in California are currently investigating the possibility of proposing similar legislation relating to contingent fees.

---

[2] Ibid., 7.

The actions of California's CPAs appear to be a paradox. In order to achieve self-regulation in the controversial area of fee structures, the profession sought out state legislation. This solution would not be the first one chosen if others appeared available. If sufficient numbers of CPAs disagree with the AICPA/FTC compromise, they may choose to ban commissions and/or contingent fees for *all* clients through the vehicle of state legislation. In October, 1991, AICPA Council members voted to assist state CPA societies seeking legislation to prohibit the acceptance of commissions by CPAs. This action is seen by many as an admission by the AICPA that they still oppose allowing their members to accept commissions, but changed their rules to allow such a fee structure only because they were compelled to do so by the FTC.

Cases and Questions

1. With regard to commissions and contingent fees, some observers believe that the current actions of the FTC are contrary to the thrust of congressional recommendations (see Chapters Ten and Eleven). Do you agree or disagree? Support your answer.

2. Do the actions of the FTC aid or hinder the accounting profession in its duty to self-regulate? Support your answer.

3. The CPA firm of Christopher, Paul, and Anderson was asked by management to review the financial statements of a credit union. The credit union, however, was just getting organized and could not afford the standard hourly rates that the firm normally charged. Management of the credit union suggested that the fee be set at a token minimum and that the maximum be the normal billing rate. The firm would then receive the minimum, plus a percentage of interest collected during each month, up to the maximum.

   The firm would not grant loans or enforce collection. Therefore, they did not feel that a fee based on percentage of interest was a "contingent fee," within the context of Rule 302, because the proposed fee would not be contingent upon "findings" or "results" of the service. Rather, the fee would be measured by activity and available funds.

   a. In your opinion, does the proposed fee arrangement violate Rule 302 of the Code of Professional Conduct? Why or why not?

   b. In your opinion, does the proposed fee arrangement violate the professional standards of independence, objectivity, or integrity? Why or why not?

c. What arguments might the FTC use to demonstrate that the proposed fee arrangement is in the public interest?

d. What arguments might the AICPA use to demonstrate that the proposed fee arrangement is not in the public interest?

e. In your opinion, which arguments (FTC or AICPA) have more merit?

Additional Readings

—"AICPA to Fight FTC Consent Order on Ethics Code." *Journal of Accountancy* (September, 1987): 87–88.

Berton, Lee. "A Battle Cry for America's Accountants." *Wall Street Journal* (September 23, 1987): 40.

Berton, Lee. "Accounting Group to Consider Dropping Ban on Contingency Fees and Commissions." *Wall Street Journal* (August 25, 1988): 19.

13
Public Opinion Surveys

Introduction

Chapters Ten, Eleven, and Twelve have summarized Congressional and other governmental reactions, during the last two decades, to the public accounting profession. Most of those reactions appeared to be negative. But were those governmental reactions representative of opinions of the general public or of persons with close working relationships with CPAs? The purpose of this chapter is to examine more closely the reactions and opinions of informed publics to developments within the accounting profession. Because professions serve the general public, and because society gives each profession the privileges of monopoly and self-regulation, professionals should be intensely interested in the public's perception and opinion of their profession.

The Public Oversight Board (POB), which oversees the activities of the SEC Practice Section of the AICPA Division for CPA Firms, in 1986 commissioned a survey of knowledgeable persons regarding their opinions of consulting work by CPAs and its possible impairment of audit independence and objectivity.[1] In that same year, the AICPA commissioned pollster Louis Harris to conduct an opinion survey of the general public and certain knowledgeable groups concerning a battery of issues relating to the profession. Summaries of both opinion surveys are presented next.

POB Survey

The POB commissioned Audits and Surveys, Inc., to conduct a mail survey to measure nine key publics' perceptions of the consulting issue. The key publics consisted of the following:

    125   CEOs of Fortune 1000 industrial and service companies
    136   Audit committee chairmen from Fortune 1000 companies
    170   Bank loan officers
    125   Financial analysts
    94   Investment bankers

---

[1] *Public Perceptions of Management Advisory Services Performed by CPA Firms for Audit Clients* by Audits & Surveys, Inc. Copyright © 1986 by American Institute of Certified Public Accountants, Inc. Reprinted with permission.

143	Attorneys
33	Financial writers
122	Accounting professors
111	Business school deans
1,059	Total responses (41 percent response rate)

The main purpose of the study was to determine whether the key publics perceived that consulting performed by CPAs in public practice impairs their auditing functions if performed for the same client. The questionnaire covered four topics:

1. Familiarity with the public accounting profession and with the management advisory services issue.

2. Perceived impairment of objectivity for 16 specific management advisory services performed by CPAs.

3. Attitudes toward specific issues associated with consulting and toward consulting overall.

4. How consulting is handled by companies.

Over half (54 percent) of the respondents said they were "very familiar" with the profession, and another 39 percent said they were "somewhat familiar." Fewer, however, were familiar with the consulting issue: 25 percent responded "very familiar," 45 percent were "some what familiar," and 20 percent responded "a little familiar." CEOs, audit committee chairmen, accounting professors, and business school deans were more knowledgeable on both questions than financial analysts, investment bankers, attorneys, and financial writers.

The respondents were asked to express their agreement or disagreement with the following three statements:

CPAs should be allowed to perform a full range of management advisory services because impairment of audit independence and objectivity is not a problem. (12 percent agreed.)

CPAs should be allowed to perform only those management advisory services where it is clear that audit independence and objectivity cannot be impaired. (75 percent agreed.)

CPAs should not be allowed to perform any management advisory services since there is always the possibility that audit independence and objectivity may be impaired. (9 percent agreed.)

CEOs and business school deans were more likely to say that audit independence and objectivity is not a problem. At the other extreme, financial analysts, attorneys, and financial writers were more likely to respond that there is always a possibility of impairment. There was very little association between key publics' knowledge of the profession/consulting issue and their responses to the three questions above.

Respondents were given a list of 16 consulting services that CPAs might perform and were asked to indicate how much or little each one impairs audit independence and objectivity if performed for an audit client. Results are shown in Table 13-1.

The nine services ranked most likely to impair appear to be related to corporate strategy, balance sheet, or finding and compensating management. Services least likely to be a problem include those concerned with internal company matters or limited planning.

For almost all of the nine services perceived to be most likely to impair, a smaller proportion of CEOs, compared to everyone else, saw objectivity and independence at risk. Bank loan officers were also slightly less concerned. Attorneys and financial writers were the most concerned publics.

Respondents were given a list of six statements people have made about the consulting issue, and were asked to indicate their agreement or disagreement with each.

Table 13-1. POB Questions Related to Consulting Services and Audit Independence.

Here is a list of consulting that some CPAs perform. For each one, indicate how much or little you think it impairs audit independence and objectivity if such consulting is performed for an audit client.

Great Deal/Somewhat

Negotiating mergers, acquisitions and divestitures 76%
Performing actuarial services which directly affect amounts included on the
    balance sheet 64%
Implementing a strategic plan 63%
Identifying merger and acquisition candidates 62%
Valuing assets acquired in a business combination 61%
Executive search for senior management personnel 56%
Renegotiating or redetermining price under a procurement contract 50%
Developing a strategic plan 49%
Developing an executive compensation plan........................... 47%

Very Little/Not At All

Designing and/or implementing a cash management system 63%
Performing actuarial services for the company's pension plan 64%
Developing a market feasibility study 66%
Designing and installing a computer system........................... 66%
Designing a control system for managing long-term
    construction contracts 65%
Designing a computer system 73%
Performing a plant site location study 75%

	Agree
Even though performing a single management advisory service may not impair auditor independence and objectivity, performing a series of management advisory services in the aggregate may	73%
If the personnel performing the management advisory services are not personally involved in the audit, then impairment of independence and objectivity is not an issue	29%
The larger the management advisory fees in relation to the auditing fees received from the same client, the greater the likelihood that independence and objectivity will be impaired	72%
The auditing firm should be required to represent to the audit committee or board of directors that in its opinion the performance of management advisory services did not impair audit independence and objectivity	80%
All management advisory services performed by the auditing firm should be reported in the client's annual report	68%
CPAs who perform management advisory services are better able to conduct more informed audits than those who do not perform these additional services..	38%

CEOs were more likely than any other key public to disagree with the above statements.

A final set of questions was directed to audit committee chairpersons only. Each question was answered by between 45 and 69 respondents:

	Yes
Does your audit committee review management advisory services engagements performed by your auditing firm to determine if audit independence and objectivity could be impaired?	86%
Is such review conducted before the auditing firm performs management advisory services for your company?	76%
Is such review conducted after the auditing firm performs management advisory services for your company?	42%

Has your committee ever taken the position that your auditing firm should not be used for a specific MAS assignment because it could impair the firm's independence or could be perceived as impairing independence? 20%

If all management advisory services performed by your company's auditing firm would have to be publicly reported, would you recommend that management not use the firm for management advisory services? 6%

During the past three years, how many times has your company used the management advisory services of the CPA firm that performs the annual audit?:
a. None 1%
b. Less than five times............................ 57%
c. Five times or more............................. 38%

Harris Poll

During the summer of 1986 the firm of Louis Harris and Associates conducted telephone interviews of over 3,400 people combined into two groups: the general public and 11 "special" publics. The general public consisted of the following subgroups:

1200	Selected from a national cross section.
681	Members of the public who claim to be knowledgeable about accountants and accounting.
550	People who own common stock and equities.
2431	Total

The 11 special publics consisted of the following:

167	Owners and managers of small businesses.
232	Owners and managers of medium-sized businesses.
101	Top executives of large corporations.
60	Audit committee members of large corporations.
60	Senior bank officers who are credit grantors.
60	Attorneys who are knowledgeable about financial affairs.
60	Key state and federal officials dealing with financial issues.
63	Aides to members of Congress.
40	Leading members of the media dealing with financial matters.
61	Leading academics in accounting and related fields.
67	Top security analysts.
971	Total

The survey measured and analyzed attitudes toward CPAs and the accounting profession. The objectives were to determine the following:

1. Perceptions concerning CPAs.

2. Knowledge of CPA qualifications and ethical standards.

3. Awareness of investigations of the profession.

4. Evaluations concerning the integrity of auditors and other key dimensions.

The substance of the poll covered over 100 "probe areas." A summary of the results is presented next.

Moral and Ethical Practices

Questions concerning the overall ethical climate of business revealed that 75 percent of the general public thought that the level of honesty and integrity in business dealings was getting worse. In the "special" publics, four groups thought the moral climate was getting better: officers of medium- and large-sized corporations, state and federal officials, members of the media, and academics.

The ethics and morality of 12 key leadership and professional groups were compared, and CPAs emerged at the top or close to the top among all key groups. The "special" publics gave CPAs a positive rating of 90 percent on their ethical and moral practices, whereas 9 percent ranked them negatively. Other rankings of CPAs, as well as the other key groups, follow:

	Positive-Negative Ratings			
		General Public		
	"Special" Publics	"Knowledgeable"	Stock Owners	As a Whole
CPAs	90– 9	75–20	72–16	56–21
College Professors	81–14	64–26	63–26	58–25
Bankers	78–20	67–30	68–26	59–33
Doctors	78–20	68–30	70–29	64–33
News Editors	P			P
TV Newscasters	P			P
Corporate Executives	P			N
Personal Financial Planners	N			P
Stockbrokers	N			P
U.S. Congressmen	P			N
Lawyers	N			N
Insurance Agents	N			N

P = More positive than negative ratings.
N = More negative than positive ratings.

Observation: By any standard, the reputation of CPAs and the accounting profession is high, indeed. Although the remainder of this study reveals areas that require attention, nonetheless any suggestion that CPAs and the accounting profession are highly vulnerable and have little reservoir of good will to tap simply is not in accord with the hard facts.[1]

---

[2] Louis Harris and Associates, Inc. 1986. *A Survey of Perceptions, Knowledge, and Attitudes Toward CPAs and the Accounting Profession*, 4–5. Copyright © 1986 by American Institute of Certified Public Accountants, Inc. Reprinted with permission.

Performance

A summary of questions relating to performance follows:

	Positive Ratings	
	"Special" Publics	General Public
The accounting profession is performing better today than it ever has in the past.	75%	75%
A CPA has to be well-trained and educated before he or she can earn that designation.	90%	90%
CPA firms exercise independent and objective judgment in performing audits of company financial statements.	90%	75%
One of the services a good auditor renders is to be a 'business advisor' to clients.	67%	67%

Observation: A substantial number of all of the publics polled perceive CPAs and the accounting profession in a positive light. It is widely recognized that CPAs must be highly trained and qualified, that public accounting firms exercise independent and objective judgment in making audits, and that a good auditor can also serve as a management advisor to clients. All in all, these cover some of the most critical and important ground rules and practices of CPAs. Satisfaction is summed up in the fact that over 9 in 10 of all categories surveyed credit the accounting profession with performing better today than ever before. It adds up to a deep appreciation of the solid professionalism associated with CPAs and the accounting profession.[3]

Three Kinds of Accountants

A summary of questions relating to types of accountants and types of functions performed by CPAs follows:

Observation: It is apparent from these results that all of the groups surveyed make a critical distinction between an accountant who is a CPA and one who is not. Among CPA accountants, it is also evident that top billing is reserved for those who work in independent public accounting firms, although CPAs who work directly in corporations are highly regarded as well.[4]

Attributes

How CPAs measure on several key attributes is examined next.

---

[3] Ibid., 5.

[4] Ibid., 6.

	"Special" Publics	"Knowledgeable"	Positive-Negative Ratings General Public Stock Owners	As a Whole
Honesty	89– 9	75–21	78–18	61–28
Competence	86–12	75–20	76–19	65–24
Reliability	85–13	74–22	75–20	65–25
Objectivity	79–20	67–26	70–23	56–29
Concern for the public interest in their work	55–43	54–42	53–42	52–38
Creativity	39–57	56–35	55–35	50–34

Observation: On balance, when all of the attributes tested are viewed as a whole, CPAs are very well rated, indeed, on such pivotal dimensions as honesty, competence, reliability, and objectivity. These are basic characteristics on which CPAs not only do well, but receive very high praise. The two problem areas deal with the creativity of the profession, implying types who do things "strictly by the book" and are "too literal-minded," and with concern for the public interest. Questions about conducting their work with the public interest in mind should raise some concern about the extent to which CPAs might be willing to compromise on strict principle. The possible confusion between public interest and public service suggests that this criticism be carefully evaluated. In any event, it remains only a minority view among the key publics. But, if not watched and tended to, it could erode an incredibly positive reaction that all of the groups have to CPAs and the accounting profession.[5]

Challenges from the Outside

A series of questions was asked to determine to what degree the various publics were aware of investigations of the profession by Congress or federal agencies, and what problems CPAs faced. Harris concluded with the following:

Observation: Large majorities believe CPAs are well qualified, are objective, highly competent, honest, and reliable. However, those who believe there are problems are vocal and outspoken about their feelings. This roster of criticisms, expressed by a minority, must be taken seriously, if only for the reason that when a profession is as highly regarded as is accounting today, there must be the accompanying concern that far more is expected of the profession than it can ever fulfill. In turn, this can lead to some real criticism when something less than ideal performance is observed.[6]

Another series of questions related to regulation of the profession follows.

---

[5] Ibid., 8.
[6] Ibid., 9.

	"Special" Publics	"Knowledgeable"	Positive-Negative Ratings General Public Stock Owners	As a Whole
Oppose stricter governmental regulation of independent auditors	72–23	50–37	45–42	56–38

Observation: Although the leadership groups who are knowledgeable and sophisticated about the accounting profession do not see the need for tighter regulation of CPAs and independent auditors, nonetheless there is a growing tendency among the less knowledgeable public for more regulation. In turn, this requires those in charge of the system of accountability that has been established to do both an effective job of making certain the highest standards of professionalism are maintained without governmental intervention and also of communicating accurately and fully just how that system of accountability is working.[7]

Qualifications and Preparation

A series of questions assessed the publics' knowledge of qualifications a CPA must have to obtain and keep certification. Harris summarized the findings in his observation.

Observation: The high standards of threshold requirements to become a CPA and then the steps which must be followed to maintain that status obviously are quite well known to both the public and more articulate leadership groups. The confidence in what it takes to become a CPA obviously contributes to the overall high regard in which CPAs are held. If there is to be movement in any direction, the key groups would like to see more required. The exception: to require a post-graduate degree in order to become a Certified Public Accountant.[8]

Enforcement of Professional Standards

Harris also assessed the publics' knowledge of peer review and enforcement procedures.

Observation: Although they are not entirely sure of the precise system of enforcing standards in the profession, it is plainly evident that big majorities of all groups want a tough and effective system. Despite there being relatively high confidence in the way the enforcement system now works, there is a continuing sense that still more ought to be done. In turn, this suggests that steps be taken to tighten the

---

[7] Ibid., 10.

[8] Ibid., 11.

current system, and make it more effective. By the same token, there is evidence that much more should be done to communicate the system of discipline and enforcement that now exists.[9]

Services CPAs Ought to Offer

Harris also asked about the appropriateness of consulting by CPA firms. Apparently, however, he did not distinguish between consulting for an audit client and consulting for a nonaudit client. Results are summarized below.

	Positive Responses	
	"Special" Publics	General Public
Assist in computer hardware selection	50+%	50+%
Assist in computer software selection design	50+%	50+%
General management consulting	70%	70%
Educational programs	77%	60%
Actuarial services	70%	50+%
Service bureaus for record keeping	70%	70%
Appraisal services	50%	60%
Executive search services	N	N
Packaging and selling tax shelters	N	N

N = more negative than positive

Observation: It is evident from these results that those publics most important to the accounting profession are convinced that CPAs should do more than audit. But they strongly suggest that there are distinct limits to the areas of potential operation. In turn, this means that there probably should be some orderly mechanism to determine what are the proper areas and what are not. Five areas do emerge clear-cut as fitting and proper for CPA audit firms to be in: assisting in computer hardware selection and computer software design or selection, general management consulting, bureaus for various record keeping functions. But appraisal services, executive search services, and packaging and selling tax shelters meet with real opposition.[10]

Commissions and Contingent Fees

A summary of questions relating to CPAs receiving commissions or contingent fees follows.

---

[9] Ibid., 12.
[10] Ibid., 14.

	Positive Responses	
	"Special" Publics	General Publics
Oppose commissions for providing services and products of others to:		
Audit clients	71%	50+%
Nonaudit clients	50+%	50+%
Oppose contingency fees from:		
Audit clients	68%	50+%
Nonaudit clients	55%	50+%

Observation: Clearly, both the commission and contingency fee areas are viewed negatively by these key publics. The strong overtone is that the practices smack of nonprofessional behavior for public accounting firms, even if they are perfectly legal and even common business practices for others.[11]

Nonaudit Professional Roles

CPAs were compared with other professional groups to measure the publics' confidence in the ability of CPAs to perform in several nonaudit areas. Harris summarized the results:

Observation: These results point up clearly the success of public accounting firms in nonaudit areas. They compare extremely well as tax advisors, as financial counselors to individuals, and as management consultants. However, there is one caveat to emerge. A 57–41 percent majority of the leadership groups feels that when an independent audit firm serves as an advisor to business on tax matters, management systems, or financial matters, it affects that firm's ability to be objective when auditing a client's financial statements. Roughly 6 in 10 of the other key groups shares this same view.[12]

This finding, by Harris, is even stronger evidence of erosion of the appearance of independence when auditors perform consulting than were the findings of the POB survey.

CPAs Vs. Lawyers on Tax Matters

The survey asked about three different tax problem situations and, for each, asked respondents whom they would go to first—a CPA or a lawyer:

1. On a special tax return preparation problem, over 3 in 4 among all groups, including attorneys, would go to a CPA.

2. On a special tax planning problem, over 3 in 4 of most groups would go to a CPA. The only exception: attorneys, who by 62–33 percent would go to their own.

---

[11] Ibid., 15.

[12] Ibid., 15.

3. On questions raised by tax authorities about your tax return, big majorities of all groups except two would go to the CPA first. The two exceptions, attorneys and congressional aides, would go to a tax lawyer.

To Whom Are Auditors Responsible?

A summary of a series of questions related to the audit function follows.

	"Special" Publics	Positive Responses General Public "Knowledgeable"	Stock Owners
The auditor's primary responsibilitty is to the stockholders or owners	64%	P	P
Top management has the primary responsibility for preparation of financial statements.	68%	Min	Min
CPAs have the primary responsibility for preparation of financial statements.	Min	P	P
A "clean" opinion means:			
1. The auditors believe the financial statements are reasonably reliable.	80%	80%	80%
2. The auditors found no fraud.	50+%	50+%	50+%
3. The auditors have verified that all the figures are completely accurate.	Min	50+%	50+%
4. Management is doing a competent job.	Min	67%	67%
5. The auditors certify the company as a good investment.	Min	50%	P

Min = Minority of positive responses.
P = Plurality of positive responses.

Observation: These results are at one and the same time both reassuring to the accounting profession and yet also illustrative of the enormous job that remains to be done in explaining and in educating the broad public just what an independent audit is and is not. The leadership groups are by and large sophisticated and understand correctly what a "clean" opinion means. But almost all of the general public, including those who know accountants and own securities, simply do not understand what a "clean" opinion really is. The stakes in explaining accurately what such a sign off really means are high. If not corrected, then CPA firms and the accounting profession will be highly vulnerable to be blamed for nearly anything that went wrong with a company which receives a "clean" opinion.

Indeed, when asked how effective financial statements are in communicating the risks and uncertainties facing a business, a 70–29 percent majority of the leadership groups say they are more effective than not, but 60 percent of these say "somewhat," not "highly" effective. This point was clarified even more when all of the key publics were asked if independent audit firms are responsible for detecting fraud or dishonesty in a company's operations. By 78–11 percent, a big majority of the leader groups say they are responsible *only insofar as the financial statements contain material misrepresentation,* not that they are completely responsible for detecting fraud as part of their job. The "knowledgeable" and stockowner groups agree with this view by roughly 3 to 2 margins. This exercise proves that when people are patiently taken through step by step on just what independent auditing means, their initial judgments are tempered by sober second thoughts.

The task of communication will not be easy. A 59 percent majority of the leader groups believe that when a business fails, it is not the result of a failure by the auditor to detect misrepresentation in the financial statements. But 39 percent of the leader groups and a 60–39 percent majority of both the "knowledgeable" public and stockowner public groups appear to equate a business failure with an audit failure. Thus, it is not an overstatement when 8 in 10 of all groups say "the accounting and auditing profession needs to be better understood."[13]

Conclusion

On release of the Harris Poll, members of the profession were heartened to learn that the public held them in such high esteem. After listening to testimony, often negative, at Congressional hearings, CPAs were glad to learn that their reputations were not as sullied as they had feared. Nevertheless, both the POB survey and the Harris Poll point to a number of concerns that simply cannot be ignored.

The public, even "informed" publics, often do not understand what an auditor's "clean" opinion means. The expectations gap of the 1970s is still alive and apparently thriving. The expanding scope of services performed by CPAs is troublesome to a significant portion of the public. The public is particularly concerned when nonaudit services of some magnitude are performed by CPAs for their audit clients. The POB survey, especially, shows that the public expects the profession to

---

[13] Ibid., 17–18.

regulate itself in this sensitive area. Differentiating between appropriate and inappropriate consulting appears to be the first step. Some activities, such as executive searches, certain actuarial services, and merger and acquisition services for a finders fee, are already prohibited by the SEC Practice Section, but the profession should begin a systematic analysis of consulting compatibility with attestation.

The Josephson Institute for the Advancement of Ethics is a nonprofit organization established to increase the ethical quality of the conduct of professionals in the fields of government, law, medicine, business, accounting, and journalism. As a knowledgeable outside observer of developments in the accounting profession, it had the following comments to make concerning the expansion of consulting by auditors:

> Since all the major accounting firms are vigorously expanding into new areas, including asset appraisal, strategic planning, and merger and acquisition consultation, the problem is bound to get worse. There are both real and apparent conflicts of interests which arise out of these various activities which seriously threaten the objectivity of an audit. While the accountants claim they can separate their functions, the fact is that a client who is giving an accounting firm a great deal of business has enormous leverage to influence the auditors' activities and opinions, especially in discretionary areas. Few business firms in financial trouble would hesitate to use this leverage against an auditor who refuses to "work with them" to offer a more positive picture of financial condition. Certainly, there is at least an appearance of impropriety. There is so much momentum in the direction of diversification, however, and the new businesses are so lucrative, that it is unlikely that any voluntary actions will be taken by the profession to deal with this problem.[14]

Questions

1. Under the heading "Services CPAs Ought to Offer," Harris concludes that "CPAs should do more than audit. But . . . there are distinct limits to the areas of potential operation." Contrast the above observation with his conclusion under the heading Non-Audit Professional Roles: "A 57–41 percent majority of the leadership groups feels that when an independent audit firm serves as an advisor to business on tax matters, management systems, or financial matters, it affects that firm's ability to be objective when auditing a client's financial statements. Roughly 6 in 10 of the other key groups shares this same view." Are the two conclusions contradictory? Why or why not?

---

[14] "Ethics Watch." *Easier Said Than Done* (Winter, 1988): 54.

2. Do the overall results of the POB survey and the Harris Poll contradict each other, parallel each other, or deal with separate issues? Support your answer.

3. Reconcile the headline "CPAs rank highest among professionals on Lou Harris Poll" with the fact that only 56 percent of the general public (as a whole) gave positive ratings to CPAs but the same general public gave 58 percent positive ratings to college professors, 59 percent to bankers, and 64 percent to doctors.

4. Given the importance of the public service ideal for all professions, what is the significance of Harris' reported ratings of CPAs on the attribute "Concern for the public service in their work"?

5. Both the Harris Poll and the POB Survey seem to indicate that some consulting activity is appropriate for audit clients and some is not. List the attributes and give examples of both appropriate and inappropriate consulting for audit clients.

6. If you had been constructing the Harris Poll, what additional questions would you have asked?

7. Do you agree or disagree with the Josephson Institute that "it is unlikely that any voluntary action will be taken by the profession to deal with this problem [of expansion of consulting by auditing firms]"? Explain your answer.

Additional Readings

—"How the Public Sees CPAs." *Journal of Accountancy* (December 1986): 16–34.

Briloff, A. J. "Do Management Services Endanger Independence and Objectivity?" *The CPA Journal* (August 1987): 22–29.

Appendix: Case Study Parker Bros., An Accountancy Corp.[1]

Part One

Ron is a senior manager at Parker Bros. and if the office has another good year he hopes to be admitted into the partnership. Ron is the manager on the Cuesta Holdings audit, the office's largest client. Cuesta isn't merely the largest client, no other client is anywhere near as important to the office. The Cuesta engagement generates over 20 percent of the office's billable hours. Everyone loves Cuesta. Besides the audit, Parker Bros. does a lot of tax, consulting, and compliance work for Cuesta. And, Cuesta pays full fees. When it comes to professional services Bob Long, chairman and largest stockholder of Cuesta, says "pay for the best and demand the best." He always laughs and says "I worry a lot more about my surgeon's competence than his fees. I'd be willing to pay a little extra if that would make my surgeon like me better."

Cuesta is a first-class organization. Besides contributing so much revenue to the office, Cuesta contributes a lot to charity. They also pay their employees well. Cuesta is probably the best paying company and best place to work in the area. Several former auditors have gone to work for Cuesta. During the audit, managers at Cuesta frequently take the audit staff to lunch (at nice restaurants). Bob Long wants his auditors to feel like they are part of the Cuesta team.

Cuesta Holdings is a great client but it is not an easy audit. It is a complex company (see Organizational Chart) with several subsidiaries, the largest of which is Cuesta Savings and Loan, a wholly owned subsidiary. Cuesta S & L itself has several wholly owned subsidiaries, the most important of which is Development. The following work paper gives some background information about Development.

---

[1] This case study was written by Tad Miller, Ph.D., California Polytechnic State University, San Luis Obispo. Reprinted with permission.

181

Organizational Chart of Cuesta Holdings.

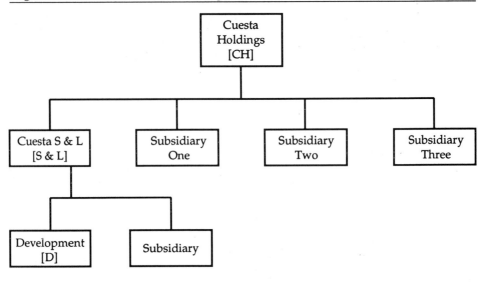

Client:	Cuesta Holdings	D1 1/2
Division:	Development	12/31/87
Audit area:	Real Estate Projects	Amy

Background memo

The Development subsidiary undertakes costly real estate projects. Real estate developers have difficulty raising enough money to build large developments. So, developers often build smaller projects that lack continuity with the surrounding neighborhoods. With access to capital, Development can buy land that has development potential but that is too costly for developers. These large parcels allow Development to locate the commercial districts, industrial parks, recreational areas and residential neighborhoods. Such planning improves traffic flow and the locations of public services. Development puts in the infrastructure for the community. Parcels are sold to real estate developers who wish to develop an area within the community. Home builders who lack the funds to build an entire neighborhood can buy lots in finished parcels. Development consists primarily of three major projects.

Tiffany Ranch

Development spent approximately $21,000,000 acquiring 2,900 acres which is called Tiffany Ranch. A park is planned along Corbett Creek. The creekside park will create a natural buffer between the industrial and residential areas. Significant portions of the infrastructure are in place in the residential sector.

On 9/30/86 Development sold 1,300 acres in Tiffany Ranch to C.C.C. Homes for $25,000,000 resulting in a $8,121,000 gain. Development has not sold any other property in Tiffany Ranch.

Parker Bros., An Accountancy Corp.

Client:	Cuesta Holdings	D1 2/2
Division:	Development	12/31/87
Audit area:	Real Estate Projects	Amy

Rancheria de la Mission

Rancheria de la Mission is the jewel in Bob Long's crown and there are no plans to sell land in Rancheria de la Mission to other developers. Rancheria de la Mission is a 20,000-acre planned community and Development intends to develop all projects in Rancheria de la Mission. Located in San Luis County, Rancheria de la Mission will capitalize on the high housing costs in Southern California. With access to the major highway and railroad arteries that link Northern and Southern California, Rancheria de la Mission will become an industrial satellite to Southern California. Reasonable land and housing costs will make Rancheria de la Mission attractive to employers and employees alike.

Mission Park

Development has acquired 8,576 acres adjacent to Rancheria de la Mission at a cost of $26,585,000. Development will plan the infrastructure for Mission Park, but this land was acquired to allow developers to build residential developments adjacent to Rancheria de la Mission.

During 1987, Development sold six tracts totalling almost 4,200 acres in Mission Park to developers for a total of $68,174,167. These sales generated gains of $46,493,000.

Miscellaneous

On 9/30/87, Development purchased 125 acres of land from Central Coast Construction for $16,306,000. The land is in Oregon and Development does not currently have any plans to develop this land.

Parker Bros., An Accountancy Corp.

Cuesta enters into complex transactions involving difficult accounting issues. The audit is made more difficult because different subsidiaries are often involved in the same transaction. For instance, when Development sells property Cuesta S & L typically lends the buyer money.

Bob Long is a good client, but he can be domineering and autocratic. He expects a lot out of his managers, his employees, and his auditors. Even though Cuesta is a big company, the company reflects Bob Long's personality. Critics say that Cuesta is an extension of his ego.

Cuesta is profit oriented and proud of it. As Bob Long says, "We don't run our business to make accountants happy, we run our business to make money." Bob Long and his managers respect Generally Accepted Accounting Principles and do their homework, but they are in business to make a profit. They don't let accounting standards stand in the way of profits and they will stretch GAAP to the limit if it increases profitability. An auditor better do his or her homework and be able to explain why an adjustment is required before asking Cuesta to record an adjusting entry.

Julie Gets Sick

Although the audit is almost complete, this is a very difficult period for Ron. Julie, the supervising senior on the Cuesta audit just had an emergency appendectomy. Julie is going to be all right but her illness substantially disrupts the audit. The audit staff at Cuesta is a good team of auditors but Julie is the only one who has a picture of the overall audit. Each member of the audit staff works on a different audit area and they may not see how their findings relate to evidence from other areas of the audit. As supervising senior, Julie pulls the work of the audit staff together. She would have reviewed every workpaper to see if the audit evidence supported the staff auditor's conclusion about her or his audit area. In addition, she would have considered whether the audit evidence obtained by each staff auditor might have implications for other areas of the audit. Now that Julie is gone, Ron will have to take a much more active role reviewing workpapers for the remainder of the audit.

Julie has already reviewed most of the workpapers and she made review comments which the audit staff are working on. At the end of an audit there are always loose ends. At this time it is important for Ron to get all those loose ends wrapped up. Bob Long likes to release earnings as early as possible, so time pressure is always a consideration on the Cuesta audit. From day one everyone assumed Cuesta would get an unqualified opinion. Mr. Johnston, the partner on the engagement, has said as much. The last time Ron talked to Julie, she told him that she hadn't found any serious problems. Sure, there had been disagreements on the audit, but nothing unusual. Cuesta presents their position better, argues longer, and stands their ground more firmly than most clients, but everyone expects that from Cuesta. No surprises have turned up.

But even with the time pressure, Ron knows he must review the workpapers thoroughly. Because Julie is gone, Ron will be the first person to have access to a complete set of workpapers. Because there is no supervising senior, Ron will be the only person to review many of the workpapers. Mr. Johnston will probably review more workpapers than usual, but certainly not all of them. So, the brunt of the additional work will fall on Ron.

It's Late Evening, Time to Go Home

Ron finds an appraisal that has apparently fallen out of the workpapers. He writes a "to-do" note for someone to put the appraisal back in the workpapers but he doesn't know whose workpapers it fell from. Ron knows that "to-do" notes don't get done unless they have a name on them, so he decides to stay a minute and attach the appraisal to the appropriate workpapers. Normally, a manager should always delegate such a task, but with the added confusion from Julie being gone, this is exactly the kind of thing that might get lost in the shuffle.

****

Robinson Appraisal Service

To: Cuesta Savings   December 28, 1987

At your request, we have appraised the 425 acre tract of undeveloped land in Mission Park. The valuation is dated as of our most recent inspection. This report is for a loan to Pacific Construction. The appraisal estimates the market value of a fee simple interest in the subject property. The legal description of this property is in the report.

Market value is defined as the most probable price at which the property will sell in a competitive market under conditions requisite to fair sale. This definition assumes:

1. Buyer and seller are motivated by self-interest.

2. Buyer and seller are well informed and acting prudently.

3. Neither buyer nor seller is under undue duress.

4. Payment is made in cash, its equivalent, or under financing terms generally available for property of this type and location on the valuation date.

We have analyzed a number of comparable sales which are discussed in the report. Based upon information available as of December 28, 1987, it is our opinion that the subject property has an estimated market value of $3,900,000,000.

This appraisal report has been made in conformity with and is subject to the requirements of the Code of Professional Ethics and Standards of Professional Conduct of the American Institute of Real Estate Appraisers and the Standards of Professional Practices and Conduct of the Society of Real Estate Appraisers.

Your attention is called to the pertinent data, exhibits, and discussions contained in the report.

We certify that, to the best of our knowledge and belief, all statements and opinions contained in this report are correct, subject to the limiting conditions which are made a part of this report.

Respectfully, Tracie Robinson

****

Ron thinks for a moment. Development negotiates the deals and sells the properties. Cuesta S & L lends the money and uses appraisals

Client: Division: Audit Area:		Cuesta Holdings Cuesta S & L Loans to R. E. Developers			S & L 1 12/31/87 Dave
Borrower	Date	Selling Price	Cash Down	Loan	Appraised Value
West Coast Homes	4/02/87	14,000,000	3,500,000v	10,500,000	8,500,000
Mission Constr	7/30/87	9,900,000	2,475,000v	7,425,000	5,400,000
Pacific Constr	8/31/87	14,997,000	[A] 0	14,997,000	5,000,000
C.C.C. Land	8/31/87	16,862,062	4,215,515v	12,646,547	8,670,000
Homes/Los Verdes	9/30/87	9,570,000	2,390,000v	7,180,000	5,365,000
Central Coast C	9/30/87	11,042,105	2,775,931v	8,266,174	5,670,000
Pacific Constr	12/29/87	6,800,000	1,700,000v	5,100,000	3,900,000

    v   down payment exceeds 20% of selling price
  [A]   this loan was not a loan to finance property purchased from Development

Parker Bros., An Accountancy Corp.

to document the collateral. Ron finds the appraisals in the Cuesta S & L binder with the "Loans to Real Estate Developers" workpapers (S & L 1) and he replaces the appraisal.

Ron notices the Dec. 29th sale date, so they were probably squeezing one more sale into 1987 income. Nothing wrong with that. Ron knows that Cuesta S & L has a policy requiring at least 20 percent down for loans secured by undeveloped land, so he subconsciously calculates that the down payment is 25 percent of the selling price.

Next Ron notices that the property which appraised for $3,900,000 is collateral for a $5,100,000 loan. The loan exceeds the collateral. That bothers Ron, so he looks further and finds a memo discussing "Loans Exceeding 80 percent of Appraised Value." Ron is pleased that Dave didn't leave this unresolved.

Client: Division: Audit area:	Cuesta Holdings Cuesta S & L Loans to R. E. Developers	S & L 2 12/31/87 Dave

"Loans Exceeding 80 Percent of Appraised Value"

Our audit tests revealed several loans which exceeded 80 percent of the collateral's appraised value. The Controller explained that Cuesta Holdings, Cuesta S & L, and Development discussed this issue in a meeting. Everyone agreed that Development should require down payments of at least 20 percent of the selling price. But even with a 20 percent down payment, the loan could exceed 80 percent of the appraised value if the selling price exceeds the appraised value. They considered their alternatives when Development had the opportunity to sell property for more than the appraised value.

1) Cuesta S & L could lend 80 percent of the appraised value and require a downpayment equal to the difference between the selling price and 80 percent of the appraised value.

2) Development could reduce selling price to the appraised value.

No. 1. No other lenders in the area require more than 20 percent down. If Cuesta S & L requires more than 20 percent down, they might lose deals. At best the buyer would obtain a loan elsewhere and Cuesta S & L would loose the interest income. At worst another lender might spoil the deal or encourage the purchaser to pay no more than the appraised value.

No. 2 was unacceptable. Development should try to make as much money as possible on every deal.

They all agreed that the appraisal should not limit the profit. If Development could get a 20 percent down payment, Cuesta S & L should lend the remaining 80 percent. This would result in some loan-to-value ratios exceeding 0.80 on Cuesta S & L's books, but everyone agreed that it would be necessary in order to maximize profits.

Bob Long said that he didn't understand why the Cuesta S & L even wanted appraisals. Development wasn't going to walk away from profit just because an appraisal was low. Even if the appraisal was correct, Development wasn't going to turn down money from a developer who hadn't done his homework and was willing to pay more for property than its appraisal value.

Parker Bros., An Accountancy Corp.

The memo makes sense to Ron, sort of. At least he can understand the reasoning behind Cuesta's actions. Then he begins to wonder who Pacific Construction is. Ron knows he has seen Pacific Construction's name on a workpaper before, but he can't remember where. Julie would know in a minute. If Ron had been reviewing all the workpapers throughout the entire audit he would remember too. But he didn't start reviewing every single work paper until Julie got sick.

Ron finally remembers. Cuesta Holdings made a couple of loans to developers. Since Cuesta S & L usually makes the loans, Ron thought this was a little out of the ordinary when he reviewed the Cuesta Holdings workpapers. But the loans were for reasonable amounts and properly documented, so Ron didn't give them much attention. Ron looks in the Cuesta Holdings binder and finds the workpaper with the loan to Pacific Construction.

Client:	Cuesta Holdings	CH 1
Division:	Cuesta Holdings	12/31/87
Audit area:	Unsecured Borrowings Lines of Credit	Tracie

Borrower	Origination Date	Amount of Loan
C.C.C. Homes	4/ 8/87	2,000,000
Pacific Constr.	12/29/87	1,700,000

Parker Bros., An Accountancy Corp.

Ron may not have given much attention to the loan when he reviewed the Cuesta Holdings binder, but he is troubled now. Cuesta Holdings loaned the money to Pacific Construction on Dec. 29th, the same day Development sold land to Pacific Construction.

Ron tries to figure this out. Loans in excess of the collateral value seemed to make sense when he read the memo. But if Pacific Construction used the line of credit to make the down payment, then Pacific didn't have any equity tied up in the property and didn't have anything to lose.

Mr. Johnston's Point of View

Cuesta's importance to Parker Bros. is evident by the fact that Mr. Johnston, the managing partner of the local office, is the audit partner for Cuesta. Ron decides to set up a meeting to discuss the Pacific Construction deal with Mr. Johnston. Mr. Johnston is good at breaking down problems and analyzing the issues. Besides, as the senior partner he should make the really tough decisions.

Ron explains the Pacific Construction situation to Mr. Johnston as they look over the workpapers. Mr. Johnston sees three issues: the line of credit, loans exceeding appraisals, and additional time for Ron to review workpapers. The big issue in Mr. Johnston's mind is whether to delay Cuesta's earnings announcement so Ron can have more time to review the workpapers. First of all, Mr. Johnston says there definitely isn't sufficient evidence to qualify the opinion. At least at this point, the opinion is not the issue. Rather, the issue is whether there is sufficient cause to delay Cuesta's earnings announcement.

At first Mr. Johnston finds the line of credit troubling. But after awhile he decides that even though it looks bad, it doesn't bother him. Pacific Construction's credit application requested a line of credit to cover fluctuations in their cash flows while houses are under construction but not yet completed. Mr. Johnston says such lines of credit are typical and it wouldn't bother him if Pacific had a line of credit with some bank in New York. In fact, he says it would have made our lives a lot easier if Pacific had gone to some New York bank for their line of credit.

Mr. Johnston does acknowledge that some auditors would disagree with him. They would argue that cash is fungible and it would be impossible to determine that Pacific Construction had not used the line of credit for the down payment. However, Mr. Johnston believes Pacific's credit application documents a legitimate business need and that Pacific does, in fact, have several developments under construction. So he can accept the line of credit.

Ron does not entirely agree with Mr. Johnston, but Mr. Johnston doesn't expect him always to agree.

Mr. Johnston is not at all troubled by loans exceeding the appraised values. First of all, Mr. Johnston agrees with the memo about loans in excess of collateral. Second, although he admits he would never write this in a workpaper, he believes continuing appreciation of land values will eliminate any exposure Cuesta S & L might have from such loans. And third, since he believes Pacific Construction used the line of credit for other purposes, Mr. Johnston believes Pacific has too much invested in the land to default on their loan.

Should we delay Cuesta's earnings announcement? Not in Mr. Johnston's mind. He does not believe the Pacific Construction sale justifies a delay. If this had come up earlier in the audit or if it didn't delay Cuesta's earnings release, Mr. Johnston would probably recommend a more thorough review of the workpapers. But at this stage of the audit, Mr. Johnston does not feel it justifies delaying Cuesta's earnings announcement.

However, Mr. Johnston believes this is Ron's decision. During an audit, the audit staff find lots of little errors that are immaterial. Mr. Johnston says he would not be aware of all these little errors, which might indicate that we failed to find a bigger audit problem. Mr. Johnston believes Ron is in the best position to decide if there is any indication of a possible problem.

Mr. Johnston doesn't believe the Pacific Construction loan justifies delaying completion of the audit. But if Ron feels there is any other indication of a problem in addition to the Pacific loan then he should spend more time reviewing the workpapers.

Ron doesn't want to hear that. He doesn't say anything to Mr. Johnston, but until he stumbled onto the Pacific Construction line of credit, this had been a pretty clean audit with fewer small errors than usual.

Parker Bros. Is a Business

Mr. Johnston says that he will support Ron's decision 100 percent. But he does want Ron to put his decision into perspective.

Bob Long has been applying more pressure than usual. At one point he asked if there was any way the audit could be completed ahead of schedule so Cuesta could release earnings. Until now, Mr. Johnston hasn't burdened Ron with all of this because he knew Ron was doing everything possible to complete the audit on time.

Bob Long is talking about getting bids from other audit firms for next year's audit. That would be the first time Cuesta has gone out for bids since Parker Bros. began auditing Cuesta. Mr. Johnston doesn't believe Cuesta will actually change auditors, he is not even sure that Cuesta will go out for bids. He thinks this is Bob Long's way of pushing for early completion of the audit and keeping the audit fees honest. But it is a sobering thought.

Ron was just two years out of college when Cuesta selected Parker Bros. as their auditors. It was a great day for Parker Bros., but Ron also knew a couple of people who worked for the predecessor auditor. When the predecessor firm lost Cuesta they pushed the audit partner into early retirement, transferred a senior manager to another office, laid off two managers and almost one-fourth of the staff in the office. In addition, three secretaries who worked for the partner and managers were let go. Promotions have been far and few between in that office and career opportunities are just starting to return to normal.

Mr. Johnston repeats himself, he will stand behind Ron's decision 100 percent. But if Ron decides it is necessary to delay the earnings release, he better let Mr. Johnston break the news to Bob Long, because Bob Long will be very upset.

Part One Questions[2]

1. What are the accounting/auditing issues in this case?

2. Would it make any difference if Pacific Construction's line of credit were with a different bank? If so, why does the source of funding affect one's ability to measure revenue?

3. Should the amount of revenue that a client contributes to an accounting firm have any bearing on the extent of the audit tests or how thoroughly the manager reviews the workpapers?

4. Mr. Johnston states that "If this had come up earlier in the audit ... [he] would probably recommend a more thorough

---

[2] Note: In addition to official guidance referenced in this text, students may want to consult the following resources:
— AICPA Professional Standards American Institute of Certified Public Accountants, New York 1991
  AU Section 334(SAS No. 45) Related Parties
  AU Section 9334 Related Parties: Auditing Interpretations of AU Section 334
— FASB Original Pronouncements, Accounting Standards, Financial Accounting Standards Board, Norwalk, Connecticut 1991
  FAS Statement No. 66 Accounting for Sales of Real Estate
  FAS Statement No. 57 Related Party Disclosures

review...." Should the stage of the audit in which the senior or manager uncovers evidence have any affect on how thoroughly they review the workpapers?

5. What are the ethical issues in this case?
6. Mr. Johnston is most likely at what stage of moral development? Support your answer.
7. How is Ron likely to respond to the fact that Mr. Johnston does not see a need to delay Cuesta's earnings announcement, if Ron is at stage three of moral development ? If he is at stage four? If he is at stage five?
8. What ethical principles should Ron be considering when he decides whether or not to delay the earnings announcement?
9. Audit staff are sometimes terminated when an office loses a large client. Should the partner(s) consider the potential hardships to their staff when dealing with a large client? Should such hardships affect the opinion issued on the financial statements?
10. If you were Ron, what would you do?

Part Two

Ron decided to delay the completion of the audit, but now he wishes he hadn't. Mr. Johnston promised to support Ron 100 percent, but Ron can tell Mr. Johnston is not completely happy with his decision. It is obvious to everyone that Bob Long is 100 percent unhappy. When Ron is working at Cuesta, he feels like he has the plague. The people at Cuesta think that Ron doesn't trust them, that he has accused them of lying.

Ron didn't even say the financial statements weren't fairly presented, he just wanted more time to review the workpapers.

Ron keeps looking at the "Loans to Real Estate Developers" workpaper (S & L 1) in the Cuesta S & L binder. In particular, he keeps coming back to all those loans in excess of appraised value. The more Ron thinks about it, the less sense they make. It just doesn't make sense for Cuesta S & L to lend more than the collateral value. Effectively the amount in excess of the collateral is an unsecured loan. Cuesta S & L charges developers the same interest rate as they charge for home mortgages. Since mortgages are fully secured, Cuesta S & L would be better off to make home mortgages. No matter how big the down payment, if the loan exceeds the value of the collateral then the developer holds an option. If the value of the land doesn't increase the developer can stop making payments and let Cuesta S & L repossess the property.

Everyone seems so sure land values will continue to increase. But, if that is true then why sell the land? When you think prices are going up you buy, you don't sell. And, when you need money you sell for cash, you don't finance the sale.

Ron asks himself, "Why did these deals happen?" Cuesta S & L would have been better off making home loans. Did the developers benefit from deals where they paid more than the appraised value? Are all of the appraisals too low? Are all the developers foolish? Ron figures the developers must be pretty smart if they can afford to make those big down payments. Now Ron looks in Development's binder at the "Real Estate Sales" workpaper (D 2).

Ron examines the gains on these sales, hoping they will answer one of his questions. Development booked some mighty big gains on these deals.

Ron is stumped by the down payments the developers made. Ron wonders where they got all that money; developers obviously make a lot more than auditors. Ron laughs to himself. No matter what Mr. Johnston says, Ron thinks Pacific Construction used the line of credit for their down payment.

Ron looks at the "Real Estate Sales" workpaper (D 2) one more time. He remembers something in the "Background Memo" (workpaper D 1) about Central Coast Construction. So Ron reads the miscellaneous section of the "Background Memo" again. On Sept. 30th Development paid Central Coast $16,306,000 for 125 acres of undeveloped land in Oregon. Ron can't find an appraisal for the land Development bought from Central Coast. On the same day, Central Coast gave Development a $2,775,931 down payment on 630 acres in Mission Park and Development booked an $8,587,000 gain on the sale. The 630 acres that Central Coast bought for $11,042,105 only appraised for $5,670,000 (see workpaper S & L 1).

Client: Division: Audit area:			Cuesta Holdings Development Real Estate Sales			D 2 12/31/87 Amy
			Sales in Mission Park			
	Date	Acres	Sales Price	Cash Down	Loan	Gain
West Coast Homes	4/02	1,000	14,000,000	3,500,000	10,500,000	11,067,000
Mission Constr	7/30	600	9,900,000	2,475,000	7,425,000	3,900,000
C.C.C. Land	8/31	963	16,862,062	4,215,515	12,646,547	13,193,000
Homes/Los Verdes	9/30	580	9,570,000	2,390,000	7,180,000	7,349,000
Central Coast C	9/30	630	11,042,105	2,775,931	8,266,174	8,587,000
Pacific Constr	12/29	425	6,800,000	1,700,000	5,100,000	2,397,000
		Parker Bros., An Accountancy Corp.				

Back to Mr. Johnston

Ron meets with Mr. Johnston again. Mr. Johnston doesn't see anything wrong with the Sept. 30th sale to Central Coast Construction. He can't believe Ron wants to treat the transaction as an exchange of similar assets. Mr. Johnston doesn't think land in Oregon and land in California need to be treated as similar assets. Mr. Johnston says there is no doubt in his mind that Cuesta can report a gain on the sale to Central Coast Construction.

Mr. Johnston says he thought Ron understood the business side of auditing better. He said that Ron needed to be more responsive to Bob Long. Cuesta pays top dollar and there is virtually no risk associated with the engagement. Who is hurt if Cuesta's financial statements are misstated? The stockholders? Bob Long wouldn't do anything to hurt the stockholders, he owns more than one-fourth of Cuesta's common stock. The top management at Cuesta (including Bob Long) owns almost three-fourths of the stock. Bob Long, top management, the employee stock ownership plan and the employee stock trust own almost 98 percent of Cuesta's stock. Mr. Johnston explains that the management at Cuesta is well aware of the circumstances surrounding these transactions. He believes we should explain the proper way to report the transactions under GAAP, but if management wants to report a transaction differently it really isn't any big deal, since they own the company. Mr. Johnston says the courts have ruled that management can't claim to have relied on the auditor's report if management knows the company's actual financial position. Bob Long and the management know Cuesta's financial position better than anyone, including Ron and himself.

Bob Long and management are doing their very best to run their company, and in Mr. Johnston's eyes they are doing a good job.

Without thinking, Ron asks about possible losses to creditors. As Ron knows, Cuesta Holdings doesn't really have any significant debt. Cuesta S & L has debt in the form of savings accounts and certificates of deposit. Mr. Johnston explains that all of these accounts are insured by the Federal Government. So even if Cuesta went bankrupt nobody would be hurt.

Mr. Johnston's patience is worn pretty thin. He says Parker Bros. may have worn out their welcome at Cuesta. In retrospect, Mr. Johnston regrets letting Ron put the firm's relationship with Cuesta in jeopardy. Mr. Johnston tells Ron to go back and wrap up the audit so Cuesta can release their earnings.

A Troubled Young Man

Ron assumes that Mr. Johnston's instructions to "go back and wrap up the audit" means that he should box up the workpapers and bring them back to Parker Bros. office. Although Mr. Johnston never actually came right out and said so, and Ron was too intimidated to ask, Ron was sure that Mr. Johnston was ready to issue an unqualified opinion.

There isn't another soul in the Parker Bros. office that evening and Ron knows he can't sleep, so he stays to straighten up the workpapers. He discovers that no one ever reviewed workpaper S & L 11. Ron notices a $75,000,000 advance to Central Coast Construction on a line of credit. Cuesta S & L loaned Central Coast all that money on Sept. 30th, the same day Development sold Central Coast 630 acres in Mission Park. Ron is so confused and frustrated that he doesn't even know if he should tell Mr. Johnston about the line of credit in the morning.

Client:	Cuesta Holdings		S & L 11
Division:	Cuesta S & L		12/31/87
Audit area:	Commercial Lending		
Borrower	Origination Date		Amount of Loan
E.R. Wells Co.	3/30/87	20,200,000	Secured by stock
C.C.C. Homes	6/30/87	30,000,000	Unsecured line of credit
Homes by Los Verdes	9/21/87	25,000,000	Unsecured line of credit
Central Coast Constr.	9/30/87	75,000,000	Unsecured line of credit
	Parker Bros., An Accountancy Corp.		

Part Two Questions[3]

1. What additional accounting/auditing issues have arisen in Part Two of this case?

2. Why is it difficult to measure revenue if an asset is exchanged for a similar asset?

3. What is the business risk to which Parker Bros. is exposed in this case? The audit risk?

4. Why does Mr. Johnston believe that Parker Bros.' business risk is minimal?

---

[3] Note: In addition to official guidance referenced in this text, students may want to consult the following resources:
— FASB Original Pronouncements, Accounting Standards (Volume II) Financial Accounting Standards Board, Norwalk, Connecticut 1991
— APB Opinion No. 29 Accounting for Nonmonetary Transactions
— "Business risk and the audit process" by Craig A. Brumfield, Robert K. Elliott and Peter D. Jacobson in the *Journal of Accountancy* (April 1983), pp. 60–68.

5. Should the existence of government insurance covering Cuesta's creditors affect the auditor's assessment of either business risk or audit risk? Should it influence the auditor's opinion?

6. Why do you think the management of Cuesta S & L was not only willing to loan large amounts in excess of appraised value, but was even willing to use other subsidiaries to advance the down payment to the purchasers?

7. What should Ron do if he believes Cuesta Holding's financial statements are materially misstated and Mr. Johnston decides to issue an unqualified opinion? Does your answer change if you know that Ron's wife is six months pregnant and he will lose his medical insurance if he loses his job?

8. Would Congressman Dingell or Congressman Wyden be interested in this case? Support your answer.

9. If all of the Treadway Commission recommendations had been in effect, how would this case be different?

Index

Accountants, role of, 117
Accounting "tricks", 118
Accounting Establishment: A Staff Study, The, 137–140
Accounting principles, 61–63. *See also* Code of Professional Conduct of the AICPA
Accounting profession, 30–31
   changes in, 106
   changes in standards, 150–151
   and expertise, 31
   federal takeover of, 137–139
   and independence, 53, 106–109
   institutional changes, 140–141
   investigation of, 145–146
   Metcalf report and, 139–140
   and monopoly, 31–32
   and public service, 32
   reforms in, 149–156
   responsibilities of versus accounting firms, 109–11
   and self-regulation, 33
Accuracy, of tax professionals, 88
Acts discreditable, 66–68
Act utilitarianism, 6–7
Advertising, 68–69
   FTC investigation of, 159–160
   by tax professionals, 89–90
Advisory services, 111–112
Afferent ethics
   versus efferent ethics, 29–30, 161–162
AICPA, 73
   division for CPA firms, 140
   division for Firms, 73
      and peer review, 74–76
      and quality review, 76–78
   DOJ antitrust action and, 158–159
   JEEP agreements and, 78
   and peer review, 74–76
   and quality review, 76–78

   Special committee on Standards of Professional Conduct for CPAs, 150
   tax professional guidance, 92
AICPA Code of Professional Conduct, and management accountants, 121
AICPA Professional Ethics Division Executive Committee, 50
Anderson Committee, contigent fees and commissions and, 160–161
APB Opinion, 63
ASB. *See* Auditing Standards Board
Association of Government Accountants Code of Ethics, 116, 126–129
Attestation services. *See also* Internal auditing
   auditor independence and consulting, 107–109
   decrease in, 106
   independence and, 44–45
   monopoly and, 31
   public interest and, 42
   scope and nature of services principle and, 47
Audit committees, Treadway recommendations on, 154–155
Auditing. *See* Attestation services
Auditing standards, changes in, 151–153
Auditing Standards Board (ASB), 151–153
Auditors, Treadway recommendations on, 155

Board of Accountancy, 38
Bodies designated by council, 51 (tab.)
Brooks, Jack, Congressman, 148

Cantor v. Detroit Edison Co., 163
Certified public accountants (CPAs).
See also Accounting profession;
Tax professional
AICPA jurisdiction, 140
and attestation services, 31–32, 47
consulting services, 110–111
and ethical issues, 2
expertise of, 31, 46
monopoly of, 31–32
public service of, 32
questions on tax returns, 94–95
responsibilities principle, 39–40
roles of, 117
and self-regulation, 33
and taxpayer estimates, 96–97
and tax returns, 95–96
 advice to clients, 101–102
 deviations from prior rulings, 97–98
 preparation errors, 99–101
 tax return standards, 92–95
and whistle blowing, 130–131
Civil penalties, 91
Client-nonclient control, independence and, 56
Client omission, and tax professionals, 88
Code of ethics, as public service, 29–30
Code of Ethics of Financial Executives Institute, 116, 121–122
Code of Professional Conduct of the AICPA, 38
Code of Professional Conduct of the AICPA. See also Accounting Principles
principles of, 39
 due care, 45–46
 integrity, 42–43
 objectivity and independence, 43–45
 public interest, 40–42, 40–42
 responsibilities, 39–40

scope and nature of services, 46–47
Cohen Commission, 141–142
 report, 108
Commission of Auditors' Responsibilities. See Cohen Commission
Commissions, 69
 FTC investigation of, 160–161
 Harris Poll on, 175
 standard changes, 150–151
Committee of Sponsoring Organizations (COSO), 156
Committee on Responsibilities in Tax Practice, 92
Competence, 61. See also Professional competence
 management accountants and, 119
Compliance with standards, 61
Confidential client information, 63–64
Confidentiality, management accountants and, 119
Conflict of interest
 independence and, 52
 Rule 102, 60
 of tax professionals, 89
Consulting process, 111
Consulting profession. See also Profession
 versus scholarly profession, 28
Consulting services
 for attest clients, 113
 and auditor independence, 107–109
 standards for, 110–113
 survey on, 168 (tab.)
Consulting services practitioner, 111
Contingent fees, 64–66
 FTC investigation of, 160–161
 Harris poll on, 175
 standard changes, 150–151
COSO. See Committee of Sponsoring Organizations

INDEX

CPA. *See* Certified public accountants
Criminal penalties, 91

Decision tree, for act utilitarianism, 6–7
Deontology. *See also* Rule deontology
  and accountants, 116, 118
Department of Justice (DOJ), antitrust action by, 158–159
Dependent persons, independence and, 58
Developmental psychology, and moral decision making, 17
Dingell, John D., Congressman, 144–146, 155–156
Discrimination, in employment, 67
DOJ. *See* Department of Justice
Drucker, Peter, 130
Due care, 45–46
Due professional care
  consulting standards, 112
  under due care principle, 46
  Rule 201, 60
Duties and restrictions, and IRS, 87–90

Efferent ethics
  versus afferent ethics, 29–30, 161–162
Egger, Roscoe, 85
Egoism, 4–5
ESM Government Securities, Inc., 145
Ethical conflict
  loyalty, 117
  resolution of, for management accountants, 120–121
Ethical dilemma, CPAs' ratings of, 40
Ethics, defined, 2
Ethics Rulings, 50
Expectations gap, 141–142
Expertise, 29
  of accounting profession, 31
  due care and, 45

Extenuating circumstances
  and moral maturity, 22
  Rule 203, 62–63

Fairness, and moral maturity, 22
Family relationships, and independence, 58–59
FASB Statements of Financial Accounting Standards, 63
FCPA. *See* Foreign Corrupt Practices Act (FCPA) of 1977
Federal Trade Commission (FTC)
  and advertising and solicitation, 159–160
  and commissions and contigent fees, 160–161
Fees, average distribution of big eight firms, 106 (tab.)
Financial executives, 118
Financial Fraud Detection and Disclosure Act of 1986, 145, 146–148
Financial interests, independence and, 55–56
Foreign Corrupt Practices Act (FCPA) of 1977, 129–130
Former practitioners, and firm independence, 51–53
Fraud
  reforms to eliminate, 149–156
  Treadway investigation of, 153–156
  Wyden investigation of, 146–148
Freedom, and rule utilitarianism, 7
FTC. *See* Federal Trade Commission

GAGAS. *See* Generally accepted government auditing standards
GAO. *See* U.S. General Accounting Office
Generally accepted government auditing standards (GAGAS), 148
General standards, 60–61

Goldfarb v. Virginia State Bar, 163
Governmental Accounting Standards Board, 59
Government Auditing Standards, 116
Grandfathered loans, independence and, 54
Group, expectations of, 22

Harris poll, 170–178
Heinz dilemma, 18–19
   level one moral maturity, 19–22
   level two moral maturity, 22–23
   level three moral maturity, 24–26
   Honorary directorships/trusteeships, independence and, 53–54
House Legislation and National Security Subcommittee, 148–149
House Subcommittee on Oversight and Investigations, 136–137, 144–146

Impersonal egoism. *See* egoism
Implementation services, 112
Independence, 43–45
   in appearance, 108–109
   auditor's, and consulting, 107–109
   in fact, 107–108
   of internal auditors, 123–125
   Rule 101, 52–60
Individual
   inner principles of, 24–26, 38
   self-focus and, 19–22
Individual rights, versus social obligations, 24
Institute of Internal Auditors Code of Ethics, 125–126
Integrity, 42–43
   conflict of interest and, 44
   management accountants and, 119–120
   Rule 102, 60

Internal auditing. *See also* Attestation services
   statement of responsibilities, 122–125
Internal Control—Integrated Framework, 156
Internal Revenue Service (IRS)
   practice before, 87–90
   tax professional regulation by, 92
   view of tax professionals, 85
IRS. *See* Internal Revenue Service

JEEP. *See* Joint Ethics Enforcement Program
Joint Ethics Enforcement Program (JEEP), 73, 778–79
Joint Trial Board, 79–80
Journal of Accountancy, Ethics Feature, 50

Kant, Immanual, 8
Kohlberg, 17–26

Law
   moral maturity and, 23
   and rule utilitarianism, 7
   and tax professionals, 90
Litigation, independence and, 55
Loans, independence and, 54

Management, Treadway recommendations on, 155
Management accountants, 118
   standards of ethical conduct for, 119–121
Management Advisory Services Executive Committee, 110
Managerial position, and independence, 57–58
MAS Practice Standards, 110
Member's firm, independence and, 57
Member, and independence, 57

Metcalf, Lee, Senator, 137–140
Monopoly, 29
    of accounting profession, 31–32
Moral decision making. *See also* Moral judgment
Moral decision making
    and developmental psychology, 17
    content versus form, 18
    group expectations and, 22–23
    inner principles and, 25–26
    and self-focus, 19–22
Morality, and rule deontologists, 8
Moral judgment, stages of, 20–21 (tab.)
Moral maturity
    level one, 19–22
    level two, 22–23
    level three, 24–26
    and principles, 38
Moral philosophy, and egoism, 5
Moss, John E., Congressman, 136–137
Moss report, 136–137
Multidimensional scaling, 39–40

Nader, Ralph, 130–131
Name, 69–70
National Commission on Fraudulent Financial Reporting, 145, 153–156
Negligence, 67
Nonattestation services
    consulting, and independence, 107–109
    expansion of, 47
Normative ethics, 3
Notaries, tax professionals as, 89
Not-for-profit organizations, independence and, 53–54

Objectivity, 43–45
    management accountants and, 120
    Rule 102, 60
Obligation, theories of, 3
Organizational structures, 124 (fig.)

Parker v. Brown, 162
PCPS. *See* Private Companies Practice Section
Peer review, 74–76
Personal behavior, Association of Government Accountants, 127–128
Personal egoism. *See* Egoism
Planning and supervision
    consulting standards, 112
    Rule 201, 60
POB. *See* Public Oversight Board
Practice, form of, 69–70
Private Companies Practice Section (PCPS), 74
Profession. *See also* Accounting profession; Consulting profession; Scholarly profession
    defined, 28
Professional competence. *See also* Competence
    Association of Government Accountants, 128
    consulting services standards, 112
    under due care principle, 46
    Rule 201, 60
Professional trust, 41–42
Public interest, 40–42
Public Oversight Board (POB), 74, 140–141
    survey by, 166–170
Public service, 29–30. *See also* Public service ideal
    of accounting profession, 32
    public interest principle and, 41
Public service ideal. *See also* Public service
    IRS view of, 85
    of tax professionals, 84, 85, 86–87
Public trust, 41–42

QR. *See* Quality review
Quality review (QR), 76–78

Raby, William L., 85
Referral fees, 69
Relationships, and moral maturity, 22
Relatives, nondependent close, and independence, 58–59
Responsibilities, 39–40
  accounting profession versus accounting firms, 109–110
  of Association of Government Accountants, 128–129
  as client advocate, 85–86
  conflicting, 84
  of internal auditors, 123
  to IRS, 85
  and tax returns, 95–96
Reviews. *See* Peer review; Quality review
Ross, David, Sir, 8
Rule 101, independence, 52–60
Rule 102
  integrity and objectivity, 60
  and tax practice, 86
Rule 201, general standards, 60–61
Rule 202, compliance with standards, 61
Rule 203, accounting principles, 61–63
Rule 301, confidential client information, 63–64
Rule 302, contingent fees, 64–66
Rule 501, acts discreditable, 66–68
Rule 502, advertising and other forms of solicitation, 68–69
Rule 503, commissions, 69
Rule 505, form of practice and name, 69–70
Rule deontology, 8–9. *See also* Deontology
  and inner principles, 38
Rules of Conduct and Interpretations, 50
Rules of the Code of Professional Conduct, 50–52. *See also* specific rules
  enforcement of, 73

Rule utilitarianism, 7–8

SAS. *See* Statements on Auditing Standards
Savings and loan industry, 145
Scarce resources
  allocation of, 32, 118
Scholarly profession, versus consulting, 28
Scope and nature of services, 46–47
SEC. *See* Securities and Exchange Commission
SEC Practice Section (SECPS), 74–75
SECPS. *See* SEC Practice Section
Securities and Exchange Commission (SEC)
  and Moss report, 136–137
  and Treadway commission, 145–146
Securities Exchange Act of 1934, 129
Self-focus, and moral maturity, 19–22
Self-regulation, 29, 73–74
  of accounting profession, 33
  compromise of, 162–164
  peer review, 74–76
  Quality review (QR), 76–78
  by tax professionals, 92
Senate Subcommittee on Reports, Accounting, and Management, 137–140
Shapiro, Leslie, 85
Sherman Antitrust Act, 162
SIC. *See* Special Investigations Committee
Significant influence, independence and, 58
Smith, Adam, and egoism, 4–5
Social obligations, versus individual rights, 24
Society
  and attest service, 31–32
  moral maturity and, 22
  moral order of
    moral maturity and, 23

moral philosophy, 5
  professions and, 29, 30 (fig.)
Society of CPAs, 38
Sociology
  accounting professional characteristics, 30–33
  professional characteristics, 29–30
  professions and, 28
Solicitation, 68–69
  FTC investigation of, 159–160
  and tax professionals, 89–90
Special Investigations Committee (SIC), 74
Spouses, independence and, 58
SRTP. *See* Statements of Responsibilities in Tax Practice
SSCS. *See* Statement on Standards for Consulting Services
Staff/support services, 112
Standards for the Professional Practice of Internal Auditing, 122
Standards of Ethical Conduct for Management Accountants, 116
State action doctrine, 162–164
State boards of accountancy, 73
Statement of Responsibilities of Internal Auditing, 116
Statement on Standards for Consulting Services No. 1 (SSCS), 110–113
Statements of Responsibilities in Tax Practice (SRTP), 92
  No. 1, 92–94
  No. 2, 94–95
  No. 3, 95–96
  No. 4, 96–97
  No. 5, 97–98
  No. 6, 99–100
  No. 7, 100–101
  No. 8, 101–102
Statements on Auditing Standards (SASs), 151–153
State societies of CPAs, 73
Substandard CPA Audits of Federal Financial Assistance Funds: The Public Accounting Profession is Failing the Taxpayers, 148–149
Sufficient relevant data
  consulting services standards, 112
  Rule 201, 60

Tax burden, allocation of, 84
Tax matters, contingent fees in, 65–66
Taxpayer
  estimates, 96–97
  penalties for, 91–92
Taxpayer refunds, negotiations of, 90
Taxpayers, CPA advice, 101–102
Tax professional. *See also* Certified public accountants (CPAs)
Tax professional
  ACPA view of, 86
  and client's omission, 88
  as client advocate, 85–86
  CPAs versus lawyers, 176–177
  duties and restrictions, 87–90
  IRS view of, 85
  penalties for, 91–92
  public service ideal of, 84, 86–87
  self-regulation, 92
Tax Reform Act of 1976, 91
Tax return positions, 92–94
Tax returns
  answers to questions, 94–95
  deviations from prior rulings, 97–98
  preparation errors, 99–101
  preparation procedures, 95–96
  use of estimates, 96–97
Tax shelters
  options, 90
  penalties and, 91
Tax system, penalties, 91–92
Teleological ethics, 4
  versus rule deontology, 8
Theories of obligation, 3
Transaction services, 112
Treadway, James C., 145, 149

Treadway commission, 129, 153–156
report, 108
Treasury Department Circular 230, 87–90

U.S. General Accounting Office (GAO), CPA audits study, 148–149
United States v. Arthur Young & Co., 41

Utilitarianism, 4, 6–8, 118. *See also* Act utilitarianism; Rule utilitarianism

Whistle-blowing, 130–131
Wyden, Ron, Congressman, 145, 146–148